Computer Software
for Schools

Computer Software for Schools

A Payne BA
Humanities

B Hutchings BSc
Computer Studies and Mathematics

P Ayre BSc
Computer Studies and Mathematics

Oriel Grammar School
Gorleston

Pitman

PITMAN BOOKS LIMITED
128 Long Acre, London WC2E 9AN

Associated Companies
Pitman Publishing Pty Ltd, Melbourne
Pitman Publishing New Zealand Ltd, Wellington

© A Payne, B Hutchings, P Ayre 1980

First published in Great Britain 1980
Reprinted 1982, 1983

Filmset at The Universities Press, Belfast Ltd. and
printed at the Pitman Press, Bath.

ISBN 0 273 01583 4

Preface

We were prompted to write this book by the fact that, when we first came to investigate the possibility of using the computer as an aid in the school, we found little published material which offered practical advice. We have set out to show (simply) what can be done and how, suggesting relationships between a programming language on the one hand and educational applications on the other. It might be argued that there are already many textbooks available on Basic, our chosen language, and with this we could not disagree. But, in answer, we would suggest that a teacher who is new to programming has to establish a link between the language and the application—in effect do two things at once. By considering both we would hope to assist in establishing that link and in providing a useful short cut. As teachers, we are also aware of the value of working from a person's experience, hence the desirability of studying Basic in the light of educational packages.

We are enthusiastic about the possibilities which the prospect of cheap computers in schools present, but it is not our intention here to argue a case for them. The applications described have been chosen for their value in demonstrating the variety of roles that the computer can assume. Their desirability will be assessed by individuals, and experience suggests that there is no reason to expect that there will be agreement on this point. We do, however, believe strongly that, where teachers accept the use of the computer as an educational aid, they should be encouraged to write their own programs, or gain an insight into the way that programs are written, rather than rely totally upon those produced by others. In this respect, we would hope to demonstrate that programming is not such a difficult task.

Although intended primarily for teachers and student teachers, the book might be considered as useful background reading for school children engaged in examination project work, to illustrate the wealth of applications which can be drawn from their immediate environment. As a text on Basic it covers the fundamental aspects of the language and can reasonably be expected to be of value to the non-teacher who is interested in learning to program.

The authors wish to thank the Headmaster, staff and students of the Oriel Grammar School for all of their help and guidance.

A. Payne
B. Hutchings
P. Ayre

Contents

1 Introduction

What can the Computer Do?

It is not easy to answer this question both briefly and meaningfully, since one condition tends to preclude the other. The problem is compounded by the fact that there are at least five answers. Further, what is a suitable answer for one potential user may be less enlightening for another. The fact that it can be used to handle a firm's payroll, calculate the interest and capital repayments on a loan, monitor stock levels and invoice customers is likely to be a more satisfactory indication of the possibilities open to someone in a commercial environment than to a teacher, especially a teacher who is not attracted by the mathematical nature of these applications. Nevertheless, the naming of specific applications can serve to demonstrate the wide range of subjects and tasks which can derive benefit from the power of the computer. Even a cursory examination of this book will indicate the broad possibilities. These include, among others, packages in history, geography, french, physics, chemistry and information retrieval in a multi-media resource context. There is a program featuring Sir Francis Drake's voyage around the world; another simulates the qualitative analysis of chemicals; a third calculates the nutritive content of meals; one produces projections of future populations; and another can be used in the study of french verbs. These applications, presented with a brief description of the aims of each program and its operating procedures, provide one insight into "what the computer can do".

There are obviously some subjects which are not represented here, but that is not to say that they are unsuitable. There simply comes a point when it is impracticable to list every possibility. One way to avoid an infinite list and at the same time answer the question is to establish application typologies. It is possible to group applications under a series of umbrella headings. The first of these is the **simulation.** These can be used in the learning environment to allow a student to role-play, perhaps with a view to establishing empathy with a character in a given situation, or to experiment with different courses of action in particular circumstances with a view to examining outcomes. Generally speaking, one simulates by using a model which approximates to reality. Not only is this often the best way to examine a subject because of the constraints of time, cost, space and the availability of, in some cases, "real" people, but the simulation is considered to be a powerful motivator.

As the name suggests, a computer can be used as a **calculating aid.** In these circumstances it can be programmed to perform calculations which would take so long, or which are so complicated, that they tax the student's mathematical skills to the point where the real issues may become blurred. It is this problem that the programs MENU and POPULATION seek to overcome.

Instruction, drill and **demonstration** represent three more types of application. As an instructor the computer can be used to supplement the role of the teacher. It can be programmed to provide descriptions of techniques, rules or other material to be mastered, set problems which test the student's understanding, and initiate remedial action as this becomes necessary. Drill exercises like VERB allow a student to practise and develop a skill through a process of repetitive assignments. These will probably include a reinforcing element which indicates the nature of an error and the appropriate corrective action. Unlike the instruction program, the drill exercise will assume some degree of understanding on the part of the user at the outset of a run. The availability of graphics facilities on microcomputers has increased the scope for demonstration programs considerably. Armies can be made to move across a map, sequences in a process animated, and graphs and tables conjured up instantly. Relatively large groups can observe the demonstration on the visual display unit, and it can be enhanced if linked to a large television set.

In addition to providing tuition, the computer can be used to **manage the learning environment,** assessing the student's progress by tests which it administers, recording the results of those tests, and then directing the student to new tasks or revision exercises. In this role one can include its diagnostic function. Here it can be programmed to analyse test results with a view to pinpointing learning difficulties so that remedial action can be taken by the teacher.

Finally, **clerical functions** can be performed. These might include producing directories of room allocation or student option lists, the retrieval of information and the keeping of records, perhaps of library transactions.

Having established that applications transcend subject boundaries and that there are a number of types of application, one might consider running some packages in order to gain first-hand experience. Afterall, "doing" is generally accepted as a more effective learning tactic than being told. On a number of occasions the authors have observed the rapid enlightenment which accompanies a run of a program. The teacher concerned very quickly sees other possibilities. "If it can do this, then it can do that." Here, then, is the third answer to the question. If you want to know what it can do, see it in action. It is with this possibility in mind that the listings for the various programs described have been included. It would be foolish to suggest that these represent the very best of what might be achieved. It is, however, hoped that they will be regarded as a useful starting place for the reader's enquiries into this vast subject. In some cases, for example the drill exercise VERB and STUDENT RECORDS, we can only offer an insight into the possibilities. It must be left to the individual to exploit these as he or she sees fit.

Perhaps a more forthright answer than any that has been offered so far would be in the form of a series of statements which describe the primary facilities and functions of the computer. It can

1 Store data.
2 Process data.
3 Perform calculations.
4 Print the data which has been stored or information which has been derived from the processing of data.
5 Perform operations which may or may not involve calculations and which may or may not be complex, repeatedly, rapidly and accurately.
6 Take decisions. (This is not to be confused with thinking or making value judgements.)

Although to the point, these statements do not necessarily offer a clear picture of the tasks that can be performed, and each requires elaboration.

By way of a fifth and last answer, and perhaps it is this which will give some substance to the above description of the computer's capabilities, one could offer instruction in a programming language. It is at this level that one really begins to get to grips with the question, "What can the computer do?"

Because each of the five approaches described gives only a partial insight into the potential role of the computer in schools, we have chosen to develop all five, sometimes implicitly, sometimes explicitly, adopting an integrated structure. The programming language **Basic** provides the necessary continuity. It is essential that this is structured and, because each program is used to illustrate a different part of the language, it has determined the order in which these appear. As far as possible it has been considered in the light of demonstrated output—see *what* has been done, now see *how*.

The Computer– a Vocabulary

Many schools have a *teletype terminal* (Fig 1.1) linked by telephone to a large computer in a college. This large computer is referred to as a *mainframe* and will be capable of supporting a large number of users at any one time. The terminal resembles an electric typewriter and it is via the keyboard that the user communicates to the computer. The user's input (anything that he/she types in) is displayed on paper. Similarly, any communication from the computer to the user is printed on the same paper. This input and output appears as a form of dialogue, and because it is on paper it is known as a *hard copy*.

Microcomputers display the input and printout on a *visual display unit* (VDU). In this case the printout is transient and at the end of a run the user does not have a copy. They can have a printer attached to them but this will almost certainly be an optional extra. The microcomputer may be a single unit (Fig 1.2) or composed of several pieces; the keyboard, VDU, processor and cassette recorders being separate items (Fig 1.3). Whatever the arrangement, the user communicates to the computer via a keyboard and it communicates to the user via the VDU.

Fig 1.1

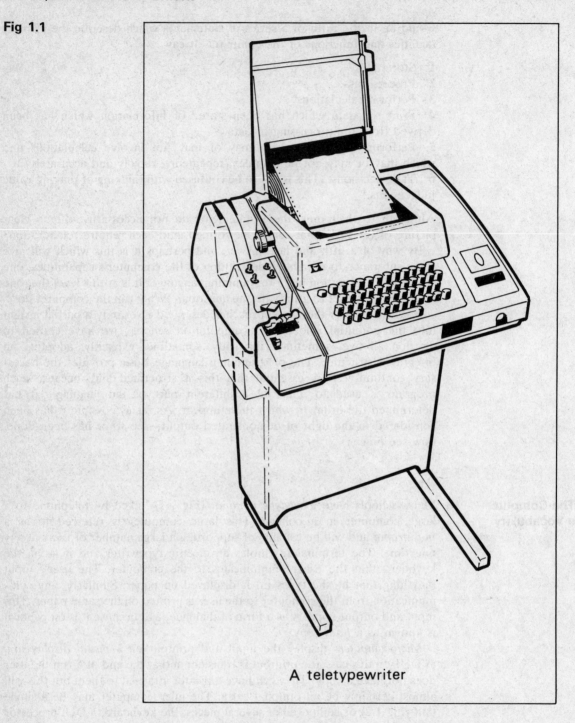

A teletypewriter

Fig 1.2

Fig 1.3

The *program* is a set of operating instructions and it, together with the language that it is written in, is known as the *software*. The computer is known as the *hardware*. Those programs that are written and run on a mainframe will almost certainly, as far as the school is concerned, be stored on *disks* which resemble large, hard gramophone records. The storage on the microcomputer will be either on *magnetic tape* in cassette form or on *mini floppy disks*. Mini floppies, as the name suggests, are floppy, rather like the promotion records given away in magazines, and will be in the region of five to eight inches in diameter. To protect them they have a card cover. When in use they are held in disk drives (Fig 1.3). Disks are considered to have advantages over tapes, not least of which is the time taken to load programs. Some disk systems use one floppy disk, others allow two. A two-disk system is more powerful than a single-disk system.

One of the early questions which most people ask is, how do you set about running a program? Each computer system and language will require the user to call up a program in a different way, but in essence it will be a simple procedure. It can be demonstrated by reference to two systems. The thing to note is the limited amount that the user has to type in. In each case the user is primarily concerned with letting the computer know which form of BASIC is required and the name of the program to be run.

Example 1   Calling up a program from a teletype terminal
First of all the mains power supply is switched on. Next the teletype is switched on by pressing a button provided for the purpose. Because the link with the computer is by telephone, the user telephones the computer. On receiving a high-pitched whistle in reply, the telephone receiver is placed in a box called an acoustic coupler and is left there while the computer is in use. (In the system operated by the authors, the key marked A and another known as the control key are pressed simultaneously.) The following user-computer dialogue ensues.

Note: The user's input follows the backward-facing arrows.

```
NORWICH CITY COLLEGE MAXIMOP SYSTEM

PLEASE LOG IN ← 1234ORIEL
TYPE PASSWORD
■ ■ ■ ■
DATE: 21/12/79 CHANNEL: 5
FOR LATEST MAXIMOP NEWS TYPE:– NEWS      (UPDATED 17/10/79)
10.44.44 ← SOBS
← OLD JOEL
← RUN
```

Each school has a logging in code and a password. The password is typed over a jumble of letters which the computer prints. The password ensures that only legitimate users have access to a school's file. The BASIC to be used is Southampton BASIC and this is referred to as SOBS. Having nominated the language, the user names the program that he wants. We precede the name of the program, JOEL, by the word OLD. The input RUN, after the last arrow, instructs the computer to begin executing the program instructions. (The figures 10.44.44 in front of SOBS is the time.)

Example 2

Now we see how to load the same program using Research Machines 12K BASIC. The system described uses dual floppy disks. The disks are marked A and B. For the purpose of this example a disk on which the BASIC is stored is put into disk drive A and another holding the program into disk drive B. To indicate the input, it has been underlined.

Again, the first thing is to switch on a mains power supply and then the computer using a key. The monitor also has to be switched on. The dialogue is as follows:

```
COS 3. O/M
→B                    ............... loads the operating system
RESEARCH MACHINES
47K CP/M VERS 1.4
A>B:                  ............... allows user to work in disk drive B
B>A:DBAS12            ............... loads the BASIC
Highest Memory?       ............... in response to this, press the return key
29576 Bytes Free
RML 12K DISC BASIC V 3.OP
READY:
LOAD "JOEL"           ............... loads the program
READY:
RUN                   ............... activates the program
```

In either system, having reached the point at which RUN has been input, there are two other courses of action that could be taken. The first is to type LIST instead of RUN. This produces a listing, a complete set of program instructions. The other possibility is to begin adding to or making changes to the program. As soon as the program has been loaded, the user can begin to input new lines or "type over" old ones. This will be necessary when a program is found to have bugs in it, or what the man in the street might call errors. Another reason for typing new lines is that the program was not typed in at one sitting, and where this happens all the user does is pick up where he/she left off.

Instead of loading a program in each case, it is possible, once the BASIC has been loaded, to begin to input a program.

Teachers and Programming

A point which must be made very clear is that TEACHERS DO NOT HAVE TO BE ABLE TO PROGRAM IN ORDER TO RUN APPLICATION PACKAGES. It is partly as a result of this misconception that many teachers have in the past expressed a reluctance to use a computer in their lessons. Programs are available from a number of sources, including colleges which both develop materials and maintain program libraries, user groups and publishers. Once obtained it is a simple matter to run a package and should demand no special knowledge of either the computer or programming, given that the program is compatible with the user's system.

Although teachers need not be able to program, there is a growing feeling that more teachers should be engaged in the production of software, bringing with them the all-important subject expertise. The hardware, it is said, is here, but the programs to run on it are not so readily available. It is with their involvement that appropriate directions and applications can be defined, and a fruitful union, in all probability a polygamous union, between computer scientists and subject teachers is anticipated. Computing skill will not be a prerequisite for participation in such an arrangement, one which has produced very successful results in the past and which no doubt will continue to do so, although it would be true to say that it might be an advantage, if only because a precise understanding of a programming language can in itself act as a stimulus for ideas. The underlying premise for such a notion, however, is that the interested subject teacher will have someone to work with.

Time and time again teachers have been encouraged and advised to make use of their "local computer expert". This may be a highly organised support service available to teachers in a particular authority, perhaps centred on a college of further or higher education. On the other hand, it may be an already overworked lecturer at a college who does not see his role as a teacher's program writer. Or, it could be the computer studies teacher in the school. This individual might be imposed upon to help by running programs and adapting or writing some. But, even if he or she is receptive to requests for assistance, there is a limit to the number of applications demands that can be satisfied, and these perhaps not very quickly.

The ability to program need not be a problem—but it can be a limitation. Although software is being developed for use by teachers with no experience of the computer, it does not follow that what is available will suit all tastes and needs. Much of what has been produced in the infancy of computer-assisted learning has been for scientific and mathematically orientated subjects and designed for A-level and post-A-level students. Where a package exists on what is considered to be a suitable topic and at an appropriate level, a teacher might be dissatisfied with the way that the subject has been handled. Unless the teacher is in a position to adapt the idea or produce a new program, there is little that can be done to remedy this situation. Nevertheless, there is a lot to be said for accepting something less than one's ideal for the sake of avoiding duplication and a waste of that scarce resource, time, which could be used for other programming projects.

Some user groups operate a system whereby an individual puts something in and then takes something out. There are ways round most problems but this one would seem to put the non-programmer at something of a disadvantage. It is difficult for such groups to establish and maintain adequate quality control since the existence of the group depends upon the continued goodwill and contributions of its members. There are numerous applications which have merit but which are unlikely to tempt the more highly organised bodies engaged in software production. Unless these materials are produced at the parochial level they will not be produced at all.

Basic

Basic is one of a number of programming languages. It was developed primarily for use in education and is widely used in schools. As with spoken languages, there are, within Basic, different dialects. Some forms offer a wider range of facilities than others. Some allow one thing but not another. Sometimes two variations of the language will allow the same function but require the use of an idiosyncratic instruction. Despite this there is sufficient common ground between the dialects to allow one to consider teaching or studying Basic as though it was a language with no variations.

A **program** is a set of instructions written in a computer language upon which the computer acts. It determines the operations that are performed, perhaps makes provision for data to be typed in during a run, and produces the output—information printed on paper or presented on a Visual Display Screen. These instructions must be presented in a way that the computer can recognise, paying regard to the vocabulary and syntax of the language. Where a person might make an accurate guess at the meaning of a badly phrased instruction, the computer won't.

Two attractive features of Basic for the beginner are the limited nature of the fundamental aspects of the language, which account for some twenty-five instructions and concepts, and the sensible names which many of these have been given. Many of the instructions are common English words which means that we are already conversant with much of the vocabulary of Basic. The only problem is to become aquainted with the few words that the computer understands and the way that it likes them to be used. The computer outputs messages to a screen or onto paper. To do this it has to print, and the instruction that it recognises is PRINT. Most of the programs in this book are what are described as **interactive programs.** They require a substantial input from the user. The instruction to permit this, and on which the computer acts, is the word INPUT. Perhaps we want the computer to carry out a certain action if a particular condition applies. To handle this we use an expression like: IF the condition applies THEN do this. Sometimes we might want the computer to go to a set of instructions and execute them before doing anything else. So that it goes to a particular line of the program, we say GO TO line whatever it is and carry out the instruction that you find there.

This ease of language extends beyond programming instructions into what are termed Basic commands. These are instructions which we give directly to the computer—they are not contained or used in a program. Two of these, LIST and RUN, have already been mentioned. Two more obvious ones are those which allow a program to be saved, and one which is no longer required to be deleted. In many versions of Basic, the instruction to

	DRAKE	GAS	POPULATION	CHEM	VERB	MENU	VILLAGE	GRADIENT	MATRIX	JOEL	SORT	TEST	CLDP
PRINT	⊘	√	√	√	√	√	√	√	√	√	√	√	√
INPUT	⊘	√	√	√	√	√	√	√	√	√	√	√	√
IF...THEN	⊘	√	√	√	√	√	√	√	√	√	√	√	√
GOTO	⊘	√	√	√	√	√	√	√	√	√	√	√	√
LET	⊘	√	√	√	√	√	√	√	√	√	√	√	√
GOSUB/RETURN	⊘					√	√		√				√
ARITHMETIC	*	⊘	√	√	*	√	√	√	√	*	*	*	*
LOOPS		⊘	√	√	√	√	√	√	√	√	√	√	√
FURTHER USE OF PRINT	⊘		√	√	√		√		√				
TAB	⊘				√	√	√	√		√			
READ/DATA			⊘	√	√	√	√			√			√
RESTORE			⊘		√		√			√			√
LISTS				⊘	√					√	√	√	
ARRAYS				⊘		√	√		√				
DIM				⊘	√	√	√			√	√		
STRING FUNCTIONS				**	⊘		√			√		√	√
ON...GOTO					⊘		√			√		√	
CONCATENATION				⊘	⊘								√
PRINT USING			**			⊘						√	
GRAPHICS									⊘				
FILES:READ										⊘		√	
RESET										⊘			
FILES:WRITE												⊘	

	DRAKE	GAS	POPULATION	CHEM	VERB	MENU	VILLAGE	GRADIENT	MATRIX	JOEL	SORT	TEST	CLDP
380Z BASIC		9K	12K	12K	12K				12K	12K	12K	XDB	
ICL-CES BASIC							√						√
SOUTHAMPTON BASIC	√	√	√	√		√		√					

* program includes a simple counting feature
** used but not explained – not an essential feature
XDB – Extended Disk BASIC

Fig 1.4

save a program is simply the word SAVE (followed by the name that we wish to give it). To delete a program, the rather elegant ERASE or the less attractive Orwellian expression UNSAVE might be used.

The chapter DRAKE deals with seven Basic instructions. It is our intention to show how readable a program can be and to establish these instructions in a context which throws some light on the relationship between them. Not only are they very easy to understand, five of them figure in all of the programs included in this book. The fact that a program can be written with so few instructions should serve to indicate the milage to be obtained from even a limited acquaintance with the language. We are sensitive to the fact that programming is often, understandably, associated with mathematics and that this makes the computer inaccessible to some people. DRAKE is almost entirely mathematics-free—the exception being a scoring mechanism which masquerades as a sum.

The Table in Fig 1.4 shows how the Basic has been structured. The Basic instructions are listed in order of appearance down the left-hand side. Across the top are the names of the packages that are described in the book. A tick indicates that the package makes use of a particular aspect of Basic. A circled tick indicates the point at which it is examined. Not all of the features are common to all forms of Basic. In particular, STRING FUNC-TIONS, PRINT USING and FILE HANDLING are not available in all Basics and, where they do appear, they are unlikely to be the same. They are included because they are important features of the language and should certainly be a consideration when purchasing a machine. Their details will vary from Basic to Basic but the principle in each case will be the same.

String functions and PRINT USING have been used in programs before consideration has been given to them. The latter is used in POPULATION and the former in CHEM and CHEMICAL. An understanding of them at these points is not critical and they can safely be left until later. In the case of the string functions in the chemistry programs they are not essential but a refinement and can, in fact, be removed from the program. The PRINT USING instruction can, it will be discovered, be replaced by what is described as a TAB statement, but with slightly less pleasing results. These two exceptions do not represent an entirely satisfactory state of affairs but it was felt that a compromise which slightly broke the Basic pattern was preferable to the inclusion of packages which were created with the sole purpose of resolving a minor contradiction. Graphics facilities, too, will vary and multiple statements on a line will not be a feature of all Basics. All of these irregular features are considered after the common ones.

The forms of Basic in which the programs have been written have been indicated at the bottom of the table.

Flowcharts

Throughout the book we have used diagrams, where possible, to describe the programming techniques employed. A standard way of illustrating the order and branching in a program is to draw a flowchart, using a standard set of symbols. Instructions or processes are enclosed in "boxes" and are

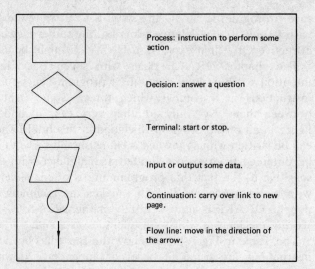

Process: instruction to perform some action

Decision: answer a question

Terminal: start or stop.

Input or output some data.

Continuation: carry over link to new page.

Flow line: move in the direction of the arrow.

Fig 1.5 Flowchart symbols

joined by arrowed lines to indicate their order. Branches occur as decisions are taken.

We have tried to follow the conventional symbols where possible, but some of the flowcharts are only "loose" constructions so we have avoided formality, indeed, some are merely block diagrams. The standard symbols we have used are shown in Fig 1.5.

Where it is useful we have included a summary of the sections of a program, and their line numbers, with the program listing. An alternative would be to include REM (remark) statements at various points of the program. These statements are ignored whilst the program is running, but add to its readability when it is listed.

Example Flowchart

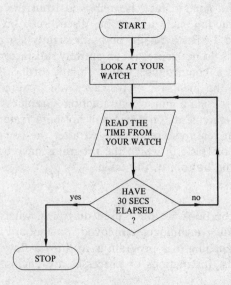

Fig 1.6

2 DRAKE: a history simulation

Introduction DRAKE is a decision-making simulation in which students are encouraged to role-play with a view to gaining an insight into an historical situation and also to establish empathy with the central character. What it offers is a controlled situation in which they can adopt an active role. As well as having the qualities of a simulation it is a data base. That is to say, the computer has stored, as well as the research of the programmer will allow, the story of Drake's voyage around the world. Unlike a conventional text, it interrupts the reader every so often and says something like, "What do you think of that?" or "What would you do next?" What we have is a dynamic text. In its limited way the book "talks" to the reader. It listens to the answer and comments upon it. We would not wish to overvalue such a program—it will hardly revolutionise the teaching of history—but what it does do is allow the information to be presented in an interesting way, and by this we mean the exercise itself, not the fact that a computer has been used.

The package, which encourages the students to draw a map and make a set of notes, under the guise of plotting a route on a Sea Chart and keeping a Captain's Log, can be used by individuals, small groups or a whole class under the direction of a teacher. It was, however, designed for groups of three or four who collectively assume the role of Drake. The decision points promote discussion within the group as the members try to persuade each other to adopt a course of action.

When the exercise has been completed a post-simulation discussion with the teacher has to be arranged. This will be valuable for consolidating what has been learnt and for exploring issues which have been raised. It can be approached in a number of ways. One possibility is to consider courses of action which were neither adopted by Drake nor offered by the computer. Usually the students have strong opinions about what Drake could have done. An examination of these often throws more light on the situation or allows one to grapple with a student's misconceptions regarding both the period and the nature of the problems. Another possibility is to pose a general question like, "What do you think was Drake's most serious problem?" This immediately raises the question of what exactly his problems were. These may have been stated explicitly or implicitly. On the face of it his problem with Doughty was one of maintaining discipline. On another level one might suggest that his problem was a personal one—the decision to execute a close friend. Opinions will differ.

One of the factors which prompted the inclusion of this simulation in the book, for it is certainly not the only way to approach the subject of teaching history with a computer, was the fact that the programming required is so elementary—yet so important—that it provides a suitable introduction to Basic in an application context. Another reason is that the simulation is built on a simple model which acts almost as a template for other history simulations of the same type. The way that it has been structured, therefore, and the description of the elements of Basic which it takes advantage of have been examined at length. We trust that non-historians will bear with this, for even if the content is of no consequence to them, the aspects of programming which are described undoubtedly will be.

Before embarking upon this description it is necessary to make a few observations concerning the structure of this chapter. It continues with a brief description of the way in which the simulation works. This is followed by the contents of the student's booklet and a specimen printout. There then comes a brief narrative of the voyage so that the reader can see the raw material from which the simulation was created and note the similarity between it and the program. The remaining pages fall into three sections: those that describe the tasks that the computer can perform and the way in which the simulation is constructed so that a teacher is in a position to write a similar program with no knowledge of a programming language; those that consider and explain the very simple programming statements that are used in the simulation; and those that contain the listing.

On the whole, listings are not meant to be read. They are provided for reference and for those who wish to use the program. On this occasion, however, we would encourage you to briefly examine the printout at this point and to compare it with the listing. There is a remarkable similarity. One is not lost in a sea of symbols or an ocean of formulae. This perhaps says something about the nature of programming. Programming is not difficult; it's what people put into programs that makes it appear so.

How the Simulation Works

The student is given a booklet (see pp. 19–22) which contains:

1 An introduction outlining the purposes of the simulation and the tasks to be performed.
2 Operating instructions.
3 Background information regarding the size of the fleet, size and quality of the crew, Drake's destination and his orders.
4 A Sea Chart on which to plot a course.
5 Pages of a Captain's Log on which to record the major events of the voyage.

During the run, the computer describes events and provides information. It also prints map coordinates which the student is instructed to plot and suggests that a note should be made in the log. These instructions are always accompanied by the instruction PLOT/LOG. At certain points in the voyage the student is invited to make a decision regarding some problem that has arisen. A solution to the problem is selected from two or three presented by the computer. These are labelled A, B or C. The computer then analyses the decision, comparing it with Drake's, and explains why it is considered to be a sensible decision or otherwise. It is often possible to say why Drake chose as he did, therefore making it possible to say why the student's choice was less appropriate. The student is then invited to continue as though the same choice had been made as by the historical character.

Sample Run

```
PLOT/LOG     SET SAIL FROM PLYMOUTH. 13TH DEC. 1577
             REACH MOGADO 27TH DEC.
             HERE YOU TRADE WITH THE MOORS. CAPTURE SPANISH
             MERCHANT SHIPS.REPLACE THE CHRISTOPHER WITH THE
             CAPTURED BENEDICT.
TYPE CON WHEN READY TO CONTINUE
-CON


PLOT/LOG     SAIL TO ISLAND OF MAYA (CAPE VERDE ISLANDS)
             CAPTURE PORTUGESE SHIP LADEN WITH PROVISIONS.
             PLACE A CREW OF 28 ON BOARD UNDER THE COMMAND
             OF YOUR CLOSE FRIEND THOMAS DOUGHTY.
TYPE CON WHEN READY TO CONTINUE
-CON


PLOT/LOG     SAIL TO RIO DE LA PLATA. ARRIVE APRIL 5TH.
             SAIL TO PORT SAINT JULIAN. ARRIVE 19TH JUNE
TYPE CON TO CONTINUE.
-CON

DECISION 1   DOUGHTY HAS BEEN STIRRING UP TROUBLE AMONGST
             THE CREW. HE HAS TRIED TO UNDERMINE YOUR
             AUTHORITY AND RAISE MUTINY ( A TREASONABLE
             OFFENCE ) AMONGST THE CREW WHO ARE ALREADY
             ANGRY AT HAVING BEEN TRICKED. DOUGHTY
             HAS PROBABLY BEEN PERSUADED TO DO THIS BY
             LORD BURGHLEY WHO WOULD LIKE THE MISSION
             TO FAIL BECAUSE HE DOESN'T WANT TO STRAIN
             RELATIONS BETWEEN ENGLAND AND SPAIN.

DO YOU [A]   SEND DOUGHTY BACK TO ENGLAND IN ONE OF THE SMALL
             SHIPS SO THAT HE CAN BE OF NO FURTHER TROUBLE.

     [B]     GIVE HIM A PUBLIC WARNING IN FRONT OF THE CREW
             TO THE EFFECT THAT ANY FURTHER TROUBLE WILL BE
             DEALT WITH SEVERELY.

     [C]     TRY DOUGHTY FOR TREASON AND EXECUTE HIM IF
             FOUND GUILTY.
TYPE A,B OR C
-C
[C]     PROBABLY A WISE DECISION.
        DRAKE THOUGHT SO.
        THE CREW WERE A ROUGH CROWD.
        DRAKE APPEARS TO HAVE THOUGHT IT NECESSARY
        TO TAKE A VERY STRONG LINE.
        HE COULDN'T AFFORD TO SHOW ANY WEAKNESS IN FRONT OF
        A DISCONTENTED CREW, EVEN IF IT INVOLVED THE DEATH
        OF HIS FRIEND. HE WOULD FIND IT DIFFICULT TO EXPLAIN
        TO THE QUEEN WHY HE HAD NOT TRIED DOUGHTY FOR
        TREASON AS IT WAS HIS DUTY.
```

```
DECISION 2      THE FLEET IS TO SAIL DOWN THE COAST
                AND THEN THROUGH THE STRAITS OF MAGELLAN
                INTO THE PACIFIC. THE STRAITS IS A DIFFICULT
                PIECE OF WATER AND ROUGH SEAS ARE EXPECTED.
DO YOU [A]      TAKE ALL THE SHIPS THROUGH.
       [B]      BREAK UP THE SWAN, THE BENEDICT AND THE
                CAPTURED PORTUGUESE VESSEL AND DISTRIBUTE THEIR
                SUPPLIES, USEFUL EQUIPMENT AND CREW AMONGST
                THE OTHER SHIPS.
TYPE A OR B.
←B
[B]  UNDER THE CIRCUMSTANCES, A GOOD DECISION.
     IT IS QUITE LIKELY THAT ONE OR MORE SHIPS WILL BE
     BADLY DAMAGED, SUNK OR SEPARATED FROM THE REST.
     IF THE SUPPLY SHIP IS LOST THIS WOULD CREATE SERIOUS
     PROBLEMS FOR THE REMAINING CREWS.
     DRAKE CLEARLY BELIEVED IT UNWISE TO HAVE ALL HIS EGGS
     IN ONE BASKET AND ORDERED THAT THE SWAN AND THE
     SMALLER SHIPS SHOULD BE BROKEN UP.


PLOT/LOG     THE PELICAN, ELIZABETH AND MARIGOLD SET SAIL
             FROM PORT ST. JULIAN 17TH. AUG. ARRIVE AT THE
             STRAITS OF MAGELLAN.


DECISION 3.  BEFORE ENTERING THE STRAITS, DECIDE
             WHICH SHIP YOU WISH TO SAIL IN.
WILL YOU SAIL IN [A] THE PELICAN.
                 [B] THE ELIZABETH.
                 [C] THE MARIGOLD.
TYPE A,B OR C.
←R
LINE ERROR
←B
[B] A GOOD CHOICE,BUT YOU MISS THE ACTION IN THE PACIFIC.
     THE FLEET RUNS INTO A GALE AND THE MARIGOLD
     IS LOST WITH ALL HANDS.
     THE PELICAN AND THE ELIZABETH BEAT THE STORM AND
     REACH THE PACIFIC ON 6TH. SEPT.
     THEY SHELTER IN A BAY.
     HOWEVER, THE PELICAN (NOW NAMED THE GOLDEN HIND)
     DRIFTS FROM HER MOORING AND IS FORCED SOUTH WHERE
     SHE REACHES CAPE HORN (P7/8) ON 28TH OCT.
PLOT/LOG       ENTRY INTO PACIFIC AND GOLDEN HIND'S JOURNEY
               TO CAPE HORN.
TYPE CON WHEN READY TO CONTINUE.
←CON
THE ELIZABETH WAITS FOR YOU TO REAPPEAR AND THEN, WHEN
YOU DON'T TURN UP, SHE RETURNS TO ENGLAND.


PLOT/LOG     DEPART CAPE HORN 30TH OCT.
             SAIL NORTH. SUPPLIES RUNNING LOW.
             SEARCH VARIOUS ISLANDS FOR FOOD. NO LUCK.
             EVENTUALLY ENCOUNTER AN INDIAN.(N/M7).
             HE INDICATES THAT HE CAN TAKE YOU TO
             A PLACE WHERE THERE IS FOOD.


DECISION 4      DO YOU A) TRUST HIM AND FOLLOW (HE MIGHT
                          LEAD YOU INTO A TRAP.)
                       B) KILL THE INDIAN AND CONTINUE
                          YOUR SEARCH.
TYPE A OR B
←A
BOLD MOVE.THIS IS WHAT DRAKE DID.THE INDIAN DIRECTED HIM
TO VALPARAISO (PLOT M7) AND HE TOOK STORES
WINE AND CEDARWOOD FROM THIS SMALL SETTELEMENT. HE WAS
IN LUCK. THE TREASURE SHIP 'THE GRAND CAPTAIN OF THE SEA'
WAS ANCHORED THERE. HE TOOK 400LB OF GOLD FROM IT.
```

```
PLOT/LOG    SAIL NORTH TO COQUIMBO. 300 HORSEMEN
            AND 200 FOOT SOLDIERS ARE WAITING FOR YOU.
            CLEARLY YOU CAN'T RELY ON THE ELEMENT OF
            SURPRISE ANYMORE, HAVING GIVEN YOUR PRESENCE
            AWAY. SEND 14 MEN ASHORE TO COLLECT WATER.
            ONE MAN IS KILLED. YOU WITHDRAW AND PULL IN
            AT A NEARBY BAY TO BUILD A PINNACE.
TYPE CON TO CONTINUE.
←CON
PLOT/LOG    SET SAIL 19TH JAN. 1579. HEAD NORTH. LAND (L7)
            TARAPACA. TAKE SIX BARS OF SILVER FROM MEN
            YOU FIND SLEEPING.
TYPE CON TO CONTINUE.
←CON
PLOT/LOG    SAIL NORTH TO L/K 6/7
            CAPTURE 800LB. OF SILVER WHICH IS BEING TRANS-
            PORTED BY TWO MEN.
TYPE CON TO CONTINUE.
←CON
PLOT/LOG    SAIL NORTH. REACH CALLAO 10TH FEB. YOU
            FIND 12 MERCHANT SHIPS AT ANCHOR. YOU PLUNDER
            THESE, TAKING PLATE, SILK AND LINEN. THEN
            YOU CUT THE CABLES OF SHIPS IN THE HARBOUR TO
            PREVENT PURSUIT WHILST YOU TAKE OFF IN PERSUIT
            OF A TREASURE SHIP CACAFUEGO WHICH YOU LEARNT
            ABOUT AT CALLAO.
TYPE CON TO CONTINUE.
←CON
PLOT/LOG    CACAFUEGO CAPTURED(J/K5/6).SET CREW FREE.PUT
            SOME OF YOUR OWN CREW ON BOARD AND SAIL OUT TO
            SEA FOR TWO DAYS BEFORE TRANSFERRING BOOTY
            TO YOUR OWN SHIP.
TYPE CON TO CONTINUE.
←CON
DECISION 5  YOU HAVE NO MORE ROOM FOR TREASURE.
            YOUR TASK IS TO GET HOME SAFELY.
DO YOU [A] SAIL WEST, OUT ACROSS THE PACIFIC WITH THE
            INTENTION OF SAILING RIGHT ROUND THE WORLD.
       [B] SAIL SOUTH THROUGH THE STRAITS AND RETURN
            HOME AS QUICKLY AS POSSIBLE BY A KNOWN ROUTE.
       [C] SAIL NORTH IN THE HOPE OF FINDING THE PACIFIC
            END OF THE NORTHWEST PASSAGE AND THUS GO HOME
            ACROSS THE NORTH ATLANTIC. SUCH A DISCOVERY ON
            TOP OF YOUR SUCCESS TO DATE WOULD ADD GREATLY
            TO YOUR PRESTIGE.
TYPE A, B OR C.
←C
[C] AN ADVENTUROUS MOVE. THE PASSAGE WAS BELIEVED TO EXIST
    BY A GREAT MANY PEOPLE. DRAKE DECIDED TO HEAD NORTH TO
    DISCOVER THE OUTLET OF THE NW. PASSAGE.


PLOT/LOG    SAIL NORTH TO F/E2/3. THE TEMPERATURE
            HAS FALLEN CONSIDERABLY AND IS AT
            AN UNBEARABLE LEVEL. YOU ARE FURTHER
            NORTH THAN THE OUTLETS ARE SUPPOSED TO BE.
TYPE CON TO CONTINUE.
←CON
PLOT/LOG    RETURN TO F2/3 (ON COAST). CLAIM TERRITORY
            FOR THE QUEEN. CALL IT NEW ALBION.
            MEET FRIENDLY INDIANS. STAY WITH THEM FOR
            5 WEEKS
TYPE CON TO CONTINUE.
←CON
TIME TO MOVE ON.
DO YOU [D] SET OFF ACROSS THE PACIFIC.
       [E] RETURN VIA THE STRAITS OF MAGELLAN.
TYPE D OR E.
```

```
←E
A BAD MOVE. YOU WILL ALMOST CERTAINLY BE TAKEN BY
     SPANISH MEN OF WAR WHICH WILL BE WAITING FOR YOU
     TO RETURN. IF YOU SHOULD BE FORTUNATE ENOUGH TO SLIP
     THROUGH THEM YOU WILL STILL HAVE TO NEGOTIATE
     THE VERY DANGEROUS MAGELLAN STRAITS.
     DRAKE DECIDED TO SAIL ACROSS THE PACIFIC.
     HE SET OFF ON JULY 21ST. PASSED THROUGH G1 AND I27
     AND SIGHTED
     THE PHILIPPINES FROM (X) ON 16TH OCT.
PLOT/LOG THESE DETAILS.
TYPE CON TO CONTINUE.
←CON
PLOT/LOG    SAIL TO THE ISLAND OF TERNATE IN THE
              MOLUCCAS, THE HOME OF THE SPICE
              PLANTATIONS. NO ENGLISH SHIPS HAVE REACHED THEM
              BEFORE. THE PORTUGUESE HAVE JUST BEEN EXPELLED
              AND YOU ARE ABLE TO MAKE A TRADE AGREEMENT
              WITH THE KING. HE GIVES YOU SIX TONS OF CLOVES.
TYPE CON TO CONTINUE.
←CON
PLOT/LOG    SET SAIL NOV. 19TH. ANCHOR OFF THE CELEBES
              AT CRAB ISLAND ON 10TH. DEC. FROM HERE ON THERE
              WILL BE DANGER OF ATTACK BY PORTUGUESE
              NAVAL VESSELS AND PIRATE SHIPS.
TYPE CON TO CONTINUE.
←CON
PLOT/LOG    SET SAIL 12TH. DEC.
              RUN AGROUND (K23) JAN. 9TH 1580
TYPE CON TO CONTINUE.
←CON
DECISION 6 YOU MUST REFLOAT THE SHIP QUICKLY.
              IT MIGHT SINK AT ANY TIME. IN ORDER TO REFLOAT
              YOU MUST LIGHTEN THE SHIP.
DO YOU ORDER MEN TO THROW OVERBOARD:-
[A] SIX TONS OF CLOVES AND 4 CANNONS.
[B] 3 TONS OF CLOVES, 8 CANNONS, THEN TREASURE AND MEAL
     UNTIL SHE REFLOATS.
[C] CANNON UNTIL SHE FLOATS. (THIS WILL MEAN A LOSS OF 14
     CANNONS).
TYPE A, B OR C.
←B
[B] A WISE CHOICE.
     DRAKE SEEMS TO HAVE FAVOURED A BALANCE, REALIZING THAT
     HE MUST KEEP A SUFFICIENT NUMBER OF GUNS TO ENSURE HIS
     SAFETY AND THAT HE COULD RETAIN AN ADEQUATE
     AMOUNT OF TREASURE TO MAKE THE VOYAGE PROFITABLE. THE
     CLOVES WERE VERY VALUABLE AND
     SHOWED PROOF OF HIS TRADE AGREEMENT AND THE GOOD WILL
     OF THE KING.

PLOT/LOG    SAIL TO JAVA
              SAIL TO CAPE OF GOOD HOPE.
              SAIL TO SIERRA LEONE. ARRIVE
              22ND. JULY.
              TAKE ON WATER, FRUITS AND OYSTERS.
PLOT/LOG    SAIL FOR HOME. REACH PLYMOUTH 28TH SEPT. 1580.
TYPE CON TO CONTINUE.
←CON
EACH OF YOUR CHOICES HAS BEEN MARKED. THE COURSES
OF ACTION TAKEN BY DRAKE CARRY THE HIGHEST MARKS. THE
OTHER MARKS ARE AWARDED DEPENDING UPON HOW SENSIBLE YOUR
CHOICES WERE.
IF ALL YOUR DECISIONS WERE THE SAME AS DRAKE'S, YOU COULD
SCORE 27 MARKS.
YOUR SCORE IS 23  OUT OF 27.
STOPPED AT LINE 3820
```

Student Booklet: DRAKE

Contents

1

Introduction

A This is a simulation in which you (your group) assume
   the role of Francis Drake on a voyage which he began
   in 1577.

B On page 7 is some background information which you
   must read before you begin the simulation.

C The simulation is run in SOBS and is code named
   DRAKE.

D As soon as it receives the instruction to run, the computer
   will begin to print out information concerning your
   voyage. This information will relate to three things:
   (i) your route, (ii) details of significant events,
   (iii) decisions to be taken by you.

   The information concerning the route and events of
   importance will be preceded by the instruction PLOT/
   LOG. On this signal you must plot the course on your
   Sea Chart and write a brief description of events,
   departures and ports of call in the Captain's Log.

2

Operating Instructions

Plot

You/one of your team must plot the course of your ship by joining all the places/locations that you visit. Some of these places are marked on the Sea Chart, others are given grid references. These must be worked out. Each such point will be referred to by a letter and a number. Letters run down the left-hand side of the Chart and numbers run across the bottom. The positions to plot occur where lines drawn through these points from left to right (for letters) and up and down (for numbers) cross.

Examples

(1) O3= position **O**

(2) N 4/5= position **Z**
(i.e. on line N from left to right and cut by a line drawn from top to bottom half way between 4 and 5).

(3) L/K 2 = position **X**
(on line from left to right half-way between K and L and cut by a line drawn from top to bottom through 2).

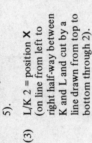

Con

After giving you the instruction PLOT/LOG, the computer will print TYPE CON WHEN READY TO CONTINUE. When ready, type the three letters CON and then press the red ACCEPT key. The computer will then print out more instructions.

Decisions

At several points in the simulation you will be faced with a problem and you will have to make a decision. The information previously printed out or contained on page 7 of this booklet may help you to take that decision. However, although there are some clues, you are in many ways being asked, "What would you do if you really found yourself in this position? How would you behave?" Rather than take pot-luck, try to think of the arguments for and against a course of action. Be sure in your own mind why you take the action that you do.

To make your task easier, the computer will present you not only with the problem but also with some possible courses of action — each identified by a letter (A, B or C). When you have made up your mind, press the appropriate key (A, B or C) and then press the red ACCEPT key. The computer will then analyse your decision, pointing out its strengths and/or weaknesses.

Should you make a wrong decision — i.e. not the same as that of the real Drake — plot your course and keep your log just as though you had made the same choice as Drake.

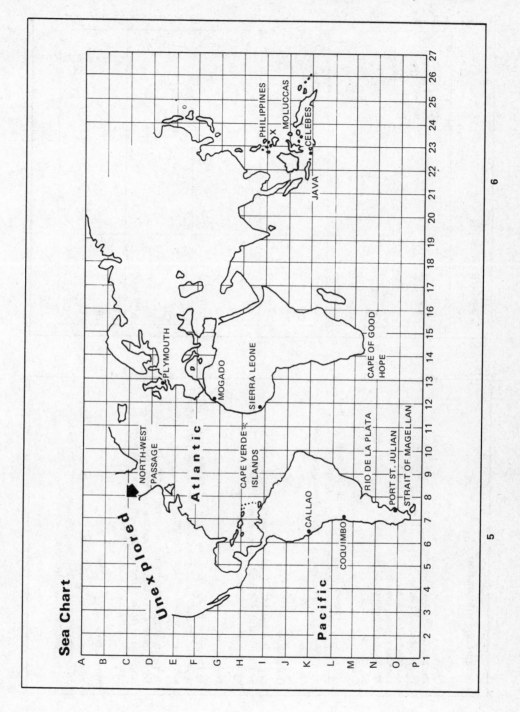

Sea Chart

Captain's Log

DEPART/ARRIVE	EVENTS	TREASURE TAKEN
FROM ON TO ARRIVED		
FROM ON TO ARRIVED		
FROM ON TO ARRIVED		
FROM ON TO ARRIVED		
FROM ON TO ARRIVED		

8-12

Background Information

Fleet

The Pelican, 120 tons, 18 guns.
The Elizabeth, 80 tons.
The Marigold, 30 tons.
The Christopher, 15 tons.
The Swan (Store ship), 50 tons.

Crew

160 men. They agreed to sail with you in the belief that the fleet was sailing for Turkey. They include a few gentlemen but the majority are very rough and very tough. They respect firm discipline.

Destination

The Pacific. You will sail via the Magellan Straits which have been negotiated only once before — some 50 years ago. In these waters, winter conditions exist all year round.

Orders

1) To explore the Pacific (crossed only once before — a difficult voyage which holds, in all probability, a host of unknown dangers) and open up trade for England in these waters.

2) To attack Spanish ships and settlements on the Pacific side of South America. The truce between England and Spain is breaking down and so Queen Elizabeth favours this action. However, in public she will deny any knowledge of it.

Motivation

You have a score to settle with the Spaniards for their treachery on a previous occasion. You and your crew look forward to bringing home some Spanish treasure.

7

The Narrative

On 13th December 1577, Drake set sail from Plymouth with a fleet of five ships. They included the Pelican of 120 tons and carrying 18 guns, the Elizabeth of 80 tons, the Marigold of 30 tons, the Christopher of 15 tons, and the store ship Swan of 50 tons. The crew of 160 men had signed on in the belief that the fleet was sailing for Turkey.

Drake's orders were to explore the Pacific with a view to promoting English trade in those waters and to attack Spanish ships and settlements on the Pacific side of South America.

On 27th December, he reached Mogado on the Moroccan coast. Here he traded with the Moors and captured some Spanish merchant ships. The Christopher was replaced by the captured Benedict. From Mogado, they sailed to the island of Maya where a Portugese ship carrying provisions was captured. A crew of twenty eight men was placed on board under the command of Drake's close friend Thomas Doughty.

On 5th April, they reached the River Plate and then sailed on to Port Saint Julian which they reached on 19th June. Doughty had been stirring up trouble amongst the crew and was trying to undermine Drake's authority. He had probably been persuaded to do this by Lord Burghley who was concerned about the effect that the operation would have on Anglo-Spanish relations. Drake had Doughty tried for treason and he was found guilty and executed.

Before leaving Port Saint Julian on 17th August, the Swan and the smaller vessels were broken up and the supplies, men and equipment were distributed between the Pelican, the Elizabeth and the Marigold.

These three ships sailed to the Straits of Magellan where, during a gale, the Marigold was lost with all hands. The Pelican and the Elizabeth beat the storm and reached the Pacific on 6th September. The Pelican, now renamed the Golden Hind, and the Elizabeth sought shelter in a bay. In the bad weather, the Golden Hind drifted from her moorings and was forced south where she reached Cape Horn on 28th October. After waiting for the Golden Hind to reappear, the Elizabeth set sail for England.

After departing from Cape Horn on 30th October, Drake searched a number of islands for food and water but with little success. Eventually he encountered an Indian who indicated that he could take Drake to a place where he could replenish his stores. This turned out to be Valparaiso which he reached on 5th December. As well as taking wine, stores and cedar-wood from the settlement, he captured "The Grand Captain Of The Sea" which had gold bullion on board.

He then sailed north to Coquimbo where 300 horsemen and 200 foot soldiers were waiting for him, having had news of his presence in the Pacific. He sent 14 men ashore, one of whom was killed. Drake withdrew and pulled in at a nearby bay where his crew built a pinnace. On 19th January, 1579, he headed north and landed at Tarapaca where he took six bars of silver from two sleeping men. He then sailed north again and was able to capture 800 pounds of silver which was being transported by two men.

On 10th February, the Golden Hind sailed into Callao harbour to find twelve merchant ships at anchor. From these Drake took plate, silk and linen and then cut the cables of all the ships in harbour to prevent pursuit while he took off after the treasure ship Cacafuego which he had learnt about at Callao. The ship was duly captured and some of Drake's crew put on board. It was sailed out to sea for two days before the treasure was transferred to the Golden Hind. After this adventure Drake's ship had no more room for bullion and he decided to strike out for home. To return via the southern route was out of the question as the whole coast was alerted to his presence in the Pacific. He decided to try to find the Pacific outlet of the North-West Passage which many believed to exist. In this he was unlucky. Having sailed north further than the outlet was supposed to have been, he sailed back along the coast of America and landed at a place which he claimed for Queen Elizabeth, naming it New Albion.

He stayed there, in the company of friendly Indians, for five weeks and then, on 21st July, he struck out across the Pacific. He sighted the Philippines on 16th October and sailed on to the island of Ternate in the Moluccas, the home of the spice plantations. The Portugese had just been expelled from the islands and no English ship had been there before. Drake was able to turn this to his advantage and established a trade agreement with the king who presented him with six tons of cloves.

He set sail on 19th November and anchored off the Celebes at Crab Island on 10th December. He left on 12th December and ran aground on 9th January 1580. In order to refloat, he had his men throw overboard three tons of cloves, eight cannon and some treasure.

The rest of the voyage home was uneventful. The ship called at the islands of Sarativa and Java and then sailed, via the Cape of Good Hope, to Sierra Leone and then on to Plymouth which he reached on 28th September 1580.

Drake's Route

Fig 2.1

The Printer

The computer is capable of simply printing the "facts" as they are depicted in the narrative. This in itself is not necessarily desirable, since a book would serve the purpose well enough. However, it is important that the computer can print because with this facility it can be programmed to ask questions, give answers and provide information, which in some cases may be an analysis of the answer to its own question. Consequently, it can be programmed to give map references and instruct the student to plot these on a map which is provided as part of the simulation. It can also describe events as they take place and instruct the student to make a note in the Captain's Log.

Example

PLOT/LOG   SET SAIL FROM PLYMOUTH 13TH DEC. 1577
                  REACH MOGADO 27TH DEC.
                  HERE YOU TRADE WITH THE MOORS. CAPTURE SPANISH
                  MERCHANT SHIPS. REPLACE THE CHRISTOPHER WITH
                  THE CAPTURED BENEDICT.
TYPE CON WHEN READY TO CONTINUE

The Decision Maker

The computer can be programmed to present the student with a decision-making situation. It can be programmed to say, "In this situation, would you do A, B or C?" The student responds by selecting and pressing one key, followed by the ACCEPT key or its equivalent. The computer can be further programmed to analyse the student's decision. In the simplest terms it can be told to say, "Correct" or "Incorrect," or "Good decision" or "Bad decision." It can also be programmed to explain why the decision was good or bad.

Example
I The computer prints:

DOUGHTY HAS BEEN STIRRING UP TROUBLE
AMONGST THE CREW . . . .
. . . .
DO YOU: A . . . .
          OR   B . . . .
          OR   C . . . .

II The student selects his/her response, e.g. A
III The computer then evaluates the response. It has been told:
  If the student chooses A, then print . . . .
  If the student chooses B, then print . . . .
  If the student chooses C, then print . . . .

The Problem

We apparently have a problem. If the student chooses C, all well and good because this is what actually happened. The computer can be programmed to acknowledge this "correct" response.

Should the student choose A or B, the computer apparently has to be programmed to give the results of a course of action which did not take place. Clearly, the history at this point becomes a fiction and the simulation is destined to fail as a teaching device.

The perverse nature of this situation is illustrated in Fig. 2.2.

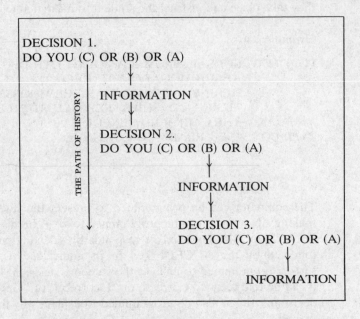

Fig. 2.2

The student begins by giving the "incorrect" response B. This triggers a sequence of bogus information, options and analysis.

The Key

This ever-increasing departure from the truth need not take place. The analysis of the "wrong" response can be constructed so that it explains why it is an unwise choice, what actually happened and why. The student is encouraged to suspend his/her disbelief and is instructed to continue as though a "correct" decision had been made, thus allowing the chronological sequence of events to unfold. This principle is demonstrated in Fig. 2.3, the Simulation Sequence.

**The Simulation
Sequence**

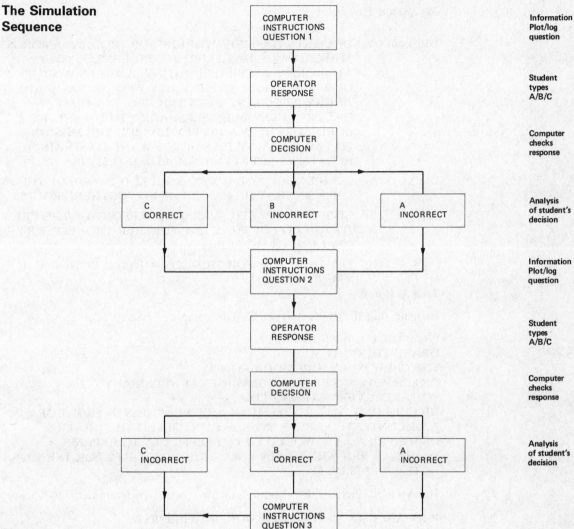

Fig 2.3

A Worked Example

DECISION 1.   DOUGHTY HAS BEEN STIRRING UP TROUBLE AMONGST THE CREW. HE HAS TRIED TO UNDERMINE YOUR AUTHORITY AND RAISE MUTINY (A TREASONABLE OFFENCE) AMONGST THE CREW WHO ARE ALREADY ANGRY AT HAVING BEEN TRICKED. DOUGHTY HAS PROBABLY BEEN PERSUADED TO DO THIS BY LORD BURGHLEY WHO WOULD LIKE THE MISSION TO FAIL BECAUSE HE DOESN'T WANT TO STRAIN RELATIONS BETWEEN ENGLAND AND SPAIN.

DO YOU (A)   SEND DOUGHTY BACK TO ENGLAND IN ONE OF THE SMAL SHIPS SO THAT HE CAN BE OF NO FURTHER TROUBLE.

(B)   GIVE HIM A PUBLIC WARNING IN FRONT OF THE CREW TO THE EFFECT THAT ANY FURTHER TROUBLE WILL BE DEALT WITH SEVERELY.

(C)   TRY DOUGHTY FOR TREASON AND EXECUTE HIM IF FOUND GUILTY.

Type A, B or C

Imagine that the student types C. The computer prints:

PROBABLY A WISE DECISION.
DRAKE THOUGHT SO.
THE CREW WERE A ROUGH CROWD.
DRAKE APPEARS TO HAVE THOUGHT IT NECESSARY
TO TAKE A VERY STRONG LINE.
HE COULDN'T AFFORD TO SHOW ANY WEAKNESS IN FRONT OF
A DISCONTENTED CREW, EVEN IF IT INVOLVED THE DEATH
OF HIS FRIEND. HE WOULD FIND IT DIFFICULT TO EXPLAIN
TO THE QUEEN WHY HE HAD NOT TRIED DOUGHTY FOR TREASON,
AS IT WAS HIS DUTY.

If A is selected the computer has been programmed to print:

PROBABLY AN UNWISE DECISION. IN THE FIRST
PLACE, THIS WOULD HAVE DEPLETED THE
FLEET AND CREW.
THE CREW WERE A ROUGH CROWD.
DRAKE APPEARS TO HAVE THOUGHT . . . .

The printout continues as for option C, ending with

AS IT WAS HIS DUTY.

Had B been selected the printout would have been as follows:

PROBABLY AN UNWISE MOVE.
THE CREW WERE A ROUGH CROWD.
DRAKE APPEARS TO HAVE THOUGHT . . . .

It continues as for options A and C, ending with

AS IT WAS HIS DUTY.

Note how basically the same analysis can be given for each student response. Whatever the outcome, the student has been instructed in the work booklet to proceed as if he/she had taken the same action as the real Drake.

Putting the two features together, the information given by the computer and the decision-making facility, gives the basis for the simulation.

The Decision Points

Six decision-making situations were incorporated into this simulation.

1 What should be done regarding Doughty's attempt at mutiny?
2 Should the Swan be broken up?
3 Which ship would the student like to sail the Straits of Magellan in? (Although in all probability this was not a decision which faced Drake, it does provide an opportunity for further student involvement since each ship suffered a different fate.)
4 Should Drake trust the Indian who offers to take him and his crew to a place where they can replenish their stores?
5 Which route should Drake take to get back to England?
6 What should he throw overboard in order to refloat when the ship runs aground?

Information Pertinent to the Decision

It is important that information which has some bearing on the decision to be taken should be made available to the student if possible. In the case of DRAKE this is done in the background information section of the booklet and in the printout prior to a decision. For example, before the first decision the student is told that the crew are a rough crowd, that they resented being tricked into undertaking the voyage, that mutiny was a treasonable offence, and that Doughty was a close friend of Drake. However, bearing in mind that one of the aims of the simulation is to stimulate student involvement in the history, the student is, in many ways being asked, "How would you have reacted in these situations? What would you have done? Could you have ordered the death of your friend? Would you have overvalued treasure to the point where you jeopardised the safety of yourself and others?" The student must not, therefore, necessarily expect to be able to deduce the "right" answers from a set of carefully arranged clues.

Where clues are given, it is possible that they have not been presented as part of the simulation. A study of Magellan's voyage some time before the Drake simulation might well have some bearing on the way that the student reacts to certain decisions. Obviously Drake would have been aware of the details of that voyage too. To some extent the way that background information is handled and introduced will depend upon the interests and imagination of the teacher concerned.

Scoring

The computer can be programmed to give a numerical value to each of the student's decisions, to memorise those values, to add them up, and to print them at the end of the simulation, comparing that score to the one achieved by the real Drake.

The scoring is arranged so that the course of action taken by the real Drake is always given the highest mark, the most sensible of the remaining choices the intermediate mark, and the least sensible choice the lowest mark.

In this simulation the weighting was as follows:

Decision 1	A	1 mark		
	B	2 marks		
	C	4 marks		
Decision 2	A	2 marks		
	B	4 marks		
Decision 3	A	4 marks		
	B	2 marks		
	C	Zero		
Decision 4	A	4 marks		
	B	2 marks		
Decision 5	A	3 marks	D	3 marks
	B	1 mark	E	1 mark
	C	4 marks		
Decision 6	A	Zero		
	B	4 marks		
	C	2 marks		

Using this weighting it is possible to score a maximum of 27 marks. Other than giving an indication of how well the student did in relation to the real Drake, the scoring routine has no significance—but this does not make it unimportant because students like to have an indication of the measure of their success. The feature might be used as a motivator, perhaps encouraging competition between groups for the title of "Best Captain".

The Double Decision

The normal process looks like Fig 2.4. Sometimes there would seem to be scope for a double decision where, having selected A, B or C, the student is then invited to make a second decision, choosing between the two possibilities previously rejected.

In DRAKE, such an opportunity presents itself with regard to the decision number 5, "Which route should Drake take back to England?" The possibilities open to Drake were

A   Return via the Pacific.
B   Return via the Straits of Magellan.
C   Return via the North-West Passage, if it exists.

What Drake actually decided to do was to sail North (C). When he had no success in finding the outlet of the supposed passage he sailed out across the Pacific, the southern route always being out of the question.

If the student chooses B or A, it seems necessary to comment on the

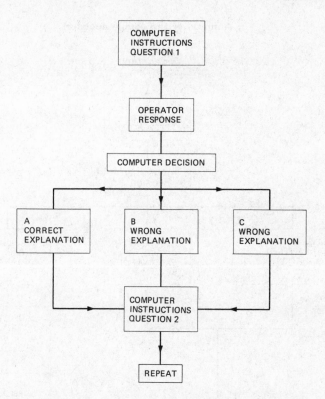

Fig 2.4

merits and demerits of that choice and to say what actually happened, finally instructing the student to sail North. However, if the choice was C, an historically correct response, it leaves us with an opportunity to force another decision, as must have faced the real Drake after he had sailed North and realised that he could not find the passage, by obliging the student to then decide between B and A, only then explaining why the southern route was out of the question.

The Double Decision is illustrated in Figs 2.5 and 2.6. Both are block-charts of the process. The second includes details from the text of DRAKE.

A model of the double decision

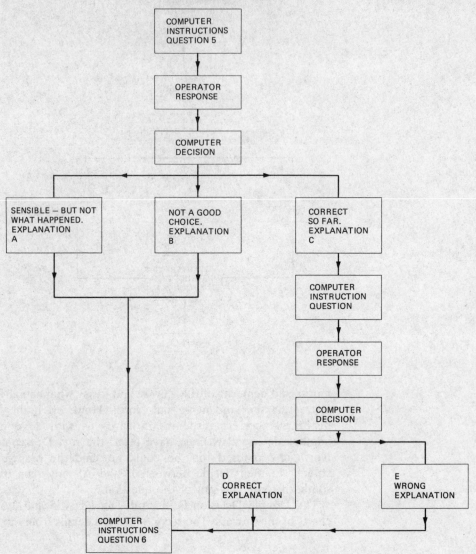

Fig 2.5

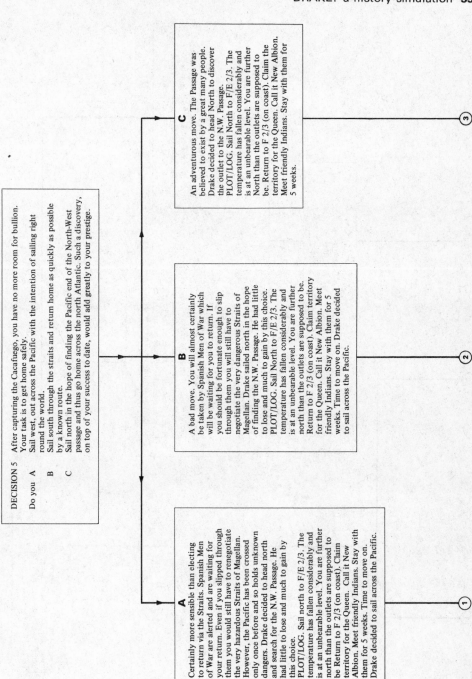

DECISION 5   After capturing the Cacafuego, you have no more room for bullion.
              Your task is to get home safely.

Do you   A   Sail west, out across the Pacific with the intention of sailing right
               round the world.

          B   Sail south through the straits and return home as quickly as possible
               by a known route.

          C   Sail north in the hope of finding the Pacific end of the North-West
               passage and thus go home across the north Atlantic. Such a discovery,
               on top of your success to date, would add greatly to your prestige.

A

Certainly more sensible than electing to return via the Straits. Spanish Men of War are alerted and are waiting for your return. Even if you slipped through them you would still have to renegotiate the very hazardous Straits of Magellan. However, the Pacific has been crossed only once before and so holds unknown dangers. Drake decided to head north and search for the N.W. Passage. He had little to lose and much to gain by this choice.

PLOT/LOG. Sail north to F/E 2/3. The temperature has fallen considerably and is at an unbearable level. You are further north than the outlets are supposed to be. Return to F 2/3 (on coast). Claim territory for the Queen. Call it New Albion. Meet friendly Indians. Stay with them for 5 weeks. Time to move on. Drake decided to sail across the Pacific.

B

A bad move. You will almost certainly be taken by Spanish Men of War which will be waiting for you to return. If you should be fortunate enough to slip through them you will still have to negotiate the very dangerous Straits of Magellan. Drake sailed north in the hope of finding the N.W. Passage. He had little to lose and much to gain by this choice.

PLOT/LOG. Sail North to F/E 2/3. The temperature has fallen considerably and is at an unbearable level. You are further north than the outlets are supposed to be. Return to F 2/3 (on coast). Claim territory for the Queen. Call it New Albion. Meet friendly Indians. Stay with them for 5 weeks. Time to sail across the Pacific.

C

An adventurous move. The Passage was believed to exist by a great many people. Drake decided to head North to discover the outlet to the N.W. Passage.

PLOT/LOG. Sail North to F/E 2/3. The temperature has fallen considerably and is at an unbearable level. You are further North than the outlets are supposed to be. Return to F 2/3 (on coast). Claim the territory for the Queen. Call it New Albion. Meet friendly Indians. Stay with them for 5 weeks.

①   ②   ③

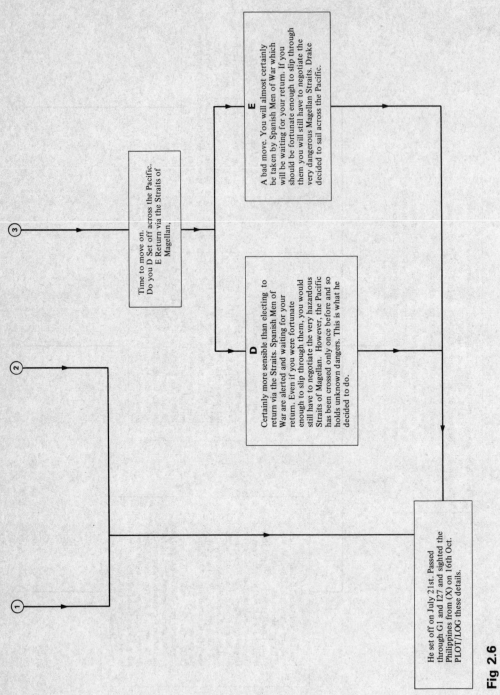

Fig 2.6

Basic

**The PRINT
Statement**

The first instruction that we shall consider is **PRINT**. It is very important and will figure in all programs because it determines the output to the printer on the teletype terminal or to the VDU. The majority of statements in DRAKE are PRINT statements. If, having observed operational procedures necessary prior to writing a program, we type PRINT and follow this with a sentence, the computer will note that at the appropriate moment it must print the contents of that line for the benefit of the person running the program. All of the output in the specimen run emanates from PRINT statements.

In addition to the word PRINT there are two other conventions to be observed when typing the sentence into the computer:

1 Each line of the program, whether or not it contains a PRINT statement, must begin with a line number. The computer operates on the instructions sequentially, unless instructed to do otherwise. It works through from the lowest to the highest line number. It is usual to increment the line numbers in tens. This allows us to introduce other lines into the program at a later stage if we wish, but there is no reason why they should not increase in ones, twos, fives, or whatever.
2 The second convention to remember is that all sentences must be enclosed by double quotation marks.

Example
20 PRINT "PLOT/LOG   SET SAIL FROM PLYMOUTH 13TH. DEC. 1577"
30 PRINT "   REACH MOGADO 27TH DEC."

If the line number is left out, the contents of that line are not retained as part of the program. Omitted quotation marks means that the program will not run. Some systems advise you of this as soon as you have asked the computer to accept the line, others do not let you know until you try to run the program.

We must have a means of letting the computer know that we have finished inputting a line. What we do is to press a specially marked key which does this job for us. On a terminal linked to an ICL 1900 series machine, this key is marked ACCEPT and you will see this referred to in many of the student's booklets accompanying the programs in this book. Other systems have a key marked RETURN. However it is marked there will be such a key. After pressing it, the line will be accepted and the computer will be ready to receive the next instruction.

The INPUT Statement

Because we are posing questions of the student and expecting answers there needs to be a way to communicate to the computer that it is to wait for and accept a message from the student. What could be more obvious than the statement **INPUT**. It will always be accompanied by a letter. This letter will have to be accompanied by a dollar or pound sign if what is to be typed in is a letter, word or combination of letters and numbers. All of the student input in DRAKE is a single letter or CON in order to continue.

Examples
70 PRINT "TYPE CON WHEN READY TO CONTINUE"
80 INPUT A£

460 PRINT "TYPE A,B OR C"
470 INPUT Q£

What the instruction is saying is, "Wait for someone to type something in and, when they do, label it with the letter accompanying the INPUT statement." Hereafter, until instructed to do otherwise, the computer will accept that A£ and Q£ refer to what has been typed in. The pound sign appears in the DRAKE program because it was written in a version of Basic called Southampton BASIC (SOBS). Other programs in the book use a dollar sign. The Research Machines 380Z uses a dollar sign. The fact that one is used rather than another is of no consequence.
Any of the letters of the alphabet could be used instead of A and Q.

The IF . . . THEN Control Statement

We have printed a message and accepted a reply. Now we need to be able to tell the computer what action to take depending upon the input. For example, where a student has been invited to input A, B or C, we need to be able to tell the computer what message to print if the input is A, what if the input is B, and what if the input is C. An **IF** control statement is used. Remember, the computer refers to the user's input by a letter accompanied by a pound sign. We do the same. The statement looks like this:

480 IF Q£ = "C" THEN 520
490 IF Q£ = "B" THEN 650
500 IF Q£ = "A" THEN 680

The first instruction is saying, "If Q£ (the name we have given to the input) is equal to C then go to line 520 and carry out the instruction there, which in this case is

520 PRINT "(C) PROBABLY NOT A WISE DECISION"

The other two IF statements behave in the same way, directing the computer under certain conditions to lines 650 and 680.

There is another convention to be observed here. If the input is what is called **alphanumeric** (i.e. anything other than a number to be used in a calculation), which A, B, C and CON clearly are, that with which Q£ or A£ is to be compared must be put in double quotation marks. If, when the computer reads an IF statement, the condition does not apply, it simply falls through and considers the next statement.

Instead of inviting the student to type in A, B or C in order to communicate a decision, the computer might have been programmed to print:

DECISION 1 DO YOU 1)............
2)............
3)............
TYPE 1, 2 OR 3

In this situation the variable in the INPUT statement does not require a pound or dollar sign. A letter unaccompanied by pound or dollar will be interpreted by the computer as a signal that a number is to be input.

Example
460 PRINT "TYPE 1, 2 OR 3"
470 INPUT Q

The computer, however, will not accept any input which is not a number.

The IF statement functions in the same way as before, but this time the letter, as in the input statement, does not take a pound or dollar sign and the value to which it is compared is not enclosed by quotation marks.

Example
480 IF Q = 3 THEN 520
490 IF Q = 2 THEN 650
500 IF Q = 1 THEN 680

We could, it should be noted, treat the numbers as alphanumeric characters and use INPUT Q£ and IF Q£ = "1" THEN 680.

The GOTO Control Statement

It was pointed out above that, if a condition in an IF statement did not apply, the computer would move on to the next instruction. What would happen if a student decided to type D or E or DON'T KNOW in response to an invitation to TYPE A, B or C? The answer is that the computer would carry on quite happily executing the instructions which followed the IF statements. We can avoid this by using a **GOTO** instruction. It does what it says. If the computer comes across this instruction accompanied by a line number, it goes to the line in question and executes the instruction which it finds there.

Example
```
460 PRINT "TYPE A, 'B OR C"
470 INPUT Q£
480 IF Q£ = "C" THEN 520
490 IF Q£ = "B" THEN 650
500 IF Q£ = "A" THEN 680
510 GOTO 460
```

It will not let you continue until A or B or C has been typed.

GOTO is not used exclusively in this role. It is a key statement which allows us to jump about the program, sometimes back a few lines, other times forwards. Very often, as in DRAKE, it is used to divert the computer from a piece of program or to jump back so that a piece of the program can be used again.

Consider this very simple example which is not drawn directly from the program.

```
10 PRINT "DOUGHTY HAS BEEN STIRRING UP TROUBLE"
20 PRINT "DO YOU A) SEND HIM HOME"
30 PRINT "          B) GIVE HIM A WARNING"
40 PRINT "          C) TRY HIM FOR TREASON"
50 PRINT "TYPE A, B OR C"
60 INPUT Q£
70 IF Q£ = "A" THEN 110
80 IF Q£ = "B" THEN 130
90 IF Q£ = "C" THEN 150
100 GOTO 50
110 PRINT "PROBABLY AN UNWISE DECISION"
120 GOTO 160
130 PRINT "AN UNWISE DECISION"
140 GOTO 160
150 PRINT "PROBABLY A WISE DECISION"
160 PRINT "THE FLEET IS TO SAIL SOUTH"
```

What would happen if the GOTO statements were not at lines 120 and 140? If the input at line 60 was C, nothing untoward would happen. But if the student had selected A, the output would have looked like this:

PROBABLY AN UNWISE DECISION
AN UNWISE DECISION
PROBABLY A WISE DECISION
THE FLEET IS TO SAIL SOUTH

By using GOTO this has been avoided. The program is written so that only the appropriate message will be printed, the others being by-passed.

The other way that it has been used is to allow us to use a piece of the program out of sequence. We shall develop the above program a little to illustrate this.

110 PRINT "PROBABLY AN UNWISE DECISION"
112 PRINT "DRAKE'S CREW WERE ROUGH AND"
113 PRINT "NEEDED FIRM DISCIPLINE. IT"
114 PRINT "WAS DRAKE'S DUTY TO TRY DOUGHTY"
120 GOTO 170
130 PRINT "AN UNWISE DECISION"
140 GOTO 112
150 PRINT "PROBABLY A WISE DECISION"
160 GOTO 112
170 PRINT "THE FLEET IS TO SAIL SOUTH"

New lines have been added: 112 to 114. The GOTO statements on lines 120 and 140 have been altered. A GOTO statement appears on line 160, and the previous contents of that line now appear on line 170.

Whatever is chosen, A, B or C, the student will be presented with the contents of lines 112 to 114. We could have programmed this information three times, but the GOTO statement has saved us the effort.

Not Equal To

The symbol to represent not equal to is < >.

It is often very convenient to phrase an IF statement as: IF A£ is not equal to something THEN go to this line. It is used in this way with the invitation to type CON to continue. If the input is not CON we want the user to type again. The sequence looks like this.

70 PRINT "TYPE CON TO CONTINUE"
80 INPUT Q£
90 IF Q£ < > "CON" THEN 70

Line 100 and subsequent lines will only be reached if the user types CON.

The LET Assignment Statement

When we input a letter, number, word or combination of characters and numbers, we **assign a variable** to it in order to give it a name. Remember that pure numbers require no pound or dollar sign, all other input does. This is not the only way to assign variables. A more obvious way is to use a **LET** statement. The statement can look like this:

LET B£ = "TYPE CON TO CONTINUE"

or like this:

LET B = 150

The second of the two examples shows the way that it would be used for a number to be used in a calculation. The first shows its use in what is called a **character string**. This will be composed of a letter, a word, some other character, a number not to be used in a calculation or some combination of these. The character string will be enclosed by double quotation marks in the LET statement.

Had B£ been established as "TYPE CON TO CONTINUE" at the beginning of the program we could have used it in the relevant print statements. Line 70, for example, could have read:

70 PRINT B£

Thus we could have economised on program size and typing time—a little. The LET statement has not been used this way in DRAKE but it is very important and will figure prominently in all of the programs which follow.

The way that it has been used is to assign a variable to a pure number, one which we wish to use in a simple calculation. Each of the options at the decision points is worth a number of marks. Each time a student inputs a decision we have to add the appropriate mark to a running total. This involves a small sum. The student (group) begins with a score of zero. As the simulation progresses we have to increment this by 1, 2, 3 or 4, depending upon the input. The symbol for addition is +. We can use it in the LET statement.

Example
LET T = 1
LET Q = 2
LET Z = T + Q   the result of this is 3

In the simulation we use only the variable T. T begins at line 10 as zero:

10 LET T = 0

If a student gives a response worth 1 point, we can say LET T = T + 1. This is the same as saying, now let T equal old T plus 1 (LET T = 0 + 1). If next time we want to add 2 to our running total, new T becomes old T plus 2 (LET T = 1 + 2).

The problem is in arranging for T to be incremented correctly and at the right moment. One way to do this is to use a subroutine.

The Subroutine

A **subroutine** is part of the program which is self-contained and in essence, if not literally, is detached from the main body of the program. It is there so that whenever that piece of program is required it can be dipped into, the relevant actions taken, and the computer returned to the main body of the program. The subroutines in DRAKE appear between lines 3740 and 3810.

```
3740 LET T = T + 1
3750 RETURN
3760 LET T = T + 2
3770 RETURN
3780 LET T = T + 3
3790 RETURN
3800 LET T = T + 4
3810 RETURN
```

After each input there is an instruction which reads GOSUB followed by a line number.

Example
```
530 GOSUB 3800
660 GOSUB 3760
710 GOSUB 3740
```

These instructions are interpreted to mean go to line .....

On arrival at the line included in the GOSUB statement, T is incremented. RETURN sends the computer back to the instruction immediately after the GOSUB instruction which it has just left. The value T can then be printed in line 3720.

3720 PRINT " YOUR SCORE IS ";T;"OUT OF 27."

The subroutines in DRAKE have allowed us to present the principle by using simple content. A more usual way to increment T would have been to use a LET statement in place of each of the GOSUB instructions.

Presentation of Output

Several assigned variables, and text, may be printed on a line by listing the items in a PRINT statement. The items are separated by either commas or semicolons and each has a different effect. The comma causes the print line to be broken up into 5 zones of 15 characters, and used after one item results in the following one being printed at the start of the next zone.

Example 1
```
LET X = 2
LET Y = 5
PRINT X,Y
```

The assigned variables X and Y will be printed as

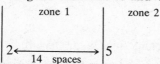

Example 2
LET A$ = "NUMBER IS"
LET B = 23
PRINT A$,B

The printout would be

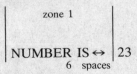

When the semicolon is used as a separator then the printing continues across the line without spaces between items. Most versions of Basic make an exception to this rule by automatically putting spaces before and after numeric items. This is done to facilitate the mixing of text and numbers. A further exception occurs in SOBS BASIC where the semicolon breaks the printing into zones of three-character width, but it is still convenient to think of the semicolon as causing the printing to "bunch up"

Example
LET A$ = "NUMBER IS"
LET B = 23
PRINT A$;B

The printout looks like this:

NUMBER IS 23

Text, assigned variables, commas and semicolons can all be used in one PRINT statement, depending on how the programmer designs his output. In DRAKE line 3720 reads

3720 PRINT " YOUR SCORE IS ";T;"OUT OF 27."

Blank Lines in the Printout

The presentation and readability of the printout can be improved by putting blank lines between sections. These have been used in DRAKE and it involves the simplest form of the PRINT instruction, where nothing follows the word PRINT.

Example
290 PRINT
300 PRINT

This results in two blank lines being "printed" before the next piece of text.

Program Listing

The program uses the most common features of Basic. It was written in Southampton BASIC for use on a teletype terminal allowing 72 characters to a line.

```
10   LET T=0
20   PRINT "PLOT/LOG    SET SAIL FROM PLYMOUTH. 13TH DEC. 1577"
30   PRINT "            REACH MOGADO 27TH DEC."
40   PRINT "            HERE YOU TRADE WITH THE MOORS. CAPTURE SPANISH"
50   PRINT "            MERCHANT SHIPS.REPLACE THE CHRISTOPHER WITH THE"
60   PRINT "            CAPTURED BENEDICT."
70   PRINT "TYPE CON WHEN READY TO CONTINUE"
80   INPUT A£
90   IF A£<>"CON" THEN 70
100  PRINT
110  PRINT
120  PRINT "PLOT/LOG    SAIL TO ISLAND OF MAYA (CAPE VERDE ISLANDS)"
130  PRINT "            CAPTURE PORTUGUESE SHIP LADEN WITH PROVISIONS."
140  PRINT "            PLACE A CREW OF 28 ON BOARD UNDER THE COMMAND"
150  PRINT "            OF YOUR CLOSE FRIEND THOMAS DOUGHTY."
160  PRINT "TYPE CON WHEN READY TO CONTINUE"
170  INPUT A£
180  IF A£<>"CON" THEN 160
190  PRINT
200  PRINT
210  PRINT "PLOT/LOG    SAIL TO RIO DE LA PLATA. ARRIVE APRIL 5TH."
220  PRINT "            SAIL TO PORT SAINT JULIAN. ARRIVE 19TH JUNE"
230  PRINT "TYPE CON TO CONTINUE."
240  INPUT A£
250  IF A£<>"CON" THEN 230
260  PRINT
270  PRINT "DECISION 1      DOUGHTY HAS BEEN STIRRING UP TROUBLE AMONGST"
280  PRINT "            THE CREW. HE HAS TRIED TO UNDERMINE YOUR"
290  PRINT "            AUTHORITY AND RAISE MUTINY ( A TREASONABLE"
300  PRINT "            OFFENCE ) AMONGST THE CREW WHO ARE ALREADY"
310  PRINT "            ANGRY AT HAVING BEEN TRICKED. DOUGHTY"
320  PRINT "            HAS PROBABLY BEEN PERSUADED TO DO THIS BY"
330  PRINT "            LORD BURGHLEY WHO WOULD LIKE THE MISSION"
340  PRINT "            TO FAIL BECAUSE HE DOESN'T WANT TO STRAIN"
350  PRINT "            RELATIONS BETWEEN ENGLAND AND SPAIN."
360  PRINT
370  PRINT "DO YOU [A] SEND DOUGHTY BACK TO ENGLAND IN ONE OF THE SMALL"
380  PRINT "            SHIPS SO THAT HE CAN BE OF NO FURTHER TROUBLE."
390  PRINT
400  PRINT "        [B] GIVE HIM A PUBLIC WARNING IN FRONT OF THE CREW"
410  PRINT "            TO THE EFFECT THAT ANY FURTHER TROUBLE WILL BE"
420  PRINT "            DEALT WITH SEVERELY."
430  PRINT
440  PRINT "        [C] TRY DOUGHTY FOR TREASON AND EXECUTE HIM IF"
450  PRINT "            FOUND GUILTY."
460  PRINT "TYPE A,B OR C"
470  INPUT Q£
480  IF Q£="C" THEN 520
490  IF Q£="B" THEN 650
500  IF Q£="A" THEN 680
510  GOTO 460
520  PRINT "[C]    PROBABLY A WISE DECISION."
530  GOSUB 3800
540  PRINT "            DRAKE THOUGHT SO."
550  PRINT "            THE CREW WERE A ROUGH CROWD."
560  PRINT "            DRAKE APPEARS TO HAVE THOUGHT IT NECESSARY"
570  PRINT "            TO TAKE A VERY STRONG LINE."
580  PRINT "            HE COULDN'T AFFORD TO SHOW ANY WEAKNESS IN FRONT OF"
590  PRINT "            A DISCONTENTED CREW, EVEN IF IT INVOLVED THE DEATH"
600  PRINT "            OF HIS FRIEND. HE WOULD FIND IT DIFFICULT TO EXPLAIN"
610  PRINT "            TO THE QUEEN WHY HE HAD NOT TRIED DOUGHTY FOR "
620  PRINT "            TREASON AS IT WAS HIS DUTY."
630  PRINT
```

```
640    GOTO 730
650    PRINT "[B]    PROBABLY AN UNWISE MOVE."
660    GOSUB 3760
670    GOTO 550
680    PRINT "[A]    PROBABLY AN UNWISE DECISION. IN THE FIRST "
690    PRINT "        PLACE, THIS WOULD HAVE DEPLETED THE"
700    PRINT "        FLEET AND CREW."
710    GOSUB 3740
720    GOTO 550
730    PRINT "DECISION 2    THE FLEET IS TO SAIL DOWN THE COAST"
740    PRINT "              AND THEN THROUGH THE STRAITS OF MAGELLAN"
750    PRINT "              INTO THE PACIFIC. THE STRAITS IS A DIFFICULT"
760    PRINT "              PIECE OF WATER AND ROUGH SEAS ARE EXPECTED."
770    PRINT "DO YOU [A]    TAKE ALL THE SHIPS THROUGH."
780    PRINT "       [B]    BREAK UP THE SWAN, THE BENEDICT AND THE"
790    PRINT "              CAPTURED PORTUGUESE VESSEL AND DISTRIBUTE THEIR"
800    PRINT "              SUPPLIES, USEFUL EQUIPMENT AND CREW AMONGST"
810    PRINT "              THE OTHER SHIPS."
820    PRINT "TYPE A OR B."
830    INPUT Q£
840    IF Q£="A" THEN 870
850    IF Q£="B" THEN 980
860    GOTO 820
870    PRINT "[A]    PROBABLY A BAD DECISION."
880    GOSUB 3760
890    PRINT "        IT IS QUITE LIKELY THAT ONE OR MORE SHIPS WILL BE"
900    PRINT "        BADLY DAMAGED, SUNK OR SEPARATED FROM THE REST."
910    PRINT "        IF THE SUPPLY SHIP IS LOST THIS WOULD CREATE SERIOUS"
920    PRINT "        PROBLEMS FOR THE REMAINING CREWS."
930    PRINT "        DRAKE CLEARLY BELIEVED IT UNWISE TO HAVE ALL HIS EGGS"
940    PRINT "        IN ONE BASKET AND ORDERED THAT THE SWAN AND THE "
950    PRINT "        SMALLER SHIPS SHOULD BE BROKEN UP."
960    PRINT
970    GOTO 1010
980    PRINT "[B]    UNDER THE CIRCUMSTANCES, A GOOD DECISION."
990    GOSUB 3800
1000   GOTO 890
1010   PRINT "PLOT/LOG    THE PELICAN, ELIZABETH AND MARIGOLD SET SAIL"
1020   PRINT "            FROM PORT ST. JULIAN 17TH. AUG. ARRIVE AT THE"
1030   PRINT "            STRAITS OF MAGELLAN."
1040   PRINT
1050   PRINT "DECISION 3.  BEFORE ENTERING THE STRAITS, DECIDE"
1060   PRINT "             WHICH SHIP YOU WISH TO SAIL IN."
1070   PRINT "WILL YOU SAIL IN [A] THE PELICAN."
1080   PRINT "                 [B] THE ELIZABETH."
1090   PRINT "                 [C] THE MARIGOLD."
1100   PRINT "TYPE A,B OR C."
1110   INPUT A£
1120   IF A£="A" THEN 1160
1130   IF A£="B" THEN 1370
1140   IF A£="C" THEN 1440
1150   GOTO 1100
1160   PRINT "[A]    A WISE CHOICE."
1170   GOSUB 3800
1180   PRINT "        THE FLEET RUNS INTO A GALE AND THE MARIGOLD"
1190   PRINT "        IS LOST WITH ALL HANDS."
1200   PRINT "        THE PELICAN AND THE ELIZABETH BEAT THE STORM AND"
1210   PRINT "        REACH THE PACIFIC ON 6TH. SEPT."
1220   PRINT "        THEY SHELTER IN A BAY."
1230   PRINT "        HOWEVER, THE PELICAN (NOW NAMED THE GOLDEN HIND)"
1240   PRINT "        DRIFTS FROM HER MOORING AND IS FORCED SOUTH WHERE"
1250   PRINT "        SHE REACHES CAPE HORN (P7/8) ON 28TH OCT."
1260   PRINT "PLOT/LOG    ENTRY INTO PACIFIC AND GOLDEN HIND'S JOURNEY"
1270   PRINT "            TO CAPE HORN."
1280   PRINT "TYPE CON WHEN READY TO CONTINUE."
1290   INPUT A£
1300   IF A£<>"CON" THEN 1280
```

```
1310   IF A£="B" THEN 1400
1320   IF A£="C" THEN 1460
1330   PRINT "THE ELIZABETH WAITS FOR YOU TO REAPPEAR AND THEN, WHEN"
1340   PRINT "YOU DON'T TURN UP, SHE RETURNS TO ENGLAND."
1350   PRINT
1360   GOTO 1490
1370   PRINT "[B] A GOOD CHOICE,BUT YOU MISS THE ACTION IN THE PACIFIC."
1380   GOSUB 3760
1390   GOTO 1180
1400   PRINT "YOU WAIT FOR THE GOLDEN HIND TO REAPPEAR. WHEN SHE DOESN'T"
1410   PRINT "YOU TURN BACK AND RETURN TO ENGLAND."
1420   PRINT "CONTINUE AS THOUGH YOU ELECTED TO SAIL IN THE PELICAN."
1430   GOTO 1490
1440   PRINT "[C]    THE FLEET RUNS INTO A GALE AND THE MARIGOLD"
1450   GOTO 1190
1460   PRINT "THE ELIZABETH WAITED FOR THE GOLDEN HIND TO REAPPEAR AND"
1470   PRINT "THEN, WHEN IT DIDN'T SHOW UP, SHE RETURNED TO ENGLAND."
1480   GOTO 1420
1490   PRINT "PLOT/LOG    DEPART CAPE HORN 30TH OCT."
1500   PRINT "           SAIL NORTH. SUPPLIES RUNNING LOW."
1510   PRINT "           SEARCH VARIOUS ISLANDS FOR FOOD. NO LUCK."
1520   PRINT "           EVENTUALLY ENCOUNTER AN INDIAN.(N/M7)."
1530   PRINT "           HE INDICATES THAT HE CAN TAKE YOU TO"
1540   PRINT "           A PLACE WHERE THERE IS FOOD."
1550   PRINT
1560   PRINT "DECISION 4    DO YOU A) TRUST HIM AND FOLLOW (HE MIGHT"
1570   PRINT "                       LEAD YOU INTO A TRAP.)"
1580   PRINT "                    B) KILL THE INDIAN AND CONTINUE"
1590   PRINT "                       YOUR SEARCH."
1600   PRINT "TYPE A OR B"
1610   INPUT Q£
1620   IF Q£="B" THEN 1720
1630   IF Q£="A" THEN 1650
1640   GOTO 1600
1650   PRINT "BOLD MOVE.THIS IS WHAT DRAKE DID.THE INDIAN DIRECTED HIM"
1660   GOSUB 3800
1670   PRINT "TO VALPARAISO (PLOT M7) AND HE TOOK STORES"
1680   PRINT "WINE AND CEDARWOOD FROM THIS SMALL SETTELEMENT. HE WAS"
1690   PRINT "IN LUCK. THE TREASURE SHIP 'THE GRAND CAPTAIN OF THE SEA'"
1700   PRINT "WAS ANCHORED THERE. HE TOOK 400LB OF GOLD FROM IT."
1710   GOTO 1790
1720   PRINT "[B] NOT A WISE CHOICE"
1730   GOSUB 3760
1740   PRINT "DRAKE WAS IN A DIFFICULT POSITION. HE NEEDED FRESH STORES"
1750   PRINT "AND WAS HAVING LITTLE SUCCESS HIMSELF. HE WAS OBLIGED"
1760   PRINT "TO TRUST THE INDIAN. HIS MEN WERE ARMED AND HE COULD HOPE"
1770   PRINT "TO FIGHT HIS WAY OUT OF TROUBLE. HE WAS TAKEN"
1780   GOTO 1670
1790   PRINT
1800   PRINT "PLOT/LOG    SAIL NORTH TO COQUIMBO. 300 HORSEMEN"
1810   PRINT "           AND 200 FOOT SOLDIERS ARE WAITING FOR YOU."
1820   PRINT "           CLEARLY YOU CAN'T RELY ON THE ELEMENT OF"
1830   PRINT "           SURPRISE ANYMORE, HAVING GIVEN YOUR PRESENCE"
1840   PRINT "           AWAY. SEND 14 MEN ASHORE TO COLLECT WATER."
1850   PRINT "           ONE MAN IS KILLED. YOU WITHDRAW AND PULL IN"
1860   PRINT "           AT A NEARBY BAY TO BUILD A PINNACE."
1870   PRINT "TYPE CON TO CONTINUE."
1880   INPUT A£
1890   IF A£<>"CON" THEN 1870
1900   PRINT "PLOT/LOG    SET SAIL 19TH JAN. 1579. HEAD NORTH. LAND (L7)"
1910   PRINT "           TARAPACA. TAKE SIX BARS OF SILVER FROM MEN"
1920   PRINT "           YOU FIND SLEEPING."
1930   PRINT "TYPE CON TO CONTINUE."
1940   INPUT A£
1950   IF A£<>"CON" THEN 1930
1960   PRINT "PLOT/LOG    SAIL NORTH TO L/K 6/7"
1970   PRINT "           CAPTURE 800LB. OF SILVER WHICH IS BEING TRANS-"
```

```
1980  PRINT "             PORTED BY TWO MEN."
1990  PRINT "TYPE CON TO CONTINUE."
2000  INPUT A£
2010  IF A£<>"CON" THEN 1990
2020  PRINT "PLOT/LOG   SAIL NORTH. REACH CALLAO 10TH FEB. YOU"
2030  PRINT "           FIND 12 MERCHANT SHIPS AT ANCHOR. YOU PLUNDER"
2040  PRINT "           THESE, TAKING PLATE, SILK AND LINEN. THEN"
2050  PRINT "           YOU CUT THE CABLES OF SHIPS IN THE HARBOUR TO"
2060  PRINT "           PREVENT PURSUIT WHILST YOU TAKE OFF IN PERSUIT"
2070  PRINT "           OF A TREASURE SHIP CACAFUEGO WHICH YOU LEARNT"
2080  PRINT "           ABOUT AT CALLAO."
2090  PRINT "TYPE CON TO CONTINUE."
2100  INPUT A£
2110  IF A£<>"CON" THEN 2090
2120  PRINT "PLOT/LOG   CACAFUEGO CAPTURED(J/K5/6).SET CREW FREE.PUT"
2130  PRINT "           SOME OF YOUR OWN CREW ON BOARD AND SAIL OUT TO"
2140  PRINT "           SEA FOR TWO DAYS BEFORE TRANSFERRING BOOTY"
2150  PRINT "           TO YOUR OWN SHIP."
2160  PRINT "TYPE CON TO CONTINUE."
2170  INPUT A£
2180  IF A£<>"CON" THEN 2160
2190  PRINT "DECISION 5  YOU HAVE NO MORE ROOM FOR TREASURE."
2200  PRINT "           YOUR TASK IS TO GET HOME SAFELY."
2210  PRINT "DO YOU [A] SAIL WEST, OUT ACROSS THE PACIFIC WITH THE"
2220  PRINT "           INTENTION OF SAILING RIGHT ROUND THE WORLD."
2230  PRINT "       [B] SAIL SOUTH THROUGH THE STRAITS AND RETURN"
2240  PRINT "           HOME AS QUICKLY AS POSSIBLE BY A KNOWN ROUTE."
2250  PRINT "       [C] SAIL NORTH IN THE HOPE OF FINDING THE PACIFIC"
2260  PRINT "           END OF THE NORTHWEST PASSAGE AND THUS GO HOME"
2270  PRINT "           ACROSS THE NORTH ATLANTIC. SUCH A DISCOVERY ON"
2280  PRINT "           TOP OF YOUR SUCCESS TO DATE WOULD ADD GREATLY"
2290  PRINT "           TO YOUR PRESTIGE."
2300  PRINT "TYPE A, B OR C."
2310  INPUT Q£
2320  IF Q£="C" THEN 2360
2330  IF Q£="B" THEN 2810
2340  IF Q£="A" THEN 2660
2350  GOTO 2300
2360  PRINT "[C] AN ADVENTUROUS MOVE. THE PASSAGE WAS BELIEVED TO EXIST"
2370  GOSUB 3800
2380  PRINT "   BY A GREAT MANY PEOPLE. DRAKE DECIDED TO HEAD NORTH TO"
2390  PRINT "   DISCOVER THE OUTLET OF THE NW. PASSAGE."
2400  PRINT
2410  PRINT
2420  PRINT "PLOT/LOG   SAIL NORTH TO F/E2/3. THE TEMPERATURE"
2430  PRINT "           HAS FALLEN CONSIDERABLY AND IS AT"
2440  PRINT "           AN UNBEARABLE LEVEL. YOU ARE FURTHER"
2450  PRINT "           NORTH THAN THE OUTLETS ARE SUPPOSED TO BE."
2460  PRINT "TYPE CON TO CONTINUE."
2470  INPUT A£
2480  IF A£<>"CON" THEN 2460
2490  PRINT "PLOT/LOG   RETURN TO F2/3 (ON COAST). CLAIM TERRITORY"
2500  PRINT "           FOR THE QUEEN. CALL IT NEW ALBION."
2510  PRINT "           MEET FRIENDLY INDIANS. STAY WITH THEM FOR"
2520  PRINT "           5 WEEKS"
2530  PRINT "TYPE CON TO CONTINUE."
2540  INPUT Z£
2550  IF Z£<>"CON" THEN 2530
2560  PRINT "TIME TO MOVE ON."
2570  IF Q£="A" THEN 2890
2580  IF Q£="B" THEN 2890
2590  PRINT "DO YOU [D] SET OFF ACROSS THE PACIFIC."
2600  PRINT "       [E] RETURN VIA THE STRAITS OF MAGELLAN."
2610  PRINT "TYPE D OR E."
2620  INPUT S£
2630  IF S£="D" THEN 2660
2640  IF S£="E" THEN 2810
2650  GOTO 2610
```

```
2660    PRINT "CERTAINLY MORE SENSIBLE THAN ELECTING TO RETURN VIA"
2670    IF Q£="C" THEN 2690
2680    GOSUB 3780
2690    PRINT "    THE STRAITS. SPANISH MEN OF WAR ARE ALERTED AND"
2700    PRINT "    WAITING FOR YOUR RETURN. EVEN IF YOU SLIPPED THROUGH"
2710    PRINT "    THEM YOU WOULD STILL HAVE TO RENEGOTIATE THE VERY"
2720    PRINT "    HAZARDOUS STRAITS OF MAGELLAN.HOWEVER,THE PACIFIC HAS"
2730    PRINT "    BEEN CROSSED ONLY ONCE AND HOLDS UNKNOWN DANGERS."
2740    IF Q£="A" THEN 2930
2750    PRINT "    THIS IS WHAT HE DECIDED TO DO."
2760    PRINT "    HE SET OFF ON JULY 21ST. PASSED THROUGH G1 AND I27"
2770    PRINT "    AND SIGHTED"
2780    PRINT "    THE PHILIPPINES FROM (X) ON 16TH OCT."
2790    PRINT "PLOT/LOG THESE DETAILS."
2800    GOTO 2960
2810    PRINT "A BAD MOVE. YOU WILL ALMOST CERTAINLY BE TAKEN BY  "
2820    IF Q£="A" THEN 2840
2830    GOSUB 3740
2840    PRINT "    SPANISH MEN OF WAR WHICH WILL BE WAITING FOR YOU"
2850    PRINT "    TO RETURN. IF YOU SHOULD BE FORTUNATE ENOUGH TO SLIP"
2860    PRINT "    THROUGH THEM YOU WILL STILL HAVE TO NEGOTIATE"
2870    PRINT "    THE VERY DANGEROUS MAGELLAN STRAITS."
2880    IF Q£="B" THEN 2910
2890    PRINT "    DRAKE DECIDED TO SAIL ACROSS THE PACIFIC."
2900    GOTO 2760
2910    PRINT "    DRAKE SAILED NORTH HOPING TO FIND THE N.W. PASSAGE."
2920    GOTO 2420
2930    PRINT "    DRAKE HEADED NORTH TO SEARCH FOR THE N.W. PASSAGE."
2940    PRINT "    HE HAD LITTLE TO LOSE AND MUCH TO GAIN BY THIS CHOICE."
2950    GOTO 2420
2960    PRINT "TYPE CON TO CONTINUE."
2970    INPUT A£
2980    IF A£<>"CON" THEN 2960
2990    PRINT "PLOT/LOG  SAIL TO THE ISLAND OF TERNATE IN THE"
3000    PRINT "          MOLUCCAS, THE HOME OF THE SPICE"
3010    PRINT "          PLANTATIONS. NO ENGLISH SHIPS HAVE REACHED THEM"
3020    PRINT "          BEFORE. THE PORTUGUESE HAVE JUST BEEN EXPELLED"
3030    PRINT "          AND YOU ARE ABLE TO MAKE A TRADE AGREEMENT"
3040    PRINT "          WITH THE KING. HE GIVES YOU SIX TONS OF CLOVES."
3050    PRINT "TYPE CON TO CONTINUE."
3060    INPUT A£
3070    IF A£<>"CON" THEN 3050
3080    PRINT "PLOT/LOG  SET SAIL NOV. 19TH. ANCHOR OFF THE CELEBES"
3098    PRINT "          AT CRAB ISLAND ON 10TH. DEC. FROM HERE ON THERE"
3100    PRINT "          WILL BE DANGER OF ATTACK BY PORTUGUESE"
3110    PRINT "          NAVAL VESSELS AND PIRATE SHIPS."
3120    PRINT "TYPE CON TO CONTINUE."
3130    INPUT A£
3140    IF A£<>"CON" THEN 3120
3150    PRINT "PLOT/LOG    SET SAIL 12TH. DEC."
3160    PRINT "            RUN AGROUND (K23) JAN. 9TH 1580"
3170    PRINT "TYPE CON TO CONTINUE."
3180    INPUT A£
3190    IF A£<>"CON" THEN 3170
3200    PRINT "DECISION 6 YOU MUST REFLOAT THE SHIP QUICKLY."
3210    PRINT "           IT MIGHT SINK AT ANY TIME. IN ORDER TO REFLOAT"
3220    PRINT "           YOU MUST LIGHTEN THE SHIP."
3230    PRINT "DO YOU ORDER MEN TO THROW OVERBOARD:-"
3240    PRINT "[A] SIX TONS OF CLOVES AND 4 CANNONS."
3250    PRINT "[B] 3 TONS OF CLOVES, 8 CANNONS, THEN TREASURE AND MEAL"
3260    PRINT "    UNTIL SHE REFLOATS."
3270    PRINT "[C] CANNON UNTIL SHE FLOATS. (THIS WILL MEAN A LOSS OF 14"
3280    PRINT "    CANNONS)."
3290    PRINT "TYPE A, B OR C."
3300    INPUT Q£
3310    IF Q£="A" THEN 3350
3320    IF Q£="B" THEN 3490
3330    IF Q£="C" THEN 3520
3340    GOTO 3290
```

```
3350   PRINT "[A] NOT ENOUGH. SHIP BREAKS UP BEFORE YOU CAN THROW"
3360   PRINT "    MORE OVERBOARD."
3370   PRINT "    SUNK......"
3380   PRINT "    DRAKE JETTISONED 3 TONS OF CLOVES, 8 GUNS, SOME OF THE"
3390   PRINT "    TREASURE AND SOME SUGAR AND MEAL."
3400   PRINT "    DRAKE SEEMS TO HAVE FAVOURED A BALANCE, REALIZING THAT"
3410   PRINT "    HE MUST KEEP A SUFFICIENT NUMBER OF GUNS TO ENSURE HIS"
3420   PRINT "    SAFETY AND THAT HE COULD RETAIN AN ADEQUATE"
3430   PRINT "    AMOUNT OF TREASURE TO MAKE THE VOYAGE PROFITABLE. THE"
3440   PRINT "    CLOVES WERE VERY VALUABLE AND"
3450   PRINT "    SHOWED PROOF OF HIS TRADE AGREEMENT AND THE GOOD WILL"
3460   PRINT "    OF THE KING."
3470   PRINT
3480   GOTO 3570
3490   PRINT "[B] A WISE CHOICE."
3500   GOSUB 3800
3510   GOTO 3400
3520   PRINT "[C] YOU REFLOAT BUT SINCE YOU SET SAIL WITH ONLY 18 GUNS"
3530   GOSUB 3760
3540   PRINT "    YOU ARE UNLIKELY TO BE ABLE TO PROTECT YOURSELF FROM"
3550   PRINT "    PORTUGUESE MEN OF WAR AND PIRATES."
3560   GOTO 3400
3570   PRINT "PLOT/LOG    SAIL TO JAVA"
3580   PRINT "           SAIL TO CAPE OF GOOD HOPE."
3590   PRINT "           SAIL TO SIERRA LEONE. ARRIVE"
3600   PRINT "           22ND. JULY."
3610   PRINT "           TAKE ON WATER, FRUITS AND OYSTERS."
3620   PRINT "PLOT/LOG    SAIL FOR HOME. REACH PLYMOUTH 28TH SEPT. 1580."
3630   PRINT "TYPE CON TO CONTINUE."
3640   INPUT A£
3650   IF A£<>"CON" THEN 3630
3660   PRINT "EACH OF YOUR CHOICES HAS BEEN MARKED. THE COURSES"
3670   PRINT "OF ACTION TAKEN BY DRAKE CARRY THE HIGHEST MARKS. THE"
3680   PRINT "OTHER MARKS ARE AWARDED DEPENDING UPON HOW SENSIBLE YOUR"
3690   PRINT "CHOICES WERE."
3700   PRINT "IF ALL YOUR DECISIONS WERE THE SAME AS DRAKE'S, YOU COULD"
3710   PRINT "SCORE 27 MARKS."
3720   PRINT "YOUR SCORE IS ";T;"OUT OF 27."
3730   GOTO 3820
3740   LET T=T+1
3750   RETURN
3760   LET T=T+2
3770   RETURN
3780   LET T=T+3
3790   RETURN
3800   LET T=T+4
3810   RETURN
3820   END
```

3 GAS: a simulation of Andrews' Experiment

Introduction

GAS is a simulated physics experiment and it takes particular advantage of two programming features, namely Calculations and Loops. They are combined to produce a **table of results**. Tables of results can form the basis of many educational packages, and it is the intention here to demonstrate one such application. However, the formula, figures and physics content might be rather intimidating for the non-scientific reader, especially since Andrews' Experiment, on which the simulation is based, is undertaken by sixth formers. Because of this, the Basic pages which follow set out to explain in a very simple way how the computer carries out calculations (addition, multiplication, subtraction, division and exponentiation), how loops operate, and how tables of results are generated. As a result, the non-scientist might reasonably expect to follow the GAS description, having first studied the programming techniques involved. Loops, it might be noted, are extremely important and feature in many of the programs described in this book.

The reader's ability to follow the programs in later chapters depends upon an understanding of the Basic, not on an understanding of Andrews' Experiment. The various arithmetic functions have been demonstrated in a series of short programs, the computer responding to instructions which correspond to the mathematical symbols. Each program is annotated on the right-hand side in lower case letters.

Some additional information is also given on the use of the PRINT statement which enables greater control of the printout.

Basic   *Calculations*

Program to calculate the sum of two numbers
(The symbol + means add)

```
10 PRINT "TYPE A NUMBER"
20 INPUT V                        e.g.2
30 PRINT "TYPE ANOTHER NUMBER"
40 INPUT X                        e.g.3
50 LET U = V + X                  U = 2 + 3
60 PRINT U                        Prints 5
```

50 is the important line. It shows that the computer recognises the symbol +
and that the line is constructed in an obvious form.

Program to subtract one number from another
(The symbol − means subtract)

10 PRINT "TYPE THE NUMBER TO BE SUBTRACTED FROM"	
20 INPUT U	e.g.5
30 PRINT "TYPE THE NUMBER TO BE SUBTRACTED"	
40 INPUT B	e.g.4
50 LET Z = U − B	Z = 5 − 4
60 PRINT Z	Prints 1

Program to multiply two numbers
(The symbol * means multiply)

10 PRINT "TYPE THE FIRST NUMBER"	
20 INPUT R	e.g.5
30 PRINT "TYPE THE SECOND NUMBER"	
40 INPUT T	e.g.8
50 LET F = R * T	F = 5 × 8
60 PRINT F	Prints 40

Program to divide one number by another
(The symbol / means divide)

10 PRINT "TYPE NUMBER TO BE DIVIDED"	
20 INPUT F	e.g.40
30 PRINT "WHAT IS IT TO BE DIVIDED BY?"	
40 INPUT V	e.g.2
50 LET K = F/V	K = 40 ÷ 2
60 PRINT K	Prints 20

The computer can handle a calculation on a PRINT line, thus allowing us to
dispense with the LET statement which appears in line 50 of each of the
previous programs.

Example

```
10 PRINT "TYPE A NUMBER"
20 INPUT V                      e.g.2
30 PRINT "TYPE A SECOND NUMBER"
40 INPUT X                      e.g.3
50 PRINT V+X                    Prints 5
```

Program to demonstrate exponentiation
(The symbol ↑ or ∗∗ can be used to mean "to the power of")

```
10 PRINT "TYPE A NUMBER"
20 INPUT A                      e.g.3
30 LET X = 2 ↑ A                X = 2³ or 2×2×2
40 PRINT X                      Prints 8
```

Note: line 30 could read LET $X = 2**A$.
It could also read PRINT $2 ↑ A$, combining the functions of
lines 30 and 40.

It is possible to carry out related arithmetic operations on a single line.

```
10 PRINT "HOW MANY PEOPLE ARE COMING TO THE PARTY?"
20 INPUT A                                          e.g. 50
30 PRINT "HOW MANY MINCE PIES WILL EACH EAT?"
40 INPUT B                                          e.g. 4
50 PRINT "HOW MANY PIES DO YOU WANT IN RESERVE?"
60 INPUT C                                          e.g. 50
70 LET D = (A∗B)+C                                  D = (50×4)+50
80 PRINT "YOU WILL NEED TO BUY ";D;"PIES."          ...to buy
                                                    250 pies
```

THE PREFERRED SEQUENCE

The use of brackets is important because
1 Brackets are calculated first, then
2 Exponents, then
3 Multiplication and Division, then
4 Addition and Subtraction.
N.B. If the operations in a sequence are of equal standing, then they are performed from left
to right.

Computer arithmetic also includes **comparisons**:

IF A = B THEN ... If A is equal to B then
IF A > B THEN ... If A is greater than B then
IF A < B THEN ... If A is less than B then
IF A > = B THEN ... If A is greater than or equal to B then
IF A < = B THEN ... If A is less than or equal to B then
IF A < > B THEN ... If A is not equal to B then

Comparisons are made in IF ... THEN Statements.

Example

```
 10 PRINT "TYPE IN TWO NUMBERS"
 20 INPUT A,B                         e.g. 5, 11
 30 IF A = B THEN 70
 40 IF A < B THEN 90
 50 IF A > B THEN 110
 60 GOTO 120
 70 PRINT A; "IS EQUAL TO"; B
 80 GOTO 120
 90 PRINT A; "IS LESS THAN "; B
100 GOTO 120
110 PRINT A; "IS GREATER THAN"; B
120 END
```

The program would jump from line 40 to line 90, and the printout would be

5 IS LESS THAN 11

GAS takes advantage of the ability of the computer to deal with related arithmetic operations, and centres on the use of the formula:

600 LET P = (R * T)/(U − B) − A/(U * * 2)

This operation is carried out bracket by bracket, but within a bracket, the computer will calculate

  * * first, * and / second, and + and − last.

The elements of line 600 will be handled in the order shown in Fig 3.1.

This formula is repeated several times, the value U changing each time. As a result, a table of figures can be produced. In order to get the computer to repeat the operation the required number of times in the most efficient way, what is known as a LOOP is used.

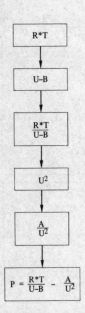

Fig 3.1 (U is calculated in line 590 LET U = V * X)

Loops

For the sake of simplicity, let us produce a program to print a multiplication table up to 12 times the number involved. The following four lines of program will cope with the first "sum":

10 PRINT " WHICH NUMBER DO YOU WANT A TABLE FOR?"	
20 INPUT A	e.g. 2
30 LET B = A ∗ 1	B = 2 × 1
40 PRINT B	Prints 2

To get the table to reach 2 × 12 we might consider continuing in the following way:

50 LET B = A ∗ 2	B = 2 × 2
60 PRINT B	Prints 4
70 LET B = A ∗ 3	B = 2 × 3
80 PRINT B	Prints 6
90 LET B = A ∗ 4	B = 2 × 4
100 PRINT B	Prints 8
etc.	

This is clearly a moderately lengthy and tedious piece of programming, even if we remove the LET statements and use, for example PRINT A ∗ 2, PRINT A ∗ 3, etc. The problem becomes more acute as the size of the table increases. Imagine the length of a program to produce a Two Times Table from 2 times 1, to 2 times 1000. By using a **LOOP** we can a) shorten the program and b) make it more flexible.

The two statements we must use are

FOR I = 1 to ?

and

NEXT I

There is a question mark in the FOR statement because in this space goes a value which is determined by the programmer or the user. In our example we will put

FOR I = 1 to 12

(because we want our program to make 12 calculations). In theory, we can use any letter of the alphabet in the I position, but letters already used should be avoided in case values are confused.

The first of these two statements is placed on the line before the part of the program which is to be repeated and the second statement immediately follows that section.

Example

```
10 PRINT "WHICH NUMBER DO YOU WANT A TABLE FOR?"
20 INPUT A
30 FOR I = 1 TO 12
40 LET B = A * I
50 PRINT B
60 NEXT I
```

The first time the computer reads line 30 it will interpret the content of that line to mean, "Let the letter I equal 1 this time and, if you come across the statement NEXT I, come back to line 30 but let I equal 2, and if you come across NEXT I again, come back to line 30 but this time let I equal 3, and so on. When at some point I is equal to 12, fall through the NEXT I instruction to the next line."

If line 30 had read FOR I = 1 to 100, the computer would perform the loop one hundred times; I increasing from 1 to 100.

This is how it works in our simple program:

```
10 PRINT "WHICH NUMBER DO YOU WANT A TABLE FOR?"
20 INPUT A                              e.g.2
30 FOR I = 1 TO 12                      I = 1
40 LET B = A * I                        B = 2 × 1
50 PRINT B                              Prints 2
60 NEXT I
```

NEXT I sends the computer back to line 30 with the following result:

```
30 FOR I = 1 TO 12                      I now equals 2
40 LET B = A * I                        B = 2 × 2
50 PRINT B                              Prints 4
60 NEXT I
```

NEXT I sends the computer back to line 30 with the following result:

```
30 FOR I = 1 TO 12                      I now equals 3
40 LET B = A * I                        B = 2 × 3
50 PRINT B                              Prints 6
60 NEXT I
```

This process will continue until I = 12 and B = 24. The I, we can see, having been defined in line 30, can be used in line 40

Using the FOR Loop to Introduce an Element of Flexibility

This can be done by

1 Making the FOR line read FOR I = 1 TO N.
2 Introducing an additional PRINT statement.
3 Introducing an additional INPUT statement.

The simple Multiplication Table program would look like this:

10 PRINT "WHICH NUMBER DO YOU WANT A TABLE FOR?"
20 INPUT A   e.g. 2
30 PRINT "HOW MANY TIMES DO YOU WANT ";A; "MULTIPLIED?"
                                              The value A will be printed as 2.
40 INPUT N   e.g. 50
50 FOR I = 1 TO N   FOR I = 1 TO 50
60 LET B = A∗I   B = 2×(value of I)
70 PRINT B   Prints value of B.
80 NEXT I   Returns program to line 50.

The program can now produce a table, the length of which is determined by the user.

Allowing the end value of a LOOP to be variable is only one example of the flexibility which is possible. The starting value can also be made variable if another INPUT statement is used.

10 PRINT " WHICH NUMBER DO YOU WANT A TABLE FOR?"
20 INPUT A   e.g.2
30 PRINT " AT WHAT VALUE SHOULD THE TABLE START?"
40 INPUT M   e.g.20
50 PRINT " AT WHAT VALUE SHOULD THE TABLE END?"
60 INPUT N   e.g.30
70 FOR I = M TO N   FOR I = 20 TO 30
80 LET B = A∗I
90 PRINT B
100 NEXT I

The result will be a table of values ranging from 2 times 20, to 2 times 30.

The STEP Value in a FOR Statement

In all of the examples of LOOPS that we have used so far, the LOOP counter has increased by one each time. If it is required that the variable should increase by some other amount, or even decrease by a regular amount, then the **STEP** value must be used.

Example 1

70 FOR S = 1 TO 10 STEP 2
S takes the values 1,3,5,7,9. The LOOP terminates when the value of S exceeds 10.

Example 2

70 FOR S = 1 TO 10 STEP 0.5
S takes the values 1,1.5, 2, . . . 9,9.5,10 and then the LOOP stops.

Example 3

70 FOR S = 10 TO 1 STEP −1
S takes the values 10,9,8,7,6,5,4,3,2,1.

The STEP value can also be a variable to increase flexibility.

Leaving the Loop

It is possible to leave the LOOP before its natural conclusion, and to re-enter if necessary, although attention should be given to the value of the variable I, if returning to the loop at a later stage.

Nesting

LOOPS can be **nested**. This happens when one LOOP is formed inside another. Care must always be taken with the choice of variable in the FOR statement to avoid duplication. With nested LOOPS, the number of times that the central LOOP is performed can be increased dramatically.

Example

```
20 FOR A = 1 TO 10 ─────────────┐
30 FOR B = 1 TO 10 ────────┐     │
40 LET X = A * B      inner      outer
50 PRINT X           loop        loop
60 NEXT B ──────────────────┘     │
70 NEXT A ────────────────────────┘
```

For each value of A, the B LOOP is performed 10 times. Altogether, 100 values of X are printed.

Further Use of the PRINT Statement

In the simulation DRAKE, the PRINT statement appeared many times, and its use was explained there as well. Sometimes it is required to keep several print items on the same line, but to print the items at different points in the program. This can be achieved by putting a **trailing comma or semicolon** at the end of a PRINT statement line. If this is done then the *next* PRINT statement will place its output on the same line, and not start a new line as is usual. The comma or semicolon has the normal item separator role for continuous or zone printing. For example

20 PRINT " MONDAY ";
30 PRINT " TUESDAY "

produces

MONDAY   TUESDAY

The trailing semicolon on line 20 causes the next print item (i.e. TUESDAY) to be printed on the same line after MONDAY.

The trailing comma or semicolon technique is used in many of the programs described here, and also as part of the PRINT USING and FORMAT statements that are described and used in the MENU package. In GAS the use is combined with the INPUT statement to produce an invitation to type directly after a question. For example

70 PRINT "WHICH GAS?";
80 INPUT Y£

produce the question

WHICH GAS ?←

and the answer is input on the same line as the question. This technique is used extensively in GAS and it helps to conserve paper and highlights the question and answer connection.

TAB Functions in PRINT Statements

When the printout is designed, commas, semicolons and spaces in quotes can be used to print the separate items in the required positions. An alternative approach is to use the **TAB** function as an item in the PRINT statement. The function controls the position of the printer across the page.

Example

TAB(45)

causes the printer to move to character position 45 across the line of output before printing the next item in the print line.

The RM 380Z version of GAS runs on a VDU screen and, to make the printout look neater, the headings for the table have been lined up using TAB functions.

540 PRINT "PRESSURE(P)";TAB(14);"VOLUME(V)";TAB(31);"P∗V"

The TAB functions are included in the list as if they were print items. They have been used widely in the programs which follow. Later a further method of controlling the printout, the PRINT USING statement, will be explained.

Why a Simulation? There is, in school science, a number of experiments which, from an educational point of view, it is desirable to perform but which a number of reasons make impossible. These reasons include lack of apparatus, lack of time or expertise, or even the fact that the experiment is dangerous. In advanced level Chemistry and Physics mention is made of the series of experiments performed by Andrews concerning the verification of Boyle's Law and the liquefaction of gases. The experiments use a number of common gases, sometimes at low temperatures and sometimes under great pressures; hence it is impossible to perform these experiments in school, although the theoretical conclusions are important. It is possible to simulate the experiments, or at least produce experimental results in a way that still enables students to experiment by choosing the temperature, pressure or volume. The students have to use their own judgement to select the results which enable them to reach the same conclusions as Andrews, the results being plotted as isotherms on a graph.

In secondary school physics, mention is made of Boyle's Law. In 1660, Boyle performed a series of experiments in which he increased the pressure on a given amount of gas, which was kept at a constant temperature, and found that the volume decreased. He found that if he doubled the pressure then the volume was halved. If the pressure was trebled then he had only one third of the volume, and so on. Expressed mathematically this meant that the pressure multiplied by the volume resulted in a constant answer, provided the temperature remained the same, i.e.

$$PV = \text{constant}$$

When the curves for different temperatures were plotted on a graph of pressure against volume the resulting isotherms looked like those in Fig 3.2.

Further theoretical work indicated that the constant value of (pressure × volume) could be determined by multiplying the temperature on the absolute scale (i.e. add 273° to the Celsius temperature) by a value known as the Gas Constant R. The equation then looked like

$$PV = RT$$

Boyle's experiments had only used low pressures and a small range of temperatures, but under ordinary conditions all the common gases followed it closely enough.

During the 19th century a number of physicists attempted to verify Boyle's Law under other than ordinary conditions. The experimental methods were more accurate than those used by Boyle, and a wider range of pressures was considered. It was found that the gases did not obey the law exactly, but that the value of (pressure × volume) depended on the pressure and was not constant. The idea of an "ideal" or "perfect" gas was used to describe a theoretical gas which would obey Boyle's Law. Real gases only approximated to the law when the pressure was small or the temperature was high. It was also found that for each gas there was a temperature, called

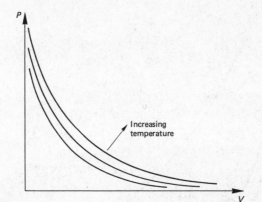

Fig 3.2 Isotherms for Boyle's Law
$PV = \text{constant}$

the Boyle Temperature, at which for small pressures the value of the (pressure × volume) did not depend on the pressure, but was constant.

Many theoretical attempts have been made to construct an equation, similar to Boyle's, which applies to real gases. One such attempt is that of Van der Waal. He considered the forces between the molecules of the gas, and the volume they take up, and arrived at a similar equation, but with an increased pressure factor and a decreased volume factor.

$$\left(P + \frac{a}{V^2}\right)(V - b) = RT$$

Here a and b are Van der Waal's constants, different for each gas. This equation predicts the results for a real gas better than Boyle's Law, but its importance is its applicability over a wide range of values rather than its accuracy. Predicted values do not agree closely with the results of experiments.

In the 1860s, Andrews performed a series of experiments measuring the pressure and volume of carbon dioxide over a range of temperatures. He plotted isotherms and obtained curves like those shown in Fig 3.3. It is Andrews' experiments that the simulation is concerned with and it is intended that the student should draw isotherms similar to those of Andrews and arrive at the same conclusions. The gases used are

Carbon dioxide
Nitrogen
Oxygen
Hydrogen

It was seen that at high temperatures Boyle's Law was nearly true. At lower temperatures a flat portion appeared, and since there the volume changed without a corresponding change in pressure, it was realised that

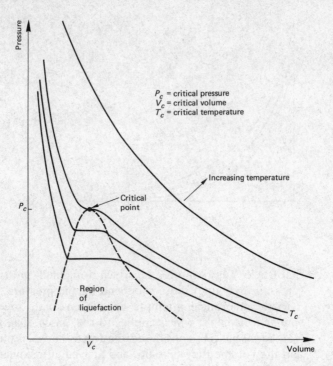

Fig 3.3 Typical isotherm graph for Andrew's Experiments

liquefaction was taking place. Also, for carbon dioxide, above the 31°C isotherm there was no flat portion, and no liquefaction was possible. This helped to explain why it had been impossible to liquefy some gases by simply increasing the pressure on them.

James Thompson (1871) suggested that the isotherms of Van der Waal's equation might be used to represent the behaviour of a real gas, and thus give isotherms such as Andrews obtained by experiment. Thompson said that the portion of the graph in Fig 3.4 between X and Y represented a mixture of liquid gas and vapour which was unstable.

The temperature above which a gas cannot be liquefied is called the critical temperature. The point on the isotherm for the critical temperature at which the gas turns to liquid is called the critical point, and this specifies the critical pressure and volume. Although Van der Waal's equation, with its two constants a and b determined experimentally, comes close to the behaviour of real gases, it is not accurate. This is particularly true in the region of the critical point.

In the simulation that follows, calculations from Van der Waal's equation have been flattened in the region X–Y to appear more like experimental results, and the volume and temperature values have been adjusted so that the critical values are accurate rather than approximate. The results of the simulation are not experimentally accurate, but they take the correct "shape" and provide accurate critical data.

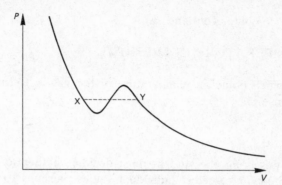

Fig 3.4 Van der Waal isotherm

Instead of being a drawback this can lead to discussion of Van der Waal's equation, usually part of the sixth form physics and chemistry teaching, when the results of a whole group are examined. Indeed, it may be important to do this, to check that all students have arrived at the correct conclusions, to compare results for different gases, and to point out the limitations of the model.

The procedure followed is this:

i) the student reads the notes provided then
ii) performs the simulation and
iii) draws the results as a graph,
iv) collects more results as required and
v) forms conclusions.

The students can work in groups and all results can be compared during a follow-up discussion.

The Student/Computer Dialogue

After the simulation program has been called up, the computer prints out the following explanation of the experiment:

THIS PROGRAM PROVIDES A SIMULATION OF ANDREWS'
EXPERIMENT FOR THE GASES OXYGEN, NITROGEN, HYDROGEN,
AND CARBON DIOXIDE. MAKE SURE YOU HAVE READ THE
INSTRUCTIONS AND BACKGROUND INFORMATION BEFORE
YOU BEGIN.

The computer then asks the question

WHICH GAS?

The student may respond with the name of one of the four gases used in this simulation. The spelling must be correct and there should be only one space between CARBON and DIOXIDE.

← CARBON DIOXIDE

The computer continues with

TEMPERATURE IN CELSIUS?

at which point the temperature of the gas in Celsius (Centigrade) can be input e.g.

← 10

At this point the student must decide whether to have a table of values printed, or to select individual values, perhaps to improve a graph. The question is simply

TABLE ? (YES OR NO)

which prompts the response.
The table printout (p. 63) of 46 lines enables an isotherm to be drawn from a selection of the points after the computer session and it is followed by the question

CONTINUE ?

Here the student can select more isotherms for the chosen gas by

← YES
TEMPERATURE IN CELSIUS?
← 20

or request another gas by

←NO
ANOTHER GAS ?

If the answer is   ← YES

then the question

WHICH GAS ?

is repeated. If the answer is   ← NO

then the program terminates and

STOPPED AT LINE 760

is printed.

PRESSURE (P)	VOLUME (V)	P*V
28.9978	0.5	14.4989
29.477	0.49	14.4437
29.9715	0.48	14.3863
30.4821	0.47	14.3266
31.0094	0.46	14.2643
31.5542	0.45	14.1994
32.1173	0.44	14.1316
32.6996	0.43	14.0608
33.3018	0.42	13.9868
33.925	0.41	13.9092
34.57	0.4	13.828
35.2378	0.39	13.7428
35.9296	0.38	13.6532
36.6462	0.37	13.5591
37.3888	0.36	13.46
18.1584	0.35	13.3554
38.9561	0.34	13.2451
39.7829	0.33	13.1284
40.6399	0.32	13.0048
41.5279	0.31	12.8737
42.4478	0.3	12.7343
43.4001	0.29	12.586
44.385	0.28	12.4278
45.4026	0.27	12.2587
46.4521	0.26	12.0775
47.5322	0.25	11.883
48.6404	0.24	11.6737
49.7729	0.23	11.4478
50.9241	0.22	11.2033
52.0856	0.21	10.938
53.1656	0.2	10.6331
53.1656	0.19	10.1015
53.1656	0.18	9.56981
53.1656	0.17	9.03815
53.1656	0.16	8.50649
53.1656	0.15	7.97484
53.1656	0.14	7.44318
53.1656	0.13	6.91153
53.1656	0.12	6.37987
53.1656	0.11	5.84822
53.1656	0.1	5.31656
53.1656	0.9E$-$1	4.7849
53.1656	0.8E$-$1	4.25325
53.1656	0.7E$-$1	3.72159
57.0095	0.6E$-$1	3.42057
141.113	0.5E$-$1	7.05567

For the non-mathematician

Numbers expressed as $0.5E-1$ are in what is called exponential form, e.g.

$$0.5E-1 = 0.5 \times 10^{-1} = 0.05$$

Student Booklet: GAS

Introduction

The following instructions will help you to use a computer simulation of Andrews' experiment. This cannot be performed in school because very high pressures are required (over 100 atmospheres).

The simulation will provide experiment results under conditions which you determine.

The program can be called up by BASIC GAS.

Operational Procedures

1 In response to the question

   WHICH GAS?

you can type OXYGEN, CARBON DIOXIDE, HYDROGEN, NITROGEN. (N.B. The names must be spelt correctly. There is only one space between CARBON and DIOXIDE.)

2 In response to

   TEMPERATURE IN CELCIUS

you can type in any temperature, but it is better to use the ranges mentioned later.

3 The question

   TABLE ? (YES OR NO)

enables either a table of values of P,V and PV **or** individual values, if preferred, to be printed. If individual values are required, the computer will reply

   INPUT VOLUME

and the volume (in litres) can be typed in.

---

4 In response to

   CONTINUE ?

you can answer YES or NO.
If you answer NO, the computer will ask

   ANOTHER GAS ?

If you answer YES the program begins again.

5 Finish by typing BYE and then LOGOUT.

The Experiment

The deviation of real gases from the gas laws bears a close relationship to the phenomenon of liquefaction. The precise conditions for the liquefaction of a gas were discovered in 1869 by Andrews, who investigated the influence of pressure and temperature upon the volume of carbon dioxide.

The apparatus used by Andrews consisted of two glass tubes, one containing carbon dioxide, the other containing air, each gas being confined by a small mercury thread. Both tubes were connected to a common compression chamber containing water to which pressure could be applied by means of screw plungers.

The upper portions of the glass tubes were maintained at the same temperatures. The volume of the carbon dioxide at different temperatures and pressures was determined. The values for the pressure were calculated from the volumes of the air.

Air

Mercury

CO_2

Water

Graphs of P against V

It might be expected that the gases satisfy Boyle's law, with smooth curves of P against V. It is suggested that you should draw these curves (isotherms) for the four gases at different temperatures.

Draw the curves for each gas on a separate graph, drawing about five curves first and adding others if you think they are necessary. Some suggestions concerning scales and ranges of values are given below. Choose your temperatures from the ranges given.

CARBON DIOXIDE

Temperatures	$10° \rightarrow 50°C$
Pressure	$40 \rightarrow 100$ atmos.
Volume	$0 \rightarrow 0.4$ litre

NITROGEN

Temperature	$-160° \rightarrow -130°C$
Pressure	$0 \rightarrow 60$ atmos.
Volume	$0 \rightarrow 0.4$ litre

OXYGEN

Temperature	$-140° \rightarrow -110°C$
Pressure	$20 \rightarrow 80$ atmos.
Volume	$0 \rightarrow 0.4$ litre

HYDROGEN

Temperature	$-250° \rightarrow -230°C$
Pressure	$0 \rightarrow 30$ atmos.
Volume	$0 \rightarrow 0.4$ litre

Although values are given every 0.01 litre, it might be best to plot pressures at :0.4; 0.35; 0.25; 0.2; 0.15; 0.1; 0.05 litres and to plot any other values which might help. Mark clearly the temperature on each isotherm.

3

You should find that below a certain temperature the curves of P agains V are no longer smooth. Instead, they begin to flatten out in the centre.

1 Try to find the temperature of the first isotherm with a horizontal portion (however small).
Note also the pressure and the volume at this horizontal part. These are referred to as the Critical Temperature, Pressure and Volume. You can compare your values with those given in textbooks.

2 Mark the points on the isotherms where the curves cease to be horizontal. Join these points, with a smooth curve, to the critical point. Mark the points where the isotherms start to be horizontal and join these to the critical point with a smooth curve. Shade carefully inside the enclosed areas.

Each isotherm portion inside this area shows the volume reducing with hardly any change in pressure. What do you think is the explanation for this?

You may be able to find the temperature, different for each gas, which gives a minimum change in the value of PV. At this temperature the gas nearly obeys Boyle's law, and so it is called the BOYLE TEMPERATURE.

References

A Textbook of Physics	R.C. Brown p469
Higher Physics	Nightingale p261
Advanced Level Physics	Nelkon and Parker p314
Heat and Thermodynamics	Roberts and Miller
New Intermediate Physics	G.R. Noaks p371 Boyle Temp. p368
Essential Principles of Physics	Whelan and Hodgson p209

4

How the Pressure is Calculated

The essential part of this simulation program is the calculation based on Van der Waal's equation, namely

$$\left(P + \frac{a}{V^2}\right)(V - b) = RT$$

or

$$P = \frac{RT}{(V - b)} - \frac{a}{V^2}$$

where P is pressure
V is volume
T is absolute temperature
R is the gas constant
a, b are Van der Waal's constants

When the isotherms are drawn for Van der Waal's equation, the critical point and the region of liquefaction are displaced so giving incorrect values for temperature, volume and pressure. It is possible to adjust the graph by first multiplying the temperature values, and then the volume values, until the critical point is correctly positioned. In the program, W is the multiplication factor for the temperature and X the factor for the volume. W and X take different values for each gas, and these are set in the program when the gas has been chosen. The values for all the constants used and the critical data are given at the end of this section.

The pressure is calculated from the volume and the temperature by

600 LET P = (R*T)/(U−B)−A/(U**2)

This line is formed from Van der Waal's equation given above but using an adjusted value for the volume U. A loop or repeating sequence enables a table of values to be printed, with the volume values ranging from 0.5 down to 0.05, decreasing in steps of 0.01.

How the Arithmetic is Performed

It has already been mentioned that arithmetic statements involve the use of LET. For example the line

590 LET U = V*X

multiplies the current value of V by X and calls the answer U. In the program this enables the volume V to be adjusted by multiplying by a factor X. The input temperature value T is adjusted twice. Firstly, the Celsius temperature is converted to the absolute scale by adding 273.

400 LET T = T+273

Notice that the result is again called T. Secondly, the graph adjustment is performed by multiplying by the factor W.

440 LET T = T * W

Again the result is called T.

The adjusted values U and T are then used to calculate the pressure.

600 LET P = (R*T)/(U − B) − A/(U**2)

This can be compared with the formula for the pressure that was given earlier. The double asterisk is used to raise U to the power 2. The values for X, W, L and the Van der Waal constants have already been assigned for the chosen gas.

A similar calculation is performed at line 560. This calculates the pressure at the critical volume and is used as the pressure S for the flat portion of the isotherm.

560 LET S = (R*T)/(2*B) − A/(9*B**2)

Theoretical work shows that

Critical volume = 3*b*   (*b* is the Van der Waal constant)

so the pressure S has been calculated with this value.

At volumes greater than the critical volume, the pressure is less than or equal to S. At volumes less than the critical volume the pressure can only be greater than or equal to S.

In this way the "peak" and "trough" of Van der Waal's equation are flattened out (Fig. 3.5):

```
560 LET S = (R*T)/(2*B) − A/(9*B**2)
   .
   .
   .
590 LET U = V*X
600 LET P = (R*T)/(U − B) − A/(U**2)
610 IF P<S THEN 650
620 IF U>(3*B) THEN 660
630 PRINT P,V,P*V
640 GOTO 670
650 IF U>(3*B) THEN 630
660 PRINT S,V,S*V
   .
   .
   .
```

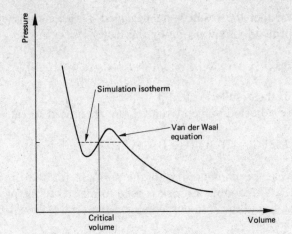

Fig 3.5 How a typical Van der Waal equation isotherm is flattened

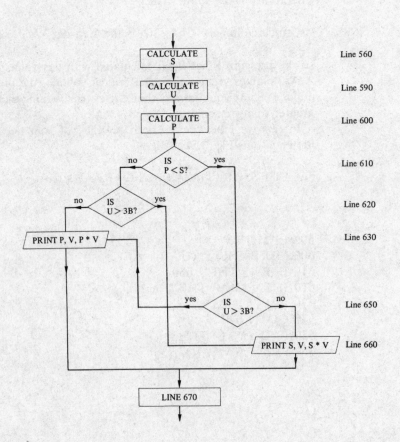

Fig 3.6

This sequence can be expressed in the form of a flowchart (Fig 3.6).

To print a table of values, a loop has been used around the calculating process:

580 FOR V = 0.5 TO 0.5E − 1 STEP −0.1E − 1
.
.
.
.
680 NEXT V
690 PRINT

Note $0.5E − 1 = 0.5 \times 10^{-1} = 0.05$

          $−0.1E − 1 = −0.1 \times 10^{-1} = −0.01$

The FOR statement marks the beginning of the loop, and the NEXT statement the end. Initially, the value of the variable V is set at 0.5 and each time round the loop the value is incremented by −0.01 (i.e. reduced by 0.01) until the final value 0.05 is reached.

The program will then proceed to line 690.

Two Limitations of the Program

If low temperatures are used in Van der Waal's equation then the results can be misleading. For example, the pressure can be calculated as zero or even negative. It is possible, however, to examine doubtful cases for each gas and find the temperature below which difficulties occur. Each gas can then be given a cut-off temperature, temperatures below this not being allowed in the simulation. The cut-off temperatures appear in the program as the variable L which takes the following values:

Gas	Cut-off temperature	L (*absolute scale*)
Carbon dioxide	−41°C	232 K
Nitrogen	−178°C	95 K
Oxygen	−157°C	116 K
Hydrogen	−247°C	26 K

The value of L is assigned when the gas is chosen, along with the other constants.

After the temperature has been chosen and converted to absolute scale it is checked to see if it is allowable.

410 IF T > = L THEN 440
420 PRINT "TEMPERATURES BELOW": (L − 273):"ARE UNRELIABLE"
430 GOTO 380

The temperature is then asked for again. If the chosen temperature is greater than or equal to the cut-off temperature, then the program proceeds to the calculations. When this is not so, a message is printed, with the calculation to take the temperature off the absolute scale included in the PRINT statement.

The pressure calculations are also unreliable when the volume is small. Values greater than 0.05 for V can be allowed. In fact, in the table this is as low as V can go. If, however, a table is not required, individual V values can be input at line 500.

A test is then made on the chosen value.

510 IF V$> = 0.5E-1$ THEN 540
520 PRINT "VOLUMES BELOW 0.05 ARE UNRELIABLE"
530 GOTO 490

The request for a volume to be input is then repeated.

The remainder of the program enables the student to use the calculation loop in the context of the simulation.

Program Summary

Lines 10–70	Simulation details.
Lines 80–140	Choosing the gas. If an unavailable gas or an incorrect spelling is used then line 140 returns the student to the question "which gas?".
Lines 150–370	Setting appropriate constant values.
Lines 380–450	Calculating absolute temperature from Celsius and setting the constant R.
Lines 460–530	Deciding table or not.
Lines 540–550	Print the table headings.
Lines 560–680	Calculations.
Lines 700–760	Deciding to continue or stop.

Program Listing: Southampton BASIC

```
10   REM ANDREWS' EXPERIMENT SIMULATION
20   PRINT "THIS PROGRAM PROVIDES A SIMULATION OF ANDREWS'"
30   PRINT "EXPERIMENT FOR THE GASES OXYGEN, NITROGEN, HYDROGEN,"
40   PRINT "AND CARBON DIOXIDE. MAKE SURE YOU HAVE READ THE"
50   PRINT "INSTRUCTIONS AND BACKGROUND INFORMATION BEFORE"
60   PRINT "YOU BEGIN."
70   PRINT "WHICH GAS ?";
80   INPUT Y£
90   IF Y£="CARBON DIOXIDE" THEN 150
100  IF Y£="HYDROGEN" THEN 210
110  IF Y£="NITROGEN" THEN 270
120  IF Y£="OXYGEN" THEN 330
130  IF Y£="STOP" THEN 760
140  GOTO 70
150  LET A=3.66
160  LET B=0.428E-1
170  LET W=1.015
180  LET X=1.363
190  LET L=232
```

```
200    GOTO 380
210    LET A=0.245
220    LET B=0.267E-1
230    LET W=0.9988
240    LET X=1.1492
250    LET L=26
260    GOTO 380
270    LET A=1.38
280    LET B=0.394E-1
290    LET W=1.005
300    LET X=1.3133
310    LET L=95
320    GOTO 380
330    LET A=1.32
340    LET B=0.312E-1
350    LET X=1.26
360    LET W=0.9927
370    LET L=116
380    PRINT "TEMPERATURE IN CELCIUS";
390    INPUT T
400    LET T=T+273
410    IF T>=L THEN 440
420    PRINT "TEMPERATURES BELOW";(L-273);"ARE UNRELIABLE"
430    GOTO 380
440    LET T=T*W
450    LET R=0.82E-1
460    PRINT "TABLE ? (YES OR NO)";
470    INPUT M£
480    IF M£="YES" THEN 540
490    PRINT "INPUT VOLUME";
500    INPUT V
510    IF V>=0.5E-1 THEN 540
520    PRINT " VOLUMES BELOW 0.05 ARE UNRELIABLE"
530    GOTO 490
540    PRINT "PRESSURE(P)","VOLUME(V)","P*V"
550    PRINT
560    LET S=(R*T)/(2*B)-A/(9*B**2)
570    IF M£<>"YES" THEN 590
580    FOR V=0.5 TO 0.5E-1 STEP -0.1E-1
590    LET U=V*X
600    LET P=(R*T)/(U-B)-A/(U**2)
610    IF P<S THEN 650
620    IF U>(3*B) THEN 660
630    PRINT P,V,P*V
640    GOTO 670
650    IF U>(3*B) THEN 630
660    PRINT S,V,S*V
670    IF M£<>"YES" THEN 690
680    NEXT V
690    PRINT
700    PRINT "CONTINUE ?";
710    INPUT Z£
720    IF Z£="YES" THEN 380
730    PRINT "ANOTHER GAS ?";
740    INPUT X£
750    IF X£="YES" THEN 70
760    END
```

Critical Data and Constants Used in the Program

Expressions for the critical values can be derived from Van der Waal's equation.

$$T_c = \frac{8a}{27Rb} \qquad V_c = 3b \qquad P_c = \frac{a}{27b}$$

W is a multiplication factor for temperature.
X is a multiplication factor for volume.
R (the gas constant) = 0.082
A and B are Van der Waal's constants.

	Carbon dioxide	*Nitrogen*	*Oxygen*	*Hydrogen*
A	3.66	1.38	1.32	0.245
B	0.0428	0.0394	0.0312	0.0267
W	1.015	1.005	0.9927	0.9988
X	1.363	1.3133	1.26	1.1492
T_c	31°C	−147°C	−119°C	−240°C
P_c	72.8 Atmos	33.5 Atmos	49.7 Atmos	12.8 Atmos
V_c	0.094 L	0.09 L	0.0742 L	0.0697 L

A version of GAS for a RM 380Z Micro

As an alternative to the SOBS BASIC version of GAS, which has been run on a teletype producing hard copy, a version which runs on a RM 380Z microcomputer is given here. This version is designed to output to a VDU screen and can be used for demonstration purposes. The program runs in 9K BASIC and some minor changes to the SOBS version had to be made. They are detailed here.

11 CLEAR 100   reserves space for the string variables used in the program.
15 PRINT CHR$(12)   "prints" a blank screen.
In SOBS, exponentiation can be written as ∗∗ or ↑, but RM 380Z 9K BASIC requires ↑. These changes have been made on lines 560 and 600.
The introduction printout has been re-written for 40 character lines, instead of the wider teletype output.
TAB functions have been used in line 540 to print the table headings, to improve the appearance of the output.

A complete listing of the program follows.

Program Listing: Research Machines 380Z 9K BASIC

```
10 REM ANDREWS' EXPERIMENT SIMULATION
11 CLEAR 100
15 PRINT CHR$(12)
20 PRINT "THIS PROGRAM PROVIDES A SIMULATION OF"
30 PRINT "ANDREW'S EXPERIMENT FOR THE GASES"
40 PRINT "CARBON DIOXIDE, OXYGEN, NITROGEN  AND"
50 PRINT "HYDROGEN. MAKE SURE THAT YOU HAVE READ"
60 PRINT "THE INSTRUCTIONS AND BACKGROUND"
65 PRINT "INFORMATION BEFORE YOU BEGIN."
67 PRINT
70 PRINT "WHICH GAS";
80 INPUT Y$
90 IF Y$="CARBON DIOXIDE" THEN 150
```

```
100 IF Y$="HYDROGEN" THEN 210
110 IF Y$="NITROGEN" THEN 270
120 IF Y$="OXYGEN" THEN 330
130 IF Y$="STOP" THEN 760
140 GOTO 70
150 LET A=3.66
160 LET B=.0428
170 LET W=1.015
180 LET X=1.363
190 LET L=232
200 GOTO 380
210 LET A=.24
220 LET B=.0267
230 LET W=.9988
240 LET X=1.1492
250 LET L=26
260 GOTO 380
270 LET A=1.38
280 LET B=.0394
290 LET W=1.005
300 LET X=1.3133
310 LET L=95
320 GOTO 380
330 LET A=1.32
340 LET B=.0312
350 LET X=1.26
360 LET W=.9927
370 LET L=116
380 PRINT "TEMPERATURE IN CELSIUS";
390 INPUT T
400 LET T=T+273
410 IF T>=L THEN 440
420 PRINT "TEMPERATURES BELOW";(L-273);"ARE UNRELIABLE"
430 GOTO 380
440 LET T=T*W
450 LET R=.082
460 PRINT "TABLE? (YES OR NO)";
470 INPUT M$
480 IF M$="YES" THEN 540
490 PRINT "INPUT VOLUME"
500 INPUT V
510 IF V>=.05 THEN 540
520 PRINT " VOLUMES BELOW 0.05 ARE UNRELIABLE"
530 GOTO 490
540 PRINT "PRESSURE(P)";TAB(14);"VOLUME(V)";TAB(31);"P*V"
550 PRINT
560 LET S=(R*T)/(2*B)-A/(9*B↑2)
570 IF M$<>"YES" THEN 590
580 FOR V=.5 TO .05 STEP -.01
590 LET U=V*X
600 LET P=(R*T)/(U-B)-A/(U↑2)
610 IF P<S THEN 650
620 IF U>(3*B) THEN 660
630 PRINT P,V,P*V
640 GOTO 670
650 IF U>(3*B) THEN 630
660 PRINT S,V,S*V
670 IF M$<>"YES" THEN 690
680 NEXT V
690 PRINT
700 PRINT "CONTINUE ?";
710 INPUT Z$
720 IF Z$="YES" THEN 380
730 PRINT "ANOTHER GAS ?";
740 INPUT X$
750 IF X$="YES" THEN 70
760 END
```

4 POPULATION: population projections

Introduction

POPULATION is a teaching package designed for fourth year geography students. As the name suggests, it forms the basis for an investigation into the population growth of countries around the world. The depth of the follow-up study is left to the individual teacher to decide and the questions which appear at the back of the booklet need not necessarily be used.

The program, which forms part of the package, makes use of the computer's ability to carry out calculations quickly and accurately and thus provides a large amount of data which the student can make use of during investigations into population growth. The program provides the student with the means of calculating the size of a population for a (student-determined) number of years into the future. The student selects the country from a list which is provided.

The countries were chosen to give a spread of average annual percentage growth rates and also to include some of the more interesting countries such as China and India. The projected population sizes are based predominately on an average annual percentage growth rate for the period 1965–1974. While it is recognised that growth rates are changing continually and that the population sizes may be incorrect for the future, the figures provided by the program will give the student an impression of the population growth that takes place when a country has a high or low growth rate.

The main aims of the package:

1 To show that the time taken to double the population is independent of the size of the population.
2 To show that as the annual percentage growth rate increases so the doubling time rapidly decreases.
3 To create a general awareness of the size of the world population and its rate of increase if population growths continue at their present rates.

It would, of course, be possible to program the microcomputer to draw the graphs for the pupil, and in a demonstration context this might be desirable. The teacher has to decide just how much the computer should do for the student. In the interests of creating an active role this may be less than that which it is capable of.

The Formula Used in the Program

The formula used in the program is the same as that used for all compound accumulation problems. The most familiar one is the compound interest calculation. The investment interest for a year is added to the capital and becomes the new capital invested for the following year. Similarly, the increase in the population is added to the population total for the beginning of the year and then becomes the new population total for the following year.

Example
An annual percentage growth rate of 10% is used for ease of calculation and illustration.

Beginning of year	Increase for that year	End of year
100 000	10 000	110 000
110 000	11 000	121 000
121 000	12 100	133 100
133 100	13 310	146 410
	etc.	

The population at the end of a year can be found by multiplying the population total for the beginning of the year by

$$\left(1 + \frac{PGR}{100}\right)$$

where PGR is 10 in the above example.

Beginning of year

100 000

$$100\,000 \times \left(1 + \frac{PGR}{100}\right)$$

End of year

$$100\,000 \times \left(1 + \frac{PGR}{100}\right) = 110\,000$$

$$\left[100\,000 \times \left(1 + \frac{PGR}{100}\right)\right] \times \left(1 + \frac{PGR}{100}\right) = 121\,000$$

Therefore, at the end of two years the total population would be

$$100\,000 \times \left(1 + \frac{PGR}{100}\right)^2 = 121\,000$$

and at the end of five years it would be

$$100\,000 \times \left(1 + \frac{PGR}{100}\right)^5 = 161\,051$$

The Scheme of Work and General Procedure

The package begins with an example projected population growth for PERU, which contains values for the population size from 1974 to 2024 in steps of five years. This set of values is plotted on a graph of population against years which appears on page 2 of the student's booklet. The student is requested to calculate from the graph the number of years it takes to increase the population by 15 million and then by another 15 million and then by a further 15 million. The aim of this is to show the student that the time taken to add another 15 million decreases as the population size grows.

When this has been completed, the student turns to page 3 of the booklet where instructions are given for the student to carry out a population projection on a country of his/her choice. This projection is performed using the computer terminal. The list of countries from which selection is made also appears on page 3.

On completion of the projection the student turns to page 4 where instructions are given to carry out two further projections on the same country. The difference this time is that the student selects two annual percentage growth rates. It is suggested that the student uses one above and one below the value given by the computer for the first projection.

Having obtained three sets of results the student plots the three graphs on the graph paper provided on page 4 of the booklet. Having completed this task, the student then calculates, from the graphs, the **doubling time** for each annual percentage growth rate.

The student now collects a set of results, which show the percentage growth rate and their corresponding doubling time, for other countries, from other members of the group. Having collected this set of results, the student plots these values on the graph paper provided on page 5. The graph represents annual percentage growth rate against doubling time.

The final part of the package consists of a set of questions which are designed to test the student's understanding of the package and also to stimulate further work and discussion on the subject of world population and its associated problems.

The Program

The program for POPULATION is fairly straightforward and contains four main sections. In the first section the program accepts choices made by the student with regard to country, final projection year, number of years between each population figure, and asks the student whether he/she wishes to submit a percentage growth rate.

In the second section the computer prints out a summary of the conditions pertaining to the population projection. It contains the base year, the annual percentage growth rate, and the period over which the average is based. It may also include a second annual percentage growth rate, for information purposes only, for a period which extends further back from the base year. If the student selects an annual percentage growth rate, then only this percentage and the base year would appear in the summary.

Population Projection for Peru

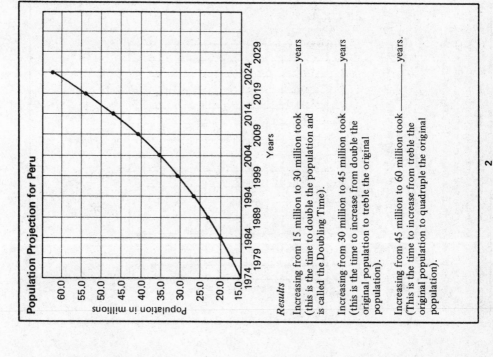

Results

Increasing from 15 million to 30 million took _____ years (this is the time to double the population and is called the Doubling Time).

Increasing from 30 million to 45 million took _____ years (this is the time to increase from double the original population to treble the original population).

Increasing from 45 million to 60 million took _____ years. (This is the time to increase from treble the original population to quadruple the original population).

2

Student Booklet: POPULATION

Example Projected Population Growth of Peru (15 million in 1974)

Projected population growth for PERU with base year 1974, assuming a continued annual growth rate of 2.9% – as was the annual average for the years 1965-74. The average annual growth rate for the period 1960-74 was 2.9% per annum.

Population (millions)	Date	Population (millions)	Date
15.0	1974	30.6	1999
17.3	1979	35.3	2004
19.9	1984	40.7	2009
23.0	1989	46.9	2014
26.5	1994	54.1	2019
		62.4	2024

On page 2 you will see the projected population growth plotted on a graph. The population in 1974 was 15 million. Calculate how many years it would take to increase to 30 million. Then find how many years it would take to increase from 30 million to 45 million and then how many years to increase from 45 million to 60 million.

Record your results below the graph in the appropriate positions and then turn to page 3 for further instructions.

1

When you have a satisfactory set of results you carry out two further projections, using the same country and projection year but choosing your own annual percentage increase. Select one above the percentage increase given by the computer and one below.

e.g. For PERU which was 2.9% you might select 1.9% and 3.9%.

Using the 3 sets of results, plot the 3 curves on the same graph labelling each with the percentage and calculate the doubling time in each case. (Plot below).

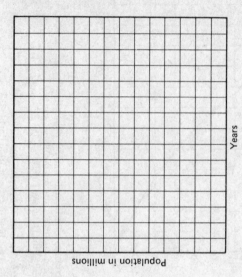

Population in millions

Years

4

How to Obtain Figures for a Population Projection

Now carry out your own projection, using the computer terminal for a country of your choice from the list given. The computer will want to know the following information.

1) Code number of country (see below)
2) Projection to which year
3) Interval between the years printed.

WHICH COUNTRY? TYPE CODE NUMBER
→20

PROJECTION TO WHICH YEAR?
TYPE A NUMBER NOT GREATER THAN 2500.
→2040

AT WHAT INTERVALS? ONE YEAR? MORE?
TYPE A WHOLE NUMBER
→5

DO YOU WISH TO INPUT AN ANNUAL PERCENTAGE INCREASE?
TYPE YES OR NO.
→NO

20 is the code number of the country. 2040 is the last year of the projection. 5 is every 5 years, e.g. 1974, 1979, 1984, etc.

Choose a sensible interval. Too many or too few figures in your table might make plotting difficult. On your first projection you do not want to insert your own annual percentage increase and so you type NO to that question.

Code	Country	Code	Country	Code	Country
1	Argentina	10	Egypt	19	Pakistan
2	Austria	11	France	20	Peru
3	Bahrain	12	India	21	Republic of
4	Belgium	13	Israel		Philippines
5	Brazil	14	Japan	22	Saudi Arabia
6	Brunei	15	Kenya	23	Singapore
7	China	16	Kuwait	24	Sweden
8	Cuba	17	Mexico	25	Switzerland
9	Denmark	18	Norway	26	U.K.
				27	U.S.A.

3

Now collect from any 5 members of your class their 3 sets of values for annual percentage growth and doubling time. Fill in the table of results below. The first two values are given. Use your own results to complete the table.

Table of results

% growth	doubling time	% growth	doubling time
6.0	11.9		
5.0	14.3		

When you have completed the above table, draw a graph of the results on the graph paper below.

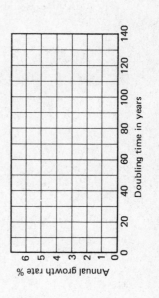

Annual growth rate %

Doubling time in years

Now answer the questions on page 6.

5

Questions

1 What can you deduce from the results that you obtained on page 2?

2 What effect did increasing the annual percentage growth rate have on the doubling time?

3 State, giving reasons, whether the size of the population has an effect on the doubling time.

4 Suggest reasons why different countries should have different annual percentage growth rates.

5 Discuss the factors which could affect the annual percentage growth rate for a particular country.

6 Suggest possible methods for reducing the annual percentage growth rate.

6

Example 1

PROJECTED POPULATION GROWTH FOR ALGERIA WITH
BASE YEAR 1974 ASSUMING A CONTINUED ANNUAL
GROWTH RATE OF 3.3 PERCENT—AS WAS THE
ANNUAL AVERAGE FOR THE YEARS 1965–74.
THE AVERAGE ANNUAL GROWTH RATE FOR THE PERIOD
1960–74 WAS 3.2 PERCENT PER ANNUM.

Example 2

THIS PROJECTION IS FOR ALGERIA AND IS BASED ON AN
ANNUAL GROWTH RATE OF 2.9 PERCENT WHICH HAS BEEN
DETERMINED BY THE STUDENT.

In the third section the program computes the table of results and prints them out. This operation is carried out within a loop and the actual PRINT statement involves a PRINT USING instruction. PRINT USING will be explained later. It is sufficient at this stage to say that it is used in order to ensure a neat lining up of columns in the table of results.

The fourth and final section contains the DATA statements which hold information about the countries available to the student. The items in the DATA statements have the following significance.

Example

1100 DATA 18,NORWAY,4.035,0.8,0.8,1977,1971–75,1965–74

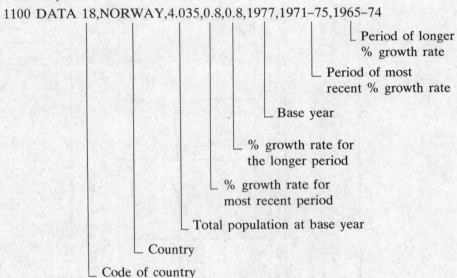

The information held in this block of DATA statements provides the necessary values for the computer to be able to perform a projection. When a student types in the code of a country, the computer reads through the DATA statements until it locates that code. It then extracts the information from that DATA line and uses it in the formula for a projection.

If desired, the range of countries can be extended. Simply continue from line 1240 in the program with the additional countries and place the END instruction after the last DATA statement. Remember to change line 100 and insert the number of countries you intend using in place of 27.

As a high number of the countries have the base year and the two periods for the annual percentage growth rates in common, these values have been incorporated into the program. The program is structured to interpret three zeros at the end of the DATA line to mean; use the values contained in the program.

Example
1100 DATA 14,JAPAN,109.67,1.2,1.1,0,0,0

There are one or two exceptions to this general rule. A case in point is the United Kingdom where there is only one annual percentage growth rate. The program recognises this by the single zero at the end of the DATA line. Note there has to be a "dummy" value (zero) placed in the position of the % growth rate for the longer period in order to satisfy the expectations of the READ statement.

Example
 110 READ A,B£,C,D,E,F,G£,H£
1220 DATA 26,UNITED KINGDOM,55.515,0.5,0,1971,1961–71,0

Research Machines 380Z Micro It is possible to run the program on this micro. If, however, the printout appears on a screen, it will mean that the student has no hard copy of projections. This will necessitate having to copy down the results from the screen. On the other hand, it may be used for demonstration purposes with a class, the output being fed to a television screen.

A listing of the program has been included for use on the Research Machines 380Z. In the case of similar microcomputers, it would only be necessary to apply minor changes to the listed program. In order to maintain the tabular form of the printout, the appropriate program statements applicable to the machines must be used. These may include ZONES, TAB statements or different forms of PRINT USING statements.

Sample Run

WHICH COUNTRY? TYPE CODE NUMBER.
←17
PROJECTION TO WHICH YEAR?
TYPE A NUMBER NOT GREATER THAN 2500.
←2020
AT WHAT INTERVALS? ONE YEAR? MORE?
TYPE A WHOLE NUMBER.
←3
DO YOU WISH TO INPUT AN ANNUAL PERCENTAGE INCREASE?
TYPE YES OR NO.
←NO

```
* * * * * * * * * * * * * * * * * * * * * * * * * * * * * * * * * * * * * * * * * * * *
```

A PROJECTED POPULATION GROWTH FOR MEXICO WITH
BASE YEAR 1974 ASSUMING A CONTINUED ANNUAL
GROWTH RATE OF 3.5 PERCENT—AS WAS THE
ANNUAL AVERAGE FOR THE YEARS 1965–74.
THE AVERAGE ANNUAL GROWTH RATE FOR THE PERIOD
1968–74 WAS 3.4 PERCENT PER ANNUM.

```
= = = = = = = = = = = = = = = = = = = = =
I                                       I
I                                       I
I      POPULATION     DATE              I
I      = = = = = = =   = = =            I
I                                       I
I      (MILLIONS)                       I
I                                       I
I            57.9     1974              I
I            64.2     1977              I
I            71.2     1980              I
I            78.9     1983              I
I            87.5     1986              I
I            97.0     1989              I
I           107.5     1992              I
I           119.2     1995              I
I           132.2     1998              I
I           146.6     2001              I
I           162.5     2004              I
I           180.2     2007              I
I           199.8     2010              I
I           221.5     2013              I
I           245.6     2016              I
I           272.3     2019              I
I                                       I
I                                       I
= = = = = = = = = = = = = = = = = = = = =
```

```
* * * * * * * * * * * * * * * * * * * * * * * * * * * * * * * * * * * * * * * * * * * *
```

DO YOU REQUIRE ANOTHER PROJECTION?
TYPE YES OR NO
←NO

Program Listing:
Southampton
BASIC

```
10    LET L£="1965-74"
20    LET K£="1960-74"
30    PRINT
40    PRINT "WHICH COUNTRY? TYPE CODE NUMBER."
50    INPUT Z
60    IF Z>27 THEN 80
70    GOTO 100
80    PRINT "THIS NUMBER IS TOO LARGE."
90    GOTO 40
100   FOR J=1 TO 27
110   READ A, B£, C, D, E, F, G£, H£
120   IF Z=A THEN 140
130   NEXT J
```

```
140   IF F<>0 THEN 160
150   LET F=1974
160   PRINT "PROJECTION TO WHICH YEAR?"
170   PRINT "TYPE A NUMBER NOT GREATER THAN 2500."
180   INPUT X
190   IF X>2500 THEN 230
200   IF X>F THEN 250
210   PRINT "THE PROJECTION STARTS FROM THE BASE YEAR";F
220   GOTO 160
230   PRINT "THIS NUMBER IS TOO LARGE."
240   GOTO 10
250   PRINT "AT WHAT INTERVALS? ONE YEAR? MORE?"
260   PRINT "TYPE A WHOLE NUMBER."
270   INPUT I
280   IF X-F<=I THEN 310
290   IF I<>INT(I) THEN 260
300   GOTO 330
310   PRINT "IMPOSSIBLE. NUMBER TOO LARGE."
320   GOTO 250
330   IF G£="0" THEN 360
340   LET L£=G£
350   LET K£=H£
360   PRINT "DO YOU WISH TO INPUT AN ANNUAL PERCENTAGE INCREASE?"
370   PRINT "TYPE YES OR NO."
380   INPUT Y£
390   IF Y£="YES" THEN 430
400   IF Y£="NO" THEN 470
410   GOTO 370
420   PRINT "THIS NUMBER IS OUT OF RANGE."
430   PRINT "TYPE A NUMBER BETWEEN 0.1 AND 6"
440   INPUT D
450   IF D>6 THEN 420
460   IF D<0.1 THEN 420
470   PRINT
480   PRINT
490   PRINT "****************************************"
500   PRINT
510   PRINT
520   IF Y£="NO" THEN 570
530   PRINT "THIS PROJECTION IS FOR ";B£;" AND IS BASED ON AN"
540   PRINT "ANNUAL GROWTH RATE OF ";D;" PERCENT WHICH HAS BEEN"
550   PRINT "DETERMINED BY THE STUDENT."
560   GOTO 640
570   PRINT "PROJECTED POPULATION GROWTH FOR ";B£;" WITH"
580   PRINT "BASE YEAR ";F;" ASSUMING A CONTINUED ANNUAL"
590   PRINT "GROWTH RATE OF ";D;" PERCENT - AS WAS THE"
600   PRINT "ANNUAL AVERAGE FOR THE YEARS ";L£;"."
610   IF K£="0" THEN 640
620   PRINT "THE AVERAGE ANNUAL GROWTH RATE FOR THE PERIOD"
630   PRINT K£;" WAS ";E£;" PERCENT PER ANNUM."
640   PRINT
650   PRINT " ======================================= "
660   PRINT " I                                     I "
670   PRINT " I                                     I "
680   PRINT " I           POPULATION    DATE    I "
690   PRINT " I           ==========    ====    I "
700   PRINT " I           (MILLIONS)            I "
710   PRINT " I                                     I "
720   FOR N=0 TO (X-F) STEP I
730   LET T=C*(1+D/100)**N
740   IF T*10-INT(T*10)>=0.5 THEN 770
750   LET Q=INT(T*10)/10
760   GOTO 800
770   LET Q=INT(T*10)/10+0.1
800   PRINT USING 810:Q,F+N
810   FORMAT" I",#####################.#,5X,####,4X,"I "
820   NEXT N
830   PRINT " I                                     I!"
840   PRINT " I                                     I "
850   PRINT " ======================================= "
```

```
860    PRINT
870    PRINT
880    PRINT "***************************************"
890    PRINT "DO YOU REQUIRE ANOTHER PROJECTION?"
900    PRINT "TYPE YES OR NO"
910    INPUT Y£
920    IF Y£="YES" THEN 950
930    IF Y£="NO" THEN 1240
940    GOTO 900
950    RESTORE
960    GOTO 10
970    DATA 1,ARGENTINA,24.646,1.5,1.5,0,0,0
980    DATA 2,AUSTRIA,7.55,0.5,0.5,0,0,0
990    DATA 3,BAHRAIN,0.245,3.1,3.4,0,0,0
1000   DATA 4,BELGIUM,9.757,0.3,0.5,1973,0,0
1010   DATA 5,BRAZIL,103.981,2.9,2.9,0,0,0
1020   DATA 6,BRUNEI,0.15,3.9,4.6,0,0,0
1030   DATA 7,CHINA,809.251,2.7,2.9,0,0,0
1040   DATA 8,CUBA,9.09,1.8,2.0,0,0,0
1050   DATA 9,DENMARK,5.05,.7,.7,0,0,0
1060   DATA 10,EGYPT,36.35,2.4,2.5,0,0,0
1070   DATA 11,FRANCE,52.16,0.8,0.9,1973,1968-75,1962-68
1080   DATA 12,INDIA,595.586,2.3,2.3,0,0,0
1090   DATA 13,ISRAEL,4.249,1.9,2.2,1972,0,0
1100   DATA 14,JAPAN,109.67,1.2,1.1,0,0,0
1110   DATA 15,KENYA,12.91,3.4,3.2,0,0,0
1120   DATA 16,KUWAIT,0.93,7.8,9.1,0,0,0
1130   DATA 17,MEXICO,57.899,3.5,3.4,0,0,0
1140   DATA 18,NORWAY,4.035,0.8,0.8,1977,1971-75,1965-74
1150   DATA 19,PAKISTAN,67.213,2.9,2.9,0,0,0
1160   DATA 20,PERU,14.953,2.9,2.9,0,0,0
1170   DATA 21,REPUBLIC OF PHILIPPINES,41.433,3.0,3.0,0,0,0
1180   DATA 22,SAUDI ARABIA,8.008,1.8,1.8,0,0,0
1190   DATA 23,SINGAPORE,2.25,1.6,2.8,1975,1970-75,1957-70
1200   DATA 24,SWEDEN,8.236,0.6,0.7,1976,0,0
1210   DATA 25,SWITZERLAND,6.44,1.1,1.2,0,0,0
1220   DATA 26,UNITED KINGDOM,55.515,0.5,0,1971,1961-71,0
1230   DATA 27,UNITED STATES OF AMERICA,203.235,1.3,0,1970,1960-70,0
1240   END
```

Program Listing:
Research Machines
380Z 12K BASIC

```
10   LET F=1974
20   LET L$="1965-74"
30   LET K$="1960-74"
40   PRINT
50   PRINT CHR$(12)
60   PRINT "WHICH COUNTRY? TYPE CODE NUMBER."
70   PRINT
80   PRINT
90   PRINT
100  PRINT
110  PRINT
120  PRINT
130  INPUT Z
140  IF Z>27 THEN 160
150  GOTO 180
160  PRINT "THIS NUMBER IS TOO LARGE."
170  GOTO 60
180  PRINT CHR$(12)
190  PRINT "PROJECTION TO WHICH YEAR?"
200  PRINT "TYPE A NUMBER NOT GREATER THAN 2500."
210  PRINT
220  PRINT
230  PRINT
240  PRINT
250  PRINT
260  INPUT X
```

```
270   IF X>2500 THEN 310
280   IF X>F THEN 330
290   PRINT "THE PROJECTION STARTS FROM THE BASE YEAR";F
300   GOTO 190
310   PRINT "THIS NUMBER IS TOO LARGE."
320   GOTO 190
330 PRINT CHR$(12)
340   PRINT "AT WHAT INTERVALS? ONE YEAR? MORE?"
350   PRINT "TYPE A WHOLE NUMBER."
360 PRINT
370 PRINT
380 PRINT
390 PRINT
400 PRINT
410   INPUT I
420   IF X-F<=I THEN 450
430   IF I<>INT(I) THEN 350
440   GOTO 470
450   PRINT "IMPOSSIBLE. NUMBER TOO LARGE."
460   GOTO 340
470   FOR J=1 TO 27
480   READ A,B$,C,D,E,F,G$,H$
490   IF Z=A THEN 510
500   NEXT J
510   IF G$="0" THEN 540
520   LET L$=G$
530   LET K$=H$
540 PRINT CHR$(12)
550   PRINT "DO YOU WISH TO INPUT AN ANNUAL"
560 PRINT "PERCENTAGE INCREASE?"
570   PRINT "TYPE YES OR NO."
580 PRINT
590 PRINT
600 PRINT
610 PRINT
620 PRINT
630   INPUT Y$
640   IF Y$="YES" THEN 680
650   IF Y$="NO" THEN 720
660   GOTO 570
670   PRINT "THIS NUMBER IS OUT OF RANGE."
680   PRINT "TYPE A NUMBER BETWEEN 0.1 AND 6"
690   INPUT D
700   IF D>6 THEN 670
710   IF D<.1 THEN 670
720   PRINT
730   PRINT
740   PRINT "*************************************"
750   PRINT
760   PRINT
770   IF F<>0 THEN 790
780   LET F=1974
790   IF Y$="NO" THEN 850
800   PRINT "THIS PROJECTION IS FOR ";B$;" AND IS"
810 PRINT "BASED ON AN ANNUAL GROWTH RATE OF"
820 PRINT D;"PERCENT WHICH HAS BEEN DETERMINED "
830 PRINT "BY THE STUDENT."
840   GOTO 940
850   PRINT "PROJECTED POPULATION GROWTH FOR"
860 PRINT B$;" WITH BASE YEAR";F
870 PRINT "ASSUMING A CONTINUED ANNUAL GROWTH RATE"
880 PRINT "OF";D;"PERCENT - AS WAS THE ANNUAL"
890 PRINT "AVERAGE FOR THE YEARS ";L$;"."
900   IF K$="0" THEN 940
910   PRINT "THE AVERAGE ANNUAL GROWTH RATE FOR THE"
920 PRINT "PERIOD ";K$;" WAS";E;"PERCENT"
930 PRINT "PER ANNUM."
940   PRINT
```

```
 950   PRINT " =========================================="
 960   PRINT " I                                         I"
 970   PRINT " I                                         I"
 980   PRINT " I                 POPULATION    DATE      I"
 990   PRINT " I                 ==========    ====      I"
1000   PRINT " I                 (MILLIONS)              I"
1010   PRINT " I                                         I"
1020   FOR N=0 TO (X-F) STEP I
1030   LET T=C*(1+D/100)↑N
1040   IF T*10-INT(T*10)>=.5 THEN 1070
1050   LET Q=INT(T*10)/10
1060 GOTO 1080
1070   LET Q=INT(T*10)/10+.1
1080   PRINT USING 1090; Q, F+N
1090 I I ####################.#     ####     I
1100   NEXT N
1110   PRINT " I                                         I"
1120   PRINT " I                                         I"
1130   PRINT " =========================================="
1140   PRINT
1150   PRINT
1160   PRINT "****************************************"
1170   PRINT "DO YOU REQUIRE ANOTHER PROJECTION?"
1180   PRINT "TYPE YES OR NO"
1190   INPUT Y$
1200   IF Y$="YES" THEN 1230
1210   IF Y$="NO" THEN 1520
1220   GOTO 1180
1230   RESTORE
1240 GOTO 10
1250   DATA 1,ARGENTINA,24.646,1.5,1.5,0,0,0
1260   DATA 2,AUSTRIA,7.55,0.5,0.5,0,0,0
1270   DATA 3,BAHRAIN,0.245,3.1,3.4,0,0,0
1280   DATA 4,BELGIUM,9.757,0.3,0.5,1973,0,0
1290   DATA 5,BRAZIL,103.981,2.9,2.9,0,0,0
1300   DATA 6,BRUNEI,0.15,3.9,4.6,0,0,0
1310   DATA 7,CHINA,809.251,2.7,2.9,0,0,0
1320   DATA 8,CUBA,9.09,1.8,2.0,0,0,0
1330   DATA 9,DENMARK,5.05,.7,.7,0,0,0
1340   DATA 10,EGYPT,36.35,2.4,2.5,0,0,0
1350   DATA 11,FRANCE,52.16,0.8,0.9,1973,1968-75,1962-68
1360   DATA 12,INDIA,595.586,2.3,2.3,0,0,0
1370   DATA 13,ISRAEL,4.249,1.9,2.2,1972,0,0
1380   DATA 14,JAPAN,109.67,1.2,1.1,0,0,0
1390   DATA 15,KENYA,12.91,3.4,3.2,0,0,0
1400   DATA 16,KUWAIT,0.93,7.8,9.1,0,0,0
1410   DATA 17,MEXICO,57.899,3.5,3.4,0,0,0
1420   DATA 18,NORWAY,4.035,0.8,0.8,1977,1971-75,1965-74
1430   DATA 19,PAKISTAN,67.213,2.9,2.9,0,0,0
1440   DATA 20,PERU,14.953,2.9,2.9,0,0,0
1450   DATA 21,REPUBLIC OF PHILIPPINES,41.433,3.0,3.0,0,0,0
1460 DATA 22,SAUDI ARABIA,8.008,1.8,1.8,1974,1965-74,1960-74
1470 DATA 23,SINGAPORE,2.25,1.6,2.8,1975,1970-75,1957-70
1480   DATA 24,SWEDEN,8.236,0.6,0.7,1976,0,0
1490   DATA 25,SWITZERLAND,6.44,1.1,1.2,0,0,0
1500   DATA 26,UNITED KINGDOM,55.515,0.5,0,1971,1961-71,0
1510   DATA 27,UNITED STATES OF AMERICA,203.235,1.3,0,1970,1960-70,0
1520   END
```

Basic

**READ and DATA
Statements**

Information that is to be processed during the running of a program can be supplied in a number of ways. It may be derived from INPUT statements or LET statements but for large quantities of information these are not very suitable. A better approach is to instruct the computer to **READ** the information either from a FILE (which is described in the chapter on Information Retrieval) or from a group of **DATA** statements. DATA statements also enable the information to be changed without having to alter the main part of the program.

The information to be processed is written on statement lines in the program and each line is headed by the word DATA. The line may contain either numeric or alphanumeric information or both. Both occur in the DATA statements of POPULATION.

Example
 970 DATA 1,ARGENTINA,24.646,1.5,1.5,0,0,0
 980 DATA 2,AUSTRIA,7.55,0.5,0.5,0,0,0
 990 DATA 3,BAHRAIN,0.245,3.4,3.4,0,0,0
1000 DATA 4,BELGIUM,9.757,0.3,0.5,1973,0,0
1010 DATA 5,BRAZIL,103.981,2.9,2.9,0,0,0
etc.

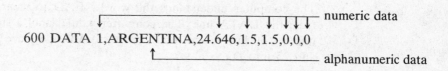

DATA statements are often placed at the end of a program although they could just as easily appear at the beginning or in the middle of the program. The computer recognizes DATA statements as containing information and therefore does not attempt to interpret them as program instructions.

Each item of information must be followed by a comma, but not the word DATA and not the last item on the line. If blank spaces are placed in the DATA line, they may or may not be ignored according to the version of Basic being used. Blank spaces within an item of alphanumeric information would not be ignored. Blank spaces within a number are not permitted and would produce an error statement by the computer.

Example (Southampton Basic)

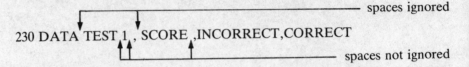

If you wished a piece of information to contain a space at the beginning or end, or to contain a comma, then you must enclose the item of information with quotation marks.

Example
240 DATA TEST 1," SCORE ","SORRY, INCORRECT",CORRECT

Without the quotation marks, SORRY,INCORRECT would be interpreted by the computer as two separate items of information.

In order for the computer to extract the information from the DATA statements (access the information) we use a READ statement in the program.

Example
10 READ A,B,C,D

.

210 DATA 10,14,19,25

The computer understands the word READ to mean extract information from the DATA line. The computer would label a store A and place the number 10 into it and then label a store B and place 14 into it, 19 into C and 25 into D.

Example
10 READ A$,B$,C$

.

210 DATA JIM,JOE,JOHN

The computer responds in a similar way for alphanumeric information labelling a store A$ and placing JIM into it, etc.

It may, however, be more convenient to READ items of information one or two at a time. The following small program illustrates this ability.

Example
10 FOR I = 1 TO 3
20 READ A,B
30 PRINT A + B
40 NEXT I
50 DATA 2,5,3,6,4,7

First time through the loop the computer reads A = 2 and B = 5 and prints
A + B which would be 7. Second time through the loop the computer reads
A = 3 and B = 6 and prints A + B which would be 9. Finally, the third time
through the loop the computer reads A = 4 and B = 7 and prints A + B which
would be 11.

You may wonder how the computer knows which line of DATA, and
which item on that line, to read when it comes across a READ statement?
When the computer runs a program containing DATA statements, it automatically forms what is known as a DATA queue. An easy way of
visualizing this is to imagine all the DATA items being placed in a long list.
The list is formulated in the order of the DATA statements and reading left
to right across any one line. The computer then places a **pointer** against the
first item of data and then as it comes across READ statements it moves the
pointer down the list. This is best illustrated by an example.

Example
 10 READ A,B,C
 20 READ E,F$,G$
 30 READ H,J
 .
 .
 .
100 DATA 210,60,17,70,STATION
110 DATA PLATFORM,19,3

The following table illustrates how the pointer progresses down the DATA
queue and also shows the values and words assigned to the various variable
names which appear in the READ statements.

Pointer →

Initially	After executing statement 10		After executing statement 20		After executing statement 30	
→ 210	210	= A	210	= A	210	= A
60	60	= B	60	= B	60	= B
17	17	= C	17	= C	17	= C
70	→ 70		70	= E	70	= E
STATION	STATION		STATION	= F$	STATION	= F$
PLATFORM	PLATFORM		PLATFORM	= G$	PLATFORM	= G$
19	19		→ 19		19	= H
3	3		3		→ 3	= J

If there had been a fourth READ statement such as 40 READ K,L, a message would be printed by the computer telling the user that the program had run out of DATA when it tried to carry out statement 40.

How the POPULATION program selects information

```
40 PRINT "WHICH COUNTRY? TYPE CODE NUMBER."
50 INPUT Z

100 FOR J = 1 TO 27
110 READ A,B$,C,D,E,F,G$,H$
120 IF Z = A THEN 140
130 NEXT J
```

The READ statement, which is inside a loop, is carried out by the computer each time the set of statements inside the loop is performed. Each time, the computer reads a complete DATA line from the block of DATA lines at the end of the program. Each item of information is stored in a separate location. Only the item A, which is the code of the country, is then compared with the code selected by the student (Z). If they are the same, the computer leaves the loop and begins the projection using the information stored in the locations. If they are different, the computer loops once more and reads a new DATA line. It places the new information into the same locations as before, replacing the previous information. The comparison is then made again.

```
970 DATA 1,ARGENTINA,24.646,1.5,1.5,0,0,0
980 DATA 2,AUSTRIA, 7.55,0.5,0.5,0,0,0
etc.
```

In this way the correct data is located and used in the processing.

RESTORE Statements

It may be necessary to read a line of DATA more than once, and this necessitates returning to the beginning of the first DATA statement, or to a particular DATA statement. This can be done by using the statement **RESTORE**, to which may be added a line number of one of the DATA statements. If the RESTORE statement has no line number after it the computer moves to the beginning of the first DATA statement in the program.

Example

In POPULATION, if the student wishes to carry out a second projection, the RESTORE statement is used without a line number to set the pointer back to the beginning of the DATA statements.

```
890 PRINT "DO YOU REQUIRE ANOTHER PROJECTION?"
900 PRINT "TYPE YES OR NO"
910 INPUT Y$
920 IF Y$ = "YES" THEN 950
930 IF Y$ = "NO" THEN 1240 (1240 end of program)
940 GOTO 900
950 RESTORE
960 GOTO 10                    (10 start of program where the
                               DATA statements are READ for
                               a second time)
```

If a program is designed to be run with several sets of data, and the user is to specify which, then it would be necessary to move the data pointer to the correct set of data. This is accomplished by following the RESTORE statement with a line number corresponding to the correct set of data.

Example

```
 10 PRINT "WHICH NOTICE DO YOU REQUIRE?"
 20 INPUT A$
 30 PRINT "HOW MANY COPIES?"
 40 INPUT B
 50 IF A$ = "A" THEN 80
 60 IF A$ = "B" THEN 100
 70 IF A$ = "C" THEN 120
 80 RESTORE 210
 90 GOTO 130
100 RESTORE 220
110 GOTO 130
120 RESTORE 230
130 READ M$
140 FOR I = 1 TO B
150 PRINT
160 PRINT
170 PRINT M$
180 PRINT
190 PRINT
200 NEXT I
210 DATA THERE WILL BE NO MAIN ASSEMBLY THIS MORNING.
220 DATA THERE WILL BE NO EARLY LUNCHES SERVED TODAY.
230 DATA THERE WILL BE NO HYMN PRACTICE TODAY.
240 END
```

According to which notice is selected (A,B or C), the RESTORE statements (80,100 and 120) will set the pointer to the correct item of data in the data queue. However, it must be noted, that for programs that have several data items on a DATA line, the RESTORE statement can only move the pointer to an item of data which appears at the beginning of a DATA line. In terms of the DATA queue, the RESTORE statement has the effect of moving the pointer to the item of data at the beginning of the line mentioned in the RESTORE instruction. It is not possible to move to any item in the DATA statement other than the first item at the beginning of the line.

Acknowledgement: the data for POPULATION was taken from the *World Bank Atlas* with the kind permission of the The World Bank (Washington D.C.).

5 CHEM: simulated qualitative analysis

Introduction

An important feature of Basic programming is the ability to create a list or an array of data items. In both cases a name is assigned to the whole collection of data and individual items can be referred to by their position in the list or array. Loops can be used to good effect with lists and "loops within loops" with arrays. The simulation program CHEM uses both of these facilities to handle its data and responses, and although the program is quite long, the actual procedure part is concise. Before the simulation is considered it is necessary to explain the list and array facilities as they are used in Basic.

Basic

Lists

A **list** in Basic may be made up of items which are either numbers or character strings, but they cannot be mixed. Each list is given a name much the same as with data variables, and each item of a list is identified by its position in the list. A list called L, which contains 5 numeric items, could be thought of like this

L

L(1)	L(2)	L(3)	L(4)	L(5)

If this list was to contain character strings it would have to be called L£.

A list can be created by the use of a READ statement, a LET statement, or an INPUT statement.

Example
```
10 FOR I = 1 TO 5
20 READ L(I)
30 NEXT I
40 DATA 2,4,6,8,10
```

As I takes the values 1, 2, 3, 4, 5 the positions in the list L are filled, so that eventually it looks like

L

L(1)	L(2)	L(3)	L(4)	L(5)
2	4	6	8	10

The list is stored, during the running of the program, until it is required. Each item of the list will retain its value unless it is changed by the program. Subsequently, $L(1) = 2$, $L(2) = 4$ etc., and $L(1) + L(2)$ would have the value 6.

A list can be created, similarly, for character strings.

Example
10 FOR I = 1 TO 5
20 READ T£(I)
30 NEXT I
40 DATA SID,ALAN,JANE,MIKE,PAUL

The list T£ would be stored until needed.

T£

T£(1)	T£(2)	T£(3)	T£(4)	T£(5)
SID	ALAN	JANE	MIKE	PAUL

A list can be created using a LET statement.

Example
20 LET S(1) = 12
30 LET S(2) = 14
40 LET S(3) = 16

The list S would then be

S

S(1)	S(2)	S(3)
12	14	16

The values would be stored until needed.
The list could have been created from an INPUT statement.

Example
10 FOR I = 1 TO 3
20 PRINT "INPUT A NUMBER"
30 INPUT S(I)
40 NEXT I

To create the list of the previous example the numbers typed in would be 12, 14 and 16.

In the program CHEM three lists are created. They are used in straightforward ways, and the following example illustrates how.

```
10 FOR I = 1 TO 4
20 READ P£(I)              Creates the list
30 NEXT I                  called P£
40 LET A£(1) = "A WHITE POWDER"
50 LET A£(2) = "GREEN CRYSTALS"     The names in
60 LET A£(3) = "BLUE CRYSTALS"      the list A£
70 LET A£(4) = A£(1)
80 PRINT "TYPE SUBSTANCE NUMBER"
90 INPUT X
100 PRINT "CHEMICAL ";X;" IS ";P£(X)
110 PRINT A£(X)
120 DATA SODIUM SULPHATE,COPPER CHLORIDE     The names in
130 DATA COPPER SULPHATE, SODIUM CHLORIDE    the list P£
140 END
```

The two lists used here will be formed as

	P£(1)	P£(2)	P£(3)	P£(4)
P£	SODIUM SULPHATE	COPPER CHLORIDE	COPPER SULPHATE	SODIUM CHLORIDE

	A£(1)	A£(2)	A£(3)	A£(4)
A£	A WHITE POWDER	GREEN CRYSTALS	BLUE CRYSTALS	A WHITE POWDER

When the program is run, the user is requested to type in a number. If 3 is typed in then the printout would be

CHEMICAL 3 IS COPPER SULPHATE
BLUE CRYSTALS

The list P£ has been created using a loop, READ, and DATA statements. List A£ has been created using LET statements.

The DIMension Statement

The number of the last item in a list is called its **dimension**. Basic automatically reserves enough storage space for a list of dimension 10, but the dimension of a larger list must be declared in a **DIM** statement which appears at the beginning of the program. A list named T which had 20 numeric items would need a line which read DIM T(20).

Example
10 DIM T(20)
20 PRINT "TYPE IN ONE NUMBER AFTER EACH ARROW"
30 FOR I = 1 TO 20
40 INPUT T(I)
50 NEXT I

Should it not be clear how many items will be in a list (perhaps because the operator will decide this factor via an INPUT statement), then a suitably large number is used to dimension it, ensuring that a reasonably large amount of space will be reserved for the list.

The first item of list T is, in fact, T(0), but it is often useful to reserve this space for some special purpose and to start the list at T(1). It certainly makes counting easier if this is done.

Arrays

The term **array** refers to a table. It helps to think of the following picture when dealing with array items.

ARRAY M

	1	2	3	4	5	6	7
1	M(1,1)	M(1,2)	M(1,3)				
2	M(2,1)	M(2,2)					
3	M(3,1)						
4						M(4,6)	
5						M(5,6)	M(5,7)

Only some of the 35 elements have been written in. The dimension of this array is (5,7), i.e. 5 rows and 7 columns. Arrays larger than 10 rows or 10 columns must be declared in a dimension statement.

Example
10 DIM M(20,100)

To read and write an array requires a "loop within a loop".

Example

```
20 FOR I = 1 TO 2
30 FOR J = 1 TO 3
40 READ M(I,J)
50 NEXT J
60 NEXT I
70 DATA 6,0,−1,2,3,7
```

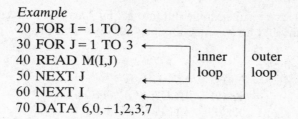

inner loop   outer loop

The table would look like this

COLUMN

		1	2	3
	1	6	0	−1
ROW	2	2	3	7

Notice that while I = 1 (i.e. row 1), J (the column number) takes the values 1, 2, 3. Then I = 2 is held while J becomes 1, 2, 3.

In fact, as with lists, the first row and column are numbered 0, so that there is an extra row and column.

It makes counting easier if the zero row and column are ignored, saving them for special use if needed.

An array is used in CHEM to enable the correct result for a test on a chemical to be printed. To demonstrate how this works we can consider two tests and three chemicals. The results are tabulated:

	SODIUM CHLORIDE	COPPER SULPHATE	MAGNESIUM CHLORIDE
SOLUBILITY IN WATER	SOLUBLE	BLUE SOLUTION	SOLUBLE
ACTION OF HEAT ON SOLID	LITTLE EFFECT	WATER OF CRYSTALISATION EVOLVED	NO APPARENT REACTION

These results can be put into a 2 by 3 array, or alternatively into a list of 5 items and a reference number put into an array.

Example
list K£

K£(1) = "SOLUBLE"
K£(2) = "BLUE SOLUTION"
K£(3) = "LITTLE EFFECT"
K£(4) = "WATER OF CRYSTALISATION EVOLVED"
K£(5) = "NO APPARENT REACTION"

array A

$A(1,1) = 1 \quad A(1,2) = 2 \quad A(1,3) = 1$
$A(2,1) = 3 \quad A(2,2) = 4 \quad A(2,3) = 5$

The numbers in this array refer to the list number of the response in K£. For example, test 1 on chemical 3 has reference number 1, which is the response "SOLUBLE". The program for this looks like

```
10 LET K£(1) = "SOLUBLE"
20 LET K£(2) = "BLUE SOLUTION"
30 LET K£(3) = "LITTLE EFFECT"
40 LET K£(4) = "WATER OF CRYSTALISATION EVOLVED"
50 LET K£(5) = "NO APPARENT REACTION"
60 FOR I = 1 TO 2
70 FOR J = 1 TO 3
80 READ A(I,J)
90 NEXT J
100 NEXT I
110 DATA 1,2,1
120 DATA 3,4,5
130 PRINT "TYPE CHEMICAL NUMBER"
140 INPUT M
150 PRINT "TYPE TEST NUMBER"
160 INPUT N
170 PRINT K£(A(M,N))
```

ARRAY A

1	2	1
3	4	5

e.g. 1

e.g. 3
e.g. SOLUBLE

In the above program, with the given input values, $M = 1$ and $N = 3$

In the array A $\quad A(1,3) = 1 \quad$ therefore

$K£(A(M,N)) = K£(A(1,3))$
$\qquad\qquad = K£(1)$
$\qquad\qquad = $ "SOLUBLE"

Much larger arrays and lists are used in CHEM, but the techniques used are the same.

The Simulation

One of the techniques taught in school chemistry is that of qualitative analysis. A substance, commonly a simple salt, is subjected to a series of tests until, by deduction, the elements present are determined. There are two distinct skills involved: the ability to perform the tests accurately and the knowledge to make the correct deductions. A computer simulation cannot replace the first of these, but it can help the student to become familiar with the test procedures and the deductions by providing the correct responses when the substances are subjected to various tests. This is what the program CHEM does. It enables the student to request the results of twenty salts subjected to eleven different tests. The student should be reminded to work systematically and not by random guesswork, since it is the learning of the procedures and the inferences that is important. In fact, a student might be encouraged to use his qualitative analysis notes for reference.

The simulation works in the following way:

1 The student selects from twenty chemicals and
2 subjects this chemical to chosen tests until
3 he/she can make an inference as to the chemical chosen.
4 If the inference is incorrect then the student can continue, or if correct can choose another chemical.

The Chemical and the Tests

In the simulation there are twenty chemicals to choose from and they can be subjected to eleven tests. There are 52 different responses and these are held in a list K£. The chemical names, all simple salts, are held in a list P£. As each chemical is chosen by the student a statement of its appearance is given. These are in the list A£.

Since 20 chemicals can be subjected to 11 tests there are 220 results, but some of these are the same. For each case a number is stored in the array A with dimensions (11,20). The number tells the computer which item in the list K£ should be printed out as the result.

The Numbers in the Array A

Chemical number

Test	1	2	3	4	5	6	7	8	9	10	11	12	13	14	15	16	17	18	19	20
1	1	43	44	44	46	50	44	44	44	44	46	44	44	44	44	44	44	44	46	46
2	2	12	5	12	39	40	5	5	12	12	41	51	25	25	5	5	5	25	38	38
3	3	13	15	3	15	13	3	14	15	3	15	24	10	11	10	3	3	15	24	11
4	4	20	18	4	19	20	4	4	16	4	22	19	16	37	4	4	4	19	19	21
5	4	17	16	4	16	17	4	4	16	4	22	16	16	23	4	4	4	26	16	21
6	5	5	5	5	38	5	5	5	5	48	5	5	5	5	5	27	5	16	52	38
7	5	5	5	5	38	5	5	5	5	48	5	16	5	5	5	27	5	5	36	30
8	6	33	6	5	38	6	32	32	5	29	5	31	45	45	5	5	31	45	38	38
9	7	5	7	5	5	7	35	35	5	5	5	34	5	5	5	5	34	5	5	5
10	8	8	8	8	8	8	8	8	8	8	8	8	9	9	8	8	8	9	8	8
11	4	16	5	16	28	5	5	5	16	5	16	5	5	5	16	5	5	5	42	28

Sample Run

MAKE SURE THAT YOU HAVE READ THE INSTRUCTIONS IN
THE BOOKLET PROVIDED. A LIST OF THE CHEMICALS
AND TESTS AVAILABLE IS PRINTED THERE.
WHICH CHEMICAL DO YOU WISH TO ANALYSE?
←1
CHEMICAL 1   A WHITE CRYSTALLINE SOLID
WHICH TEST DO YOU WANT TO DO ? ←1
CHEMICAL 1   TEST 1
SOLUBLE PRODUCING A COLOURLESS SOLUTION
WHICH TEST DO YOU WANT TO DO ? ←2
CHEMICAL 1   TEST 2
LITTLE EFFECT. SOME DECREPITATION OCCURRED
WHICH TEST DO YOU WANT TO DO ? ←3
CHEMICAL 1   TEST 3
PERSISTENT YELLOW COLOURATION
WHICH TEST DO YOU WANT TO DO ? ←4
CHEMICAL 1   TEST 4
NO PRECIPITATE WAS FORMED
WHICH TEST DO YOU WANT TO DO ? ←5
CHEMICAL 1   TEST 5
NO PRECIPITATE WAS FORMED
WHICH TEST DO YOU WANT TO DO ? ←6
CHEMICAL 1   TEST 6
NO APPARENT REACTION
WHICH TEST DO YOU WANT TO DO ? ←7
CHEMICAL 1   TEST 7
NO APPARENT REACTION
WHICH TEST DO YOU WANT TO DO ? ←8
CHEMICAL 1   TEST 8
COLOURLESS PUNGENT GAS GIVEN OFF, FUMING IN MOIST AIR
WHICH TEST DO YOU WANT TO DO ? ←9
CHEMICAL 1   TEST 9
A WHITE PRECIPITATE TURNING GREY ON STANDING
WHICH TEST DO YOU WANT TO DO ? ←10
CHEMICAL 1   TEST 10
NO RING PRODUCED
WHICH TEST DO YOU WANT TO DO ? ←11
CHEMICAL 1   TEST 11
NO PRECIPITATE WAS FORMED
WHICH TEST DO YOU WANT TO DO ? ←0
WHAT IS YOUR INFERENCE ? ←SODIUM CHLORIDE
CORRECT. DO YOU WISH TO TRY ANOTHER CHEMICAL (YES OR NO) ? ←NO
STOPPED AT LINE 1260

Choosing the Chemical

When asked to choose a chemical the student types in a number.

```
980 PRINT "WHICH CHEMICAL DO YOU WISH TO  ANALYSE?";
990 INPUT J
```

If it is certain that the student will always type a number at this point, then the program can proceed. If, however, the student types a character or word instead of a number, then the program terminates because of an error in the data type, i.e. character string instead of numeric variable.

Now the programmer has a choice. There is only a small chance that a number will not be typed in, and even if the program terminates it can easily be restarted. It is possible, though, to cover this possibility by taking the input as character and converting it to a numeric value. To do this, string handling functions are needed, so discussion of the methods is left until the chapter on the user/computer interface, after string handling functions have been explained in the chapter VERB.

The program segments

1000–1020   and   1070–1090

which calculate the numeric value of the input, can be ignored for now as they are not central to the working of the program.

Once the value J has been calculated it has to be checked to see if it is in the usable range.

1030 IF J < 1 OR J > 20 THEN 980

Line 980 is the invitation to type in a chemical number and it is repeated if the number is inappropriate. Chemical numbers are only in the range 1 to 20.

A similar process occurs when the test number I is assigned. Once again the input is taken as character and then converted to numeric. This happens in the program segment

1070–1090

The test number is checked for validity;

1100 IF I = 0 THEN 1160	An inference is to be made.
1110 IF I = 99 THEN 1220	Student wishes to end.
1120 IF I < 1 OR I > 11 THEN 1050	No such test number.

Line 1050 is the invitation to input a test number and this is repeated if necessary.

A number of the responses are too long to be typed on one line of the program. These responses are broken into two parts, which are joined together by the program. For example

860 K£(52) = L£(1) + L£(2)

The complete response, K£(52), can then be printed when appropriate. The process of "adding" character strings together is called **concatenation**, and it is mentioned again in the next chapter VERB.

The Tests

There are 20 chemicals available for analysis, all single simple inorganic compounds. When asked to choose a chemical, type a number between 1 and 20 only.

The chemical tests available are:

1 Solubility in water
2 Action of heat on solid
3 Flame test
4 Reaction with sodium hydroxide solution
5 Reaction with ammonia solution
6 Reaction with dilute hydrochloric acid
7 Reaction with dilute sulphuric acid
8 Solid with conc. sulphuric acid
9 Reaction with silver nitrate solution
10 Brown ring test
11 Reaction with barium chloride solution

When asked to choose a test, type a number between 1 and 11. The result will be given, and you can then choose another test by typing in a second number. Any number of tests can be carried out in this way. When you think you know the identity of the chemical, type 0 instead of a test number. Give your inference when it is requested. Your inference must consist of both cation and anion separated by a single space. If you wish to stop testing a chemical without giving an inference then type 99 instead of a test number.

Although you are given complete freedom in choosing the order of tests, remember that your analysis should be systematic and contain as few tests as possible.

2

Student Booklet: CHEM

Introduction

This program simulates the Qualitative Analysis which is taught in the school chemistry lessons. It is intended that students work through the tests in a systematic way as indicated in chemistry notes, and not to reach their conclusions by guesswork.

There are twenty numbered chemicals to choose from and eleven tests may be used to help identify the chemicals. Each chemical is a single inorganic compound consisting of an anion and cation.

e.g. SODIUM CHLORIDE

From the results of the tests, performed in a systematic way, the substances can be deduced.

It should be remembered that this program is not a substitute for practical experience because skill is required to perform the tests satisfactorily. Instead, it is intended to assist students to become familiar with the testing procedure and the results of the tests.

The program is called up by typing CHEM

1 In making inferences
   IRON (II) replaces FERROUS
   IRON (III) replaces FERRIC
   MANGANESE (II) is used where appropriate.
   Always leave a space between the name and the bracketed I's.

2 A single space must be left between the two parts of a name in an inference, with no full stops or other punctuation being used.

1

A Run

WHICH CHEMICAL DO YOU WISH TO ANALYSE? ←2

CHEMICAL 2   A DEEP BLUE CRYSTALLINE SOLID

WHICH TEST DO YOU WANT TO DO? ←1

CHEMICAL 2   TEST 1

SOLUBLE, BLUE SOLUTION

WHICH TEST DO YOU WANT TO DO? ←2

CHEMICAL 2   TEST 2

WATER OF CRYSTALLISATION EVOLVED

WHICH TEST DO YOU WANT TO DO? ←0

WHAT IS YOUR INFERENCE? ←COPPER SULPHATE

3

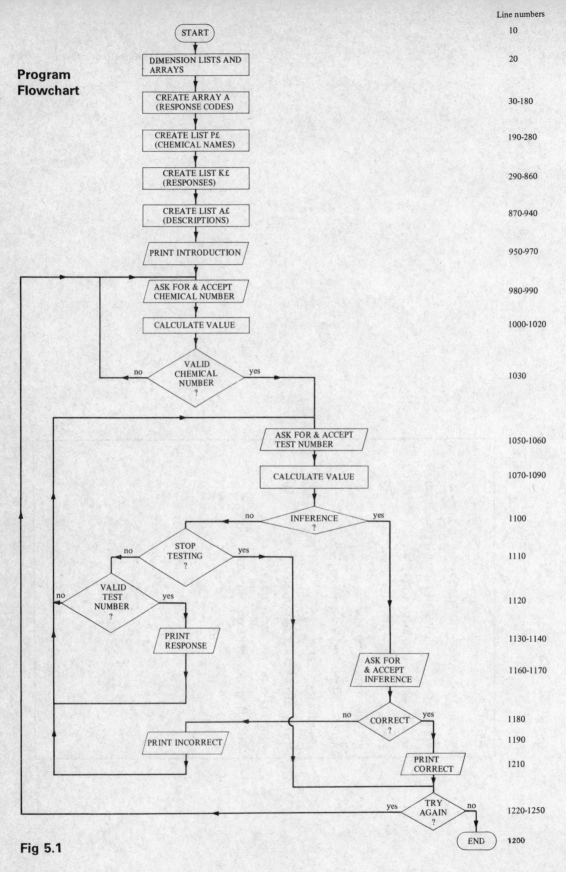

Program Flowchart

	Line numbers
START	10
DIMENSION LISTS AND ARRAYS	20
CREATE ARRAY A (RESPONSE CODES)	30-180
CREATE LIST P£ (CHEMICAL NAMES)	190-280
CREATE LIST K£ (RESPONSES)	290-860
CREATE LIST A£ (DESCRIPTIONS)	870-940
PRINT INTRODUCTION	950-970
ASK FOR & ACCEPT CHEMICAL NUMBER	980-990
CALCULATE VALUE	1000-1020
VALID CHEMICAL NUMBER ?	1030
ASK FOR & ACCEPT TEST NUMBER	1050-1060
CALCULATE VALUE	1070-1090
INFERENCE ?	1100
STOP TESTING ?	1110
VALID TEST NUMBER ?	1120
PRINT RESPONSE	1130-1140
ASK FOR & ACCEPT INFERENCE	1160-1170
CORRECT ?	1180
PRINT INCORRECT	1190
PRINT CORRECT	1210
TRY AGAIN ?	1220-1250
END	1200

Fig 5.1

104

```
10    REM QUALITATIVE ANALYSIS PROGRAM P.AYRE/8,79
20    DIM A(11,20),A£(20),K£(52),P£(20)
30    FOR I=1 TO 11
40    FOR J=1 TO 20
50    READ A(I,J)
60    NEXT J
70    NEXT I
80    DATA1,43,44,44,46,50,44,44,44,44,46,44,44,44,44,44,44,44,46,46
90    DATA2,12,5,12,39,40,5,5,12,12,41,51,25,25,5,5,5,25,38,38
100   DATA3,13,15,3,15,13,3,14,15,3,15,24,10,11,10,3,3,15,24,11
110   DATA4,20,18,4,19,20,4,4,16,4,22,19,16,37,4,4,4,19,19,21
120   DATA4,17,16,4,16,17,4,4,16,4,22,16,16,23,4,4,4,26,16,21
130   DATA5,5,5,5,38,5,5,5,5,48,5,5,5,5,5,27,5,16,52,38
140   DATA5,5,5,5,38,5,5,5,5,48,5,16,5,5,5,27,5,5,36,30
150   DATA6,33,6,5,38,6,32,32,5,29,5,31,45,45,5,5,31,45,38,38
160   DATA7,5,7,5,5,7,35,35,5,5,5,34,5,5,5,34,5,5,5
170   DATA8,8,8,8,8,8,8,8,8,8,8,9,9,8,8,8,9,8,8
180   DATA4,16,5,16,28,5,5,5,16,5,16,5,5,5,16,5,5,5,42,28
190   FOR I=1 TO 20
200   READ P£(I)
210   NEXT I
220   DATA SODIUM CHLORIDE,COPPER SULPHATE,MAGNESIUM CHLORIDE
230   DATA SODIUM SULPHATE,ZINC CARBONATE,COPPER CHLORIDE
240   DATA SODIUM IODIDE,POTASSIUM IODIDE,MAGNESIUM SULPHATE
250   DATA SODIUM SULPHITE,MANGANESE (II) SULPHATE,LEAD BROMIDE
260   DATA STRONTIUM NITRATE,IRON (II) NITRATE,LITHIUM SULPHATE
270   DATA SODIUM NITRITE,SODIUM BROMIDE,SILVER NITRATE
280   DATA LEAD CARBONATE,NICKEL CARBONATE
290   LET K£(1)="SOLUBLE PRODUCING A COLOURLESS SOLUTION"
300   LET K£(2)="LITTLE EFFECT. SOME DECREPITATION OCCURED"
310   LET K£(3)="PERSISTENT YELLOW COLOURATION"
320   LET K£(4)="NO PRECIPITATE WAS FORMED"
330   LET K£(5)="NO APPARENT REACTION"
340   LET K£(6)="COLOURLESS PUNGENT GAS GIVEN OFF, FUMING IN MOIST AIR"
350   LET K£(7)="A WHITE PRECIPITATE TURNING GREY ON STANDING"
360   LET K£(8)="NO RING PRODUCED"
370   LET K£(9)="BROWN RING PRODUCED"
380   LET K£(10)="CRIMSON COLOURATION"
390   LET K£(11)="YELLOW SPARKS PRODUCED"
400   LET K£(12)="WATER OF CRYSTALLISATION EVOLVED"
410   LET K£(13)="BLUEISH-GREEN COLOURATION"
420   LET K£(14)="LILAC COLOURATION THROUGH BLUE GLASS"
430   LET K£(15)="NO DEFINITE COLOURATION "
440   LET K£(16)="WHITE PRECIPITATE FORMED"
450   LET K£(17)="BLUE PRECIPITATE,DEEP BLUE SOLUTION FORMED WITH EXCESS"
460   LET K£(18)="WHITE PRECIPITATE FORMED, NO OTHER CHANGE"
470   LET K£(19)=K£(16)+", SOLUBLE IN EXCESS "
480   LET K£(20)="PALE BLUE PRECIPITATE TURNING BLACK ON HEATING"
490   LET K£(21)="GREEN PRECIPITATE"
500   LET K£(22)="WHITE PRECIPITATE RAPIDLY TURNING BROWN"
510   LET K£(23)="DARK MUD-GREEN PRECIPITATE TURNING BROWN AT SURFACE"
520   LET K£(24)="STEEL-BLUE COLOURED FLAME"
530   LET K£(25)=" PUNGENT ORANGE-BROWN GAS EVOLVED"
540   LET K£(26)="BROWN PRECIPITATE WHICH DISSOLVES IN EXCESS"
550   LET K£(26)=K£(26)+" AMMONIUM HYDROXIDE"
560   LET K£(27)="BROWN PUNGENT GAS EVOLVED SOLUTION TURNED BLUE"
570   LET K£(28)="FLUFFY WHITE PRECIPITATE "
580   LET K£(29)="GAS EVOLVED TURNS LEAD ACETATE PAPER BLACK"
590   LET K£(29)=K£(29)+" , AND A YELLOW PRECIPITATE"
600   LET K£(31)="RED BROWN VAPOURS PUNGENT FUMING IN AIR"
610   LET K£(32)="BLACK SOLID PRECIPITATE , VIOLET VAPOURS ON HEATING"
620   LET K£(33)="BLUE SOLID TURNS WHITE"
630   LET K£(34)="PALE YELLOW COLOURED PRECIPITATE"
640   LET K£(35)="DEEP CREAM COLOURED PRECIPITATE"
650   LET K£(37)="DIRTY GREEN PRECIPITATE"
660   LET K£(38)="ODOURLESS GAS EVOLVED TURNING LIME WATER MILKY"
670   LET K£(30)=K£(38)+", AND A GREEN SOLUTION"
680   LET K£(36)=K£(38)+", AND A "+K£(16)
690   LET K£(39)="SOLID CHANGES WHITE TO YELLOW, WHITE ON COOLING"
```

```
700   LET K£(40)="SOLID CHANGES GREEN TO LIGHT BROWN"
710   LET K£(41)="SOLID CHANGES PALE PINK TO OFF-WHITE"
720   LET K£(42)=K£(28)+", PART OF WHICH DISSOLVES ON WARMING"
730   LET K£(43)="SOLUBLE, BLUE SOLUTION"
740   LET K£(44)="SOLUBLE"
750   LET K£(45)="ACID VAPOUR BECOMING BROWN ON HEATING."
760   LET K£(46)="SPARINGLY SOLUBLE"
770   LET K£(47)="PUNGENT GAS EVOLVED ON WARMING, TURNING ACIDIFIED"
780   LET K£(48)=K£(47)+" POTASSIUM DICHROMATE  SOLUTION GREEN"
790   LET K£(49)="SOLUBLE TO GIVE A SOLUTION THAT IS PALE BLUE WHEN"
800   LET K£(50)=K£(49)+" DILUTE, AND GREEN WHEN CONCENTRATED"
810   LET L£(1)="DECREPITATION OCCURED TO FORM AN ORANGE-RED LIQUID"
820   LET L£(2)=", ON COOLING FORMS AN  OFF-WHITE TRANSLUCENT GLASS"
830   LET K£(51)=L£(1)+L£(2)
840   LET L£(1)="WHITE PRECIPITATE, SOLUBLE ON BOILING, AND COLOURLESS"
850   LET L£(2)=" GAS EVOLVED THAT  TURNS LIME WATER CLOUDY"
860   LET K£(52)=L£(1)+L£(2)
870   LET A£(1)="A WHITE CRYSTALLINE SOLID"
880   LET A£(2)="A DEEP BLUE CRYSTALLINE SOLID"
890   LET A£(4)=A£(5)=A£(15)="A WHITE POWDER"
900   LET A£(6)=A£(14)="GREEN CRYSTALS"
910   LET A£(11)="LARGE PINK CRYSTALS"
920   LET A£(20)="A GREEN POWDER"
930   LET A£(3)=A£(7)=A£(8)=A£(9)=A£(10)=A£(12)=A£(13)=A£(1)
940   LET A£(16)=A£(17)=A£(18)=A£(19)=A£(1)
950   PRINT "MAKE SURE THAT YOU HAVE READ THE INSTRUCTIONS IN"
960   PRINT "THE BOOKLET PROVIDED. A LIST OF THE CHEMICALS"
970   PRINT "AND TESTS AVAILABLE IS PRINTED THERE."
980   PRINT "WHICH CHEMICAL DO YOU WISH TO ANALYSE ?";
990   INPUT J£
1000  LET J=VAL(J£)
1010  IF LEN(J£)<2 THEN 1030
1020  LET J=J*10+VAL(J£[2,2])
1030  IF J<1 OR J>20 THEN 980
1040  PRINT "CHEMICAL ";J;" ";A£(J)
1050  PRINT "WHICH TEST DO YOU WANT TO DO ?";
1060  INPUT I£
1070  LET I=VAL(I£)
1080  IF LEN(I£)<2 THEN 1100
1090  LET I=I*10+VAL(I£[2,2])
1100  IF I=0 THEN 1160
1110  IF I=99 THEN 1220
1120  IF I<1 OR I>11 THEN 1050
1130  PRINT "CHEMICAL ";J;" TEST ";I
1140  PRINT K£(A(I,J))
1150  GOTO 1050
1160  PRINT "WHAT IS YOUR INFERENCE ?";
1170  INPUT F£
1180  IF F£=P£(J) THEN 1210
1190  PRINT "INCORRECT"
1200  GOTO 1050
1210  PRINT "CORRECT. ";
1220  PRINT "DO YOU WISH TO TRY ANOTHER CHEMICAL (YES OR NO) ?";
1230  INPUT Y£
1240  IF Y£="YES" THEN 980
1250  IF Y£<>"NO" THEN 1220
1260  END
```

An Extension to CHEM

The program CHEM has been used by individuals and by small groups. It has also been used for class instruction, and this brought the chemistry master more deeply into the project. Until that point he had advised on the suitability of the chemicals and tests, and had checked the output for inaccuracies. Using the program for himself led to new ideas being incorporated into it. Firstly, the suggestion was made that the program should be transferred to the Research Machines 380Z microcomputer since the screen output could be followed by the whole class much better than with the teletype. Secondly, since the program was to be redrafted for the RM 380Z microcomputer, the opportunity was taken to make alterations to the program. The teacher considered that certain tests and chemicals were more pertinent to the teaching programme than others, and that the inclusion of these would make the program more useful. As a consequence, the tests were changed and reduced to eight, and the unknown chemicals increased to forty.

Certainly this seems to be the most valuable way to include the computer in normal teaching, but it is not easy to arrive at this position of co-operation. In this case the programmer knew little chemistry and the subject teacher was unaware of the computer's possibilities. The explanation of how the program works was made easier by reference to the table of chemicals, tests and responses given earlier. Indeed this seems to be the key to the program, so much so that the teacher was able to read the program listing after reference to it.

The RM 380Z version, called CHEMICAL, is included here for reference, the construction being essentially the same as that of CHEM which has been described. Minor changes were required by the slightly different version of Basic used, and also because the line lengths are restricted to 40 characters on the visual display screen. The changes are given without explanation, and the program runs in 9K as well as 12K Basic.

Changes to the Program for RM 380Z Basic

10 CLEAR 1600   reserves space for the string
                  variables used in the program.
130 PRINT CHR$(12)   "prints" a blank screen.
The instructions printed at the start of the run have been designed for 40 character lines.

The substring function LEFT$(J$,2) replaces the SOBS version J$[2,2].

The tests available can be listed at any point of the program. This is necessary since there is no hard copy to refer to.

The number of chemicals available to choose from has been increased to 40, and the number of tests has been reduced to 8.

Student Booklet: CHEMICAL	380Z version

The Tests

There are 40 chemicals available for analysis; all single, simple inorganic compounds. When asked to choose a chemical type a number between 1 and 40 only.

The chemical tests available are:

1 Flame test.
2 Action of heat on solid.
3 Action of sodium hydroxide on solution of chemical.
4 Action of dilute hydrochloric acid on solution of chemical.
5 Action of dilute nitric acid and silver nitrate solution on solution of chemical.
6 Action of chlorine water and carbon tetrachloride on solution of chemical.
7 Action of dilute hydrochloric acid and barium chloride on solution of chemical.
8 Brown ring test.

When asked to choose a test, type a number between 1 and 8. The result of the test will be given, and you can choose another test. It has been assumed that the chemicals are soluble enough for the tests to be performed.

When you think you have identified the chemical, type 0 (zero) instead of a test number and give your inference when it is requested. Your inference must consist of both cation and anion, separated by a single space.

2

If you wish to display the tests available, type TESTS at any stage, and STOP if you wish to finish.

REMEMBER — WORK SYSTEMATICALLY

A Run

WHAT CHEMICAL DO YOU WISH TO ANALYSE
? 1
CHEMICAL 1 WHITE SOLID, SOLUBLE IN WATER
WHAT TEST DO YOU WANT TO DO
? 1
CHEMICAL 1 TEST 1
NO DEFINITE COLOUR
WHAT TEST DO YOU WANT TO DO
? 2
CHEMICAL 1 TEST 2
. .
. .

3

**Program Listing:
Research Machines
380Z BASIC**

```
 10 CLEAR 1600
 20 REM: CHEM MK5. P. AYRE/M. AMOS NOV '79
 30 DIM A(8,40),A$(40),K$(31),P$(40)
 40 FOR I=1 TO 8
 50 FOR J=1 TO 40
 60 READ A(I,J)
 70 NEXT J
 80 NEXT I
 90 FOR I=1 TO 40
100 READ P$(I)
110 NEXT I
120 GOTO 950
130 PRINT CHR$(12)
140 PRINT "FULL INSTRUCTIONS FOR RUNNING THIS"
150 PRINT "PROGRAM ARE PROVIDED IN A BOOKLET."
160 PRINT "THE CHEMICALS CAN BE SELECTED BY"
170 PRINT "TYPING A NUMBER BETWEEN 1 AND 40."
180 PRINT "THE TESTS AVAILABLE, AND THEIR"
190 PRINT "NUMBERS, ARE LISTED IN THE BOOKLET."
200 PRINT "FOR A LIST OF THE TESTS AVAILABLE"
210 PRINT "TYPE 'TESTS' AND PRESS THE RETURN KEY."
220 PRINT "PRESS THE 'RETURN' KEY WHEN YOU"
230 PRINT "ARE READY TO START. TYPE 'STOP' WHEN"
240 PRINT "YOU WISH TO FINISH."
250 INPUT A$
260 IF A$="STOP" THEN 1880
270 IF A$="TESTS" THEN GOSUB 1690
280 PRINT "WHAT CHEMICAL DO YOU WISH TO ANALYSE"
290 INPUT J$
300 IF J$="STOP" THEN 1880
310 IF J$="TESTS" THEN GOSUB 1690:GOTO 280
320 LET L$=LEFT$(J$,1)
330 IF L$<"0" OR L$>"9" THEN 280
340 LET J=VAL(LEFT$(J$,2))
350 IF J<1 OR J>40 THEN 280
360 PRINT CHR$(12)
370 PRINT "CHEMICAL";J;A$(J)
380 PRINT "WHAT TEST DO YOU WANT TO DO"
390 INPUT I$
400 IF I$="STOP" THEN  580
410 IF I$="TESTS" THEN GOSUB 1690:GOTO 380
420 LET L$=LEFT$(I$,1)
430 IF L$<"0" OR L$>"9" THEN 380
440 LET I=VAL(L$)
450 IF I=0 THEN 500
460 IF I<1 OR I>8 THEN 380
470 PRINT "CHEMICAL";J;"TEST";I
480 PRINT K$(A(I,J))
490 GOTO 380
500 PRINT "WHAT IS YOUR INFERENCE"
510 INPUT F$
520 IF A$="STOP" THEN 1880
530 IF F$="TESTS" THEN GOSUB 1690
540 IF F$=P$(J) THEN 570
550 PRINT "INCORRECT."
560 GOTO 380
570 PRINT "CORRECT."
580 PRINT "DO YOU WISH TO TRY ANOTHER CHEMICAL?"
590 PRINT "YES OR NO";
600 INPUT A$
610 IF A$="YES" THEN 280
620 IF A$="NO" THEN 1880
630 IF A$="TESTS" THEN GOSUB 1690
640 IF A$="STOP" THEN 1880
650 GOTO 590
660 DATA 1,2,3,4,5,6,6,1,2,3,4,5,6,6,1,2,3,4,5,6
670 DATA 6,1,2,3,4,5,6,6,1,2,3,4,5,6,2,3,4,6,3,4
680 DATA 10,7,7,7,9,8,7,10,7,7,7,8,7,9,10,7,7,11,7,9
690 DATA 8,10,7,7,7,7,7,7,10,7,7,7,7,7,11,11,7,7,8,8
```

```
700 DATA 16,12,12,12,13,14,15,16,12,12,12,13,14,15,16,12,12,12,13,14
710 DATA 15,16,12,12,12,13,14,15,16,12,12,12,13,14,12,12,12,15,12,12
720 DATA 17,17,17,17,17,17,17,17,18,17,17,17,17,18,17,17,17,17,17,17
730 DATA 17,17,17,17,17,17,17,17,17,18,17,17,17,17,17,18,17,19,19
740 DATA 21,22,22,20,20,20,21,22,20,21,22,20,22,20,20,21,22,20,22,20
750 DATA 20,22,20,20,22,21,21,22,20,22,20,21,22,20,20,22,20,20
760 DATA 24,25,26,23,23,23,24,26,23,24,25,23,25,23,23,24,25,23,25,23
770 DATA 23,25,23,23,26,24,24,25,23,26,23,24,26,26,23,23,23,26,23,23
780 DATA 27,27,27,28,27,28,27,27,29,27,27,28,27,27,29,27,27,27,27,27
790 DATA 28,27,28,28,27,27,27,27,28,27,29,27,27,27,27,28,27,29,27,27,27
800 DATA 30,30,30,30,31,30,30,30,30,30,30,30,30,31,30,30,30,31,30,31
810 DATA 30,30,30,30,30,30,30,30,30,30,30,30,30,30,31,31,30,30,30,30
820 DATA AMMONIUM CHLORIDE,LITHIUM BROMIDE,SODIUM IODIDE
830 DATA POTASSIUM SULPHATE,COPPER NITRATE,IRON (II) SULPHATE
840 DATA IRON (III) CHLORIDE,AMMONIUM IODIDE,LITHIUM CARBONATE
850 DATA SODIUM CHLORIDE,POTASSIUM BROMIDE,COPPER SULPHATE
860 DATA IRON (II) BROMIDE,IRON (III) NITRATE,AMMONIUM CARBONATE
870 DATA LITHIUM CHLORIDE,SODIUM BROMIDE,POTASSIUM NITRATE
880 DATA COPPER BROMIDE,IRON (II) NITRATE,IRON (III) SULPHATE
890 DATA AMMONIUM BROMIDE,LITHIUM SULPHATE,SODIUM SULPHATE
900 DATA POTASSIUM IODIDE,COPPER CHLORIDE,IRON (II) CHLORIDE
910 DATA IRON (III) BROMIDE,AMMONIUM SULPHATE,LITHIUM IODIDE
920 DATA SODIUM CARBONATE,POTASSIUM CHLORIDE,COPPER IODIDE
930 DATA IRON (II) IODIDE,LITHIUM NITRATE,SODIUM NITRATE
940 DATA POTASSIUM CARBONATE,IRON (III) IODIDE,SODIUM SULPHITE,POTASSIUM
SULPHITE
950 K$(1)="NO DEFINITE COLOUR"
960 K$(2)="CRIMSON COLOURATION"
970 K$(3)="PERSISTENT YELLOW COLOURATION"
980 K$(4)="LILAC COLOURATION"
990 K$(5)="APPLE GREEN COLOURATION"
1000 K$(6)="YELLOW SPARKS PRODUCED"
1010 K$(7)="NO APPARENT CHANGE"
1020 K$(8)="ACIDIC GAS EVOLVED"
1030 K$(9)="BROWN GAS EVOLVED"
1040 K$(10)="WHITE SOLID FORMED ON COOL SIDES OF TESTTUBE"
1050 K$(11)="COLOURLESS GAS EVOLVED WHICH RELIGHTS   GLOWING SPLINT"
1060 K$(12)=K$(7)
1070 K$(13)="PALE BLUE PRECIPITATE"
1080 K$(14)="DIRTY-GREEN PRECIPITATE"
1090 K$(15)="REDDISH-BROWN PRECIPITATE"
1100 K$(16)="ALKALINE GAS EVOLVED ON WARMING"
1110 K$(17)=K$(7)
1120 K$(18)="ACIDIC GAS EVOLVED, TURNING LIME-WATER   CLOUDY"
1130 K$(19)="ACIDIC GAS EVOLVED ON WARMING,          DECOLOURISING"
1140 K$(19)=K$(19)+" POTASSIUM PERMANGANATE"
1150 K$(20)=K$(7)
1160 K$(21)="WHITE PRECIPITATE TURNING GREY"
1170 K$(22)="YELLOW PRECIPITATE"
1180 K$(23)=K$(7)
1190 K$(24)="CARBON TETRACHLORIDE LAYER COLOURLESS"
1200 K$(25)="CARBON TETRACHLORIDE LAYER BROWN"
1210 K$(26)="CARBON TETRACHLORIDE LAYER PURPLE"
1220 K$(27)=K$(7)
1230 K$(28)="HEAVY WHITE PRECIPITATE"
1240 K$(29)="LIGHT FLUFFY PRECIPITATE"
1250 K$(30)="NO RING FORMED"
1260 K$(31)="BROWN RING FORMED"
1270 A$(0)=", SOLUBLE IN WATER"
1280 A$(1)="WHITE SOLID"+A$(0)
1290 A$(2)=A$(1)
1300 A$(3)="       WHITE CRYSTALLINE SOLID"+A$(0)
1310 A$(4)=A$(3)
1320 A$(5)="       BLUE CRYSTALLINE SOLID"+A$(0)
1330 A$(6)="       PALE GREEN CRYSTALLINE SOLID"+A$(0)
1340 A$(7)="       YELLOW SOLID"+A$(0)
1350 A$(8)=A$(1)
1360 A$(9)=A$(1)
1370 A$(10)=A$(3)
1380 A$(11)=A$(3)
```

```
1390 A$(12)=A$(5)
1400 A$(13)="PALE GREEN SOLID"+A$(0)
1410 A$(14)="        PALE BROWN CRYSTALLINE SOLID"+A$(0)
1420 A$(15)=A$(1)
1430 A$(16)=A$(1)
1440 A$(17)=A$(3)
1450 A$(18)=A$(3)
1460 A$(19)="LIGHT FAWN SOLID"
1470 A$(20)=A$(6)
1480 A$(21)=A$(14)
1490 A$(22)=A$(1)
1500 A$(23)=A$(1)
1510 A$(24)=A$(3)
1520 A$(25)=A$(3)
1530 A$(26)="BLUE-GREEN SOLID"+A$(0)
1540 A$(27)=A$(13)
1550 A$(28)="PALE BROWN SOLID"+A$(0)
1560 A$(29)=A$(3)
1570 A$(30)=A$(1)
1580 A$(31)=A$(1)
1590 A$(32)=A$(1)
1600 A$(33)=A$(19)
1610 A$(34)=A$(13)
1620 A$(35)=A$(1)
1630 A$(36)=A$(1)
1640 A$(37)=A$(1)
1650 A$(38)=A$(28)
1660 A$(39)=A$(3)
1670 A$(40)=A$(3)
1680 GOTO 130
1690 PRINT "THE TESTS AVAILABLE ARE:"
1700 PRINT
1710 PRINT "    1.  FLAME TEST"
1720 PRINT "    2.  ACTION OF HEAT ON SOLID."
1730 PRINT "    3.  ACTION OF SODIUM HYDROXIDE"
1740 PRINT "        ON SOLUTION OF CHEMICAL"
1750 PRINT "    4.  ACTION OF DILUTE HYDROCHLORIC"
1760 PRINT "        ACID ON SOLUTION OF CHEMICAL"
1770 PRINT "    5.  ACTION OF DILUTE NITRIC ACID"
1780 PRINT "        AND SILVER NITRATE SOLUTION"
1790 PRINT "        ON SOLUTION OF CHEMICAL."
1800 PRINT "    6.  ACTION OF CHLORINE WATER AND"
1810 PRINT "        CARBON TETRACHLORIDE ON"
1820 PRINT "        SOLUTION OF CHEMICAL"
1830 PRINT "    7.  ACTION OF DILUTE HYDROCHLORIC"
1840 PRINT "        ACID AND BARIUM CHLORIDE ON"
1850 PRINT "        SOLUTION OF CHEMICAL."
1860 PRINT "    8.  BROWN RING TEST."
1870 RETURN
1880 END
```

6 VERB: French drill exercise

Introduction

VERB was conceived as a drill exercise in which the student could practise forming the present tense of regular French verbs, while having errors pointed out as they occur, the correct verb endings explained and reinforced, and the work marked by the computer. One would expect the student to begin the session with a less than precise knowledge of the correct verb endings—although appreciating that the root has to be replaced—but, as a result of the corrective features, to experience an improvement in performance over a series of runs with verbs of the same type. Unlike some computer exercises, this one would appear to derive particular benefits from the use of a Visual Display Unit, because the absence of a hard copy in the form of paper printout obliges the student to exercise his/her memory to the full in order to make progress.

Three new features of Basic are important in the design of the program. The first is a set of functions which allows the analysis and manipulation of a character string. For this reason they are called **string functions** and the process is referred to as string handling. String functions are not available in all Basic dialects, but they are not uncommon. Where they do exist they are likely to be peculiar to the system in question. Those considered here are found in ICL-CES BASIC and the Research Machines 380Z 12K BASIC. For precise definitions of all of the string functions in these forms of Basic or those in other dialects, the appropriate Basic manuals will have to be consulted. Here we are only concerned with establishing the principle of string handling.

The other new features are the statement ON . . . GOTO, which allows multiple IF . . . THEN statements to be dispensed with, and a process known as concatenation which enables two character strings to be joined together.

String Functions

Probably more important than an understanding of what each function can do in any given form of Basic (ICL-CES BASIC boasts twenty-seven of these) is a general awareness of the kind of tasks that can be performed with them.

With the ICL-CES BASIC it is possible to do the following, among other things, to the boy's name CHRISTOPHER.

1 Count the number of letters in the name.
2 Identify the position of the first occurrence of a particular letter, perhaps the letter H.
3 Identify the position of the last occurrence of that letter.
4 Delete some part of the name, perhaps TOPHER.

5 Delete all of the occurrences of a particular letter, again the letter H.
6 Replace some part of the name with other letters. For example, replace OPHER with ABELLE.

We should be able to see from these few examples the way in which we can analyse and manipulate a character string. The next question, to put it bluntly, is, "So what?" How does the fact that one can replace parts of a word or count the number of letters in a word throw any light on the use of the computer in an educational context? VERB, fortunately, allows us to tackle this question head on. String functions are a crucial element of the program, and because of this it is a very useful peg on which to hang an examination of them.

The Nature of French Verb Endings

French verbs fall into three categories: those that end in ER; those that end in IR; and those that end in RE. For example, porter—to carry, finir—to finish, and vendre—to sell. The er, ir or re will be removed and an appropriate ending substituted.

| | | ENDINGS FOR REGULAR VERB TYPES | | |
		ER	IR	RE
JE	(I)	E	IS	S
TU	(YOU,sing.)	ES	IS	S
IL	(HE)	E	IT	NO ENDING
ELLE	(SHE)	E	IT	NO ENDING
NOUS	(WE)	ONS	ISSONS	ONS
VOUS	(YOU,pl.)	EZ	ISSEZ	EZ
ILS	(THEY,masc.pl.)	ENT	ISSENT	ENT
ELLES	(THEY,fem.pl.)	ENT	ISSENT	ENT

The verb porter would read

JE PORTE	NOUS PORTONS
TU PORTES	VOUS PORTEZ
IL PORTE	ILS PORTENT
ELLE PORTE	ELLES PORTENT

It is plain to see that if we can replace OPHER with ABELLE in the name CHRISTOPHER, we can replace ER, IR or RE with what we choose. We have a means of getting the computer to work out and create the correct form of a verb for any given pronoun. If we can do that, we can compare a student's attempt to do the same thing with the computer's answer. We can go further. Having discovered that a student's input is incorrect, the computer can examine it and determine the nature of the error and communicate this to the student, then invite a further input.

**How VERB
Operates**

1 The student is asked to select the type of verb to be practised: er, ir or re.

2 Depending upon the verb type selected, one of the following lists is printed:

FERMER	AGIR	ATTENDRE
JOUER	BATIR	DESCENDRE
PORTER	CHOISIR	ENTENDRE
RESTER	FINIR	PERDRE
TOMBER	OBEIR	VENDRE

The student chooses one of these.

3 The computer prints a cue pronoun: je, tu, il, elle, etc.

4 The student types in the verb with its appropriate ending.

5 The computer checks the student's response against the correct answer which it manufactures.

6 A correct answer is credited with one mark and the next cue pronoun is printed.

7 If the student's input is incorrect, he/she receives the message INCORRECT and is then advised of the nature of the error and invited to TRY AGAIN. Another incorrect input results in the correct answer being printed, followed by the next cue pronoun.

8 All unsuccessful attempts are noted by the computer. A second attempt which is successful is credited with one mark.

9 When all parts of the verb have been attempted, a score is printed. It is expressed as the number of correct responses out of the number of attempts.

10 If the student wishes to finish the exercise before all parts of the verb have been attempted, he/she can type AXA after any invitation to input. This leads out of the program.

A Sample Run

The output of the program is not continuous. To represent the clearing of the screen, the student/computer dialogue has been presented in a series of frames, the sequence of which is numbered.

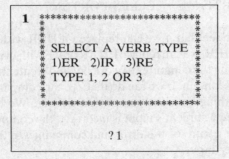

```
┌─────────────────────────────┐   ┌─────────────────────────────┐
│ 3          PORTER           │   │ 4                           │
│                             │   │                             │
│      JE ?PORE               │   │         PORTER              │
│ JE PORE IS INCORRECT        │   │                             │
│ THERE IS AN ERROR IN        │   │      TU ?PORTES             │
│ THE STEM. TRY AGAIN         │   │                             │
│ ? PORTE                     │   │                             │
│      CORRECT                │   │                             │
└─────────────────────────────┘   └─────────────────────────────┘

┌─────────────────────────────┐   ┌─────────────────────────────┐
│ 5          PORTER           │   │ 6          PORTER           │
│                             │   │                             │
│      IL ? PORTES            │   │      ELLE ? PORREZ          │
│ IL PORTES IS INCORRECT      │   │ ELLE PORREZ IS INCORRECT    │
│ REMEMBER,                   │   │ THERE IS AN ERROR IN        │
│ THE IL ENDING FOR ER        │   │ THE STEM. REMEMBER,         │
│ VERBS IS E. TRY AGAIN.      │   │ THE ELLE ENDING FOR ER      │
│ ? PORTE                     │   │ VERBS IS E. TRY AGAIN       │
│      CORRECT                │   │ ? PORTES                    │
└─────────────────────────────┘   └─────────────────────────────┘

┌─────────────────────────────┐   ┌─────────────────────────────┐
│ 7                           │   │ 8          PORTER           │
│                             │   │                             │
│                             │   │      NOUS ? PORTEZ          │
│      INCORRECT. IT          │   │ NOUS PORTEZ IS INCORRECT    │
│      SHOULD BE              │   │ REMEMBER,                   │
│      ELLE PORTE             │   │ THE NOUS ENDING FOR ER      │
│                             │   │ VERBS IS ONS. TRY AGAIN.    │
│                             │   │ ? PORTONS                   │
│                             │   │      CORRECT                │
└─────────────────────────────┘   └─────────────────────────────┘

┌─────────────────────────────┐   ┌─────────────────────────────┐
│ 9                           │   │ 10                          │
│                             │   │                             │
│      PORTER                 │   │                             │
│                             │   │ YOUR SCORE IS 4 OUT OF 9    │
│      VOUS ? AXA             │   │                             │
│                             │   │                             │
│                             │   │                             │
└─────────────────────────────┘   └─────────────────────────────┘

┌─────────────────────────────┐
│ 11                          │
│                             │
│      ANOTHER VERB?          │
│      TYPE YES OR NO         │
│        ? NO                 │
│                             │
│        OK                   │
└─────────────────────────────┘
```

Basic

An ICL-CES BASIC String Function

In ICL-CES BASIC there is a **string function** which looks as though it was designed for programs requiring the manipulation of French verbs.

REP$(A$,B$,C$)

The computer interprets this instruction to mean replace the first occurrence of B$ in A$ with C$. Let us suppose that A$ has been established as PORTER as a result of a student's response to an invitation to choose a verb to practise. The string function can be used to replace the first occurrence of "ER" with an appropriate ending. We need to be able to refer to the result of this process so we use a LET statement.

Example
LET G$ = REP$(A$,"ER","E")   i.e. G$ = "PORTE"

G$ is now the correct form of the verb PORTER when it is used with je, il and elle. The student's input R$ can be compared with G$ to test for a correct answer.

Example
260 IF G$ = R$ THEN   (number of the line which credits one mark)
270 PRINT "INCORRECT"   Only printed if G$ is not equal to R$.

If you examine the short listing which follows, you will see that the function REP$ has been used between lines 170 and 250. Except where there is an element of repetition, as with je/il/elle and ils/elles, one LET G$ = REP$(A$,B$,C$) statement has been used to work out the correct form of the verb for any given pronoun.

In the program, A$ is established by student input. In the other two cases the desired character strings (enclosed by quotation marks, note) have been written into the program in the B$ and C$ positions. The string function is flexible in that this is not the only way to set it up.

Examples
If P$ = "ER"
then LET G$ = REP$(A$,P$,"E")
is the same as LET G$ = REP$(A$,"ER","E")
and this is the same as LET G$ = REP$("PORTER","ER","E")

**Program for
Regular
ER Verbs**

This short program is presented so that the string function can be seen in an operational context.

```
 10 LET T = 0
 20 PRINT "WHICH VERB?"
 30 PRINT "PORTER,TOMBER,JOUER,REGARDER,RESTER"
 40 INPUT A$                                        Student chooses verb.

 50 FOR I = 1 TO 5
 60 READ Z$
 70 IF A$ = Z$ THEN 110                             Check to see if input valid.
 80 NEXT I
 90 PRINT "NOT A VALID VERB"
100 GOTO 350

110 RESTORE 340                                     Ready to read cue pronoun.
120 FOR J = 1 TO 8
130 READ D$                                         Reads next cue pronoun.
140 PRINT D$                                        Prints cue pronoun.

150 INPUT R$                                        Student's response.

160 ON J GOTO 170,190,170,170,210,230,250,250       Locates the piece of program
                                                    which manufactures correct
                                                    answer.
170 LET G$ = REP$(A$,"ER","E")                       for je, il, elle
180 GOTO 260
190 LET G$ = REP$(A$,"ER","ES")                      for tu
200 GOTO 260
210 LET G$ = REP$(A$,"ER","ONS")                     for nous
220 GOTO 260
230 LET G$ = REP$(A$,"ER","EZ")                      for vous
240 GOTO 260
250 LET G$ = REP$(A$,"ER","ENT")                     for ils, elles

260 IF R$ = G$ THEN 290                             Compares student response with
                                                    correct answer.
270 PRINT "INCORRECT"
280 GOTO 300
290 LET T = T + 1                                    Credits one mark for a correct
                                                    answer.
300 NEXT J                                          Returns to read and print next
                                                    cue pronoun.
310 PRINT "YOUR SCORE IS";T;"OUT OF 8"
320 DATA PORTER,TOMBER,JOUER                         Valid verbs
330 DATA REGARDER,RESTER
340 DATA JE,TU,IL,ELLE,NOUS,VOUS,ILS,ELLES           Cue pronouns.
350 END
```

ON ... GOTO

Both the program for the 380Z and the simple program using REP$ take advantage of an instruction known as **ON ... GOTO.** In the latter program it appears on line 160.

160 ON J GOTO 170,190,170,170,210,230,250,250

This is an instruction which can be used, in some instances, to replace a series of IF ... THEN statements, thus exercising a certain economy in terms of program size and typing time. Line 160 onwards could have read:

160 IF D$ = "JE" THEN 170
161 IF D$ = "TU" THEN 190
162 IF D$ = "IL" THEN 170
163 IF D$ = "ELLE" THEN 170
164 IF D$ = "NOUS" THEN 210
165 IF D$ = "VOUS" THEN 230
166 IF D$ = "ILS" THEN 250
167 IF D$ = "ELLES" THEN 250

The ON ... GOTO statement works as follows:

J will be equal to	1	when D$ is equal to	JE
J	2		TU
J	3		IL
J	4		ELLE

and so on, until J is equal to 8 and D$ is equal to ELLES.
    The ON J GOTO statement uses the value assigned to J in the loop. It means

if J = 1 then go to line 170 (i.e. the 1st number after GOTO)
if J = 2   190 (2nd   )
if J = 3   170 (3rd   )
if J = 4   170 (4th   )
etc.

$$J = 1 \quad J = 2 \quad J = 3 \quad J = 4 \quad J = 5 \quad J = 6 \quad J = 7 \quad J = 8$$

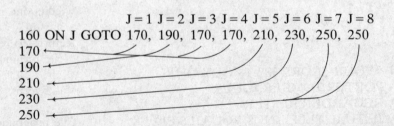

Research Machines 380Z 12K BASIC

We saw in CHEM and CHEMICAL that one was a development of the other. In this case the development related to the content of the program. It is not unrealistic to expect that developments will also take place in the way that a program is written. This is the case with VERB. It began life as a program written in ICL-CES BASIC and run on a mainframe with printed output. It is presented here as a microcomputer version which is greatly enhanced by the high speed of output and a facility which allows the VDU to be cleared at different points in the program, ensuring that the user's attention is focussed on the crucial messages. Continuous output can be something of a distraction.

The most obvious change from a programming point of view is the way that the "correct answer" has been manufactured. In the original version, as in the simple program that we have just looked at, this was achieved by using a string function, namely REP$(A$,B$,C$). When transferred to the micro a process known as concatenation was used instead.

Concatenation

Instead of the correct ending being made to replace the root, the stem of the verb is joined to the correct ending—but the structure of this routine is the same as when the string function was used.

Example
A$ = "PORT"
B$ = "ES"
LET G$ = A$ + B$
G$ becomes "PORTES", the correct form for TU

We have simply joined the two parts of the verb together by using the symbol +. Concatenation is not peculiar to the 380Z; the facility is also available in ICL-CES BASIC. The procedure is the same, but the symbol in this case is &. This process is used extensively between lines 820 and 1120 of the program.

```
820 LET G$ = S$ + "E"        S$ is the stem
830 GOTO 1130
840 LET G$ = S$ + "ES"
850 GOTO 1130
860 LET G$ = S$ + "ONS"
870 GOTO 1130
880 LET G$ = S$ + "EZ"
890 GOTO 1130
900 LET G$ = S$ + "ENT"
910 GOTO 1130
etc.
```

String Functions	Concatenation does not remove the need for string functions. They continue to play a very important part in the construction of the program, making possible the diagnosis of the nature of an error. The program uses four string functions:

> **1** LEFT$(K$,X)
> **2** RIGHT$(K$,X)
> **3** LEN(K$)
> **4** VAL(B$)

LEFT$	If we are to join the stem to the correct ending, we first have to create the stem from the infinitive. This has been achieved in the program by the LEFT$ string function.

Example
LET K$ = "PORTER"
LET S$ = LEFT$(K$,4)
S$ becomes "PORT"

The value in position X determines the number of characters on the left-hand side of the character string K$, beginning at the first, that go to make up S$.

A number or an assigned variable can be used in the X position.

Example
LET Y = 5
LET S$ = LEFT$(K$,Y)
S$ becomes "PORTE"

The creation of the stem from the infinitive takes place at line 660.

660 LET S$ = LEFT$(K$(M),X)

At this point the infinitive is held in a list, hence K$(M). The value X has been determined in the program so that the varying stem lengths can be taken into account.

RIGHT$	When an incorrect ending is used, a message advising the student of the fact is printed. One such message is contained in lines 1340 to 1360 of the listing.

1340 PRINT TAB(18);"REMEMBER."
1350 PRINT TAB(11);"THE ";D$;" ENDING FOR ";P$
1360 PRINT TAB(11);"VERBS IS ";H$;".";

D$ is the cue pronoun and is read from a data statement.
P$ is the root of the verb.
H$ is the correct ending.

At some point P$ and H$ have to be determined. Both require the use of RIGHT$.

Example
LET A$ = "PORTER"
LET P$ = RIGHT$(A$,2)
P$ becomes "ER"

This occurs at line 600 of the program.

RIGHT$ works like LEFT$ but operates on the right-hand side of the character string. The value in the X position determines the number of characters on the extreme right of the string that are to make up P$. It is a simple matter to create the root because it will always be the last two letters of A$. A$ is the student's choice of verb. K$(M) is an item in a list of acceptable verbs. A$ and K$(M) will be the same by the time that P$ is established. There is no significance in the fact that the stem is derived from K$(M) and the root from A$.

LEN

The creation of H$ involves the use of RIGHT$ and a string function LEN which determines the number of characters in a character string.

Example
LET S$ = "PORT"   S$ is the stem
LET S = LEN(S$)
S = 4 because there are 4 characters in "PORT"

Or

LET G$ = "PORTEZ"
LET G = LEN(G$)   G$ is a correct answer
G = 6 because there are 6 characters in "PORTEZ"

These two values, S and G, enable us to work out what the correct ending should be. We know that G$ is the correct answer so if we take the value S from the value G we will know the length of the correct ending. The resulting value can be used in a RIGHT$ expression.

Example
LET G = G − S   Let G = 6 − 4 = 2.
LET H$ = RIGHT$(G$,G) Let H$ = RIGHT$("PORTEZ",2).
H$ = "EZ"   H$ is the last two characters of G$.

The message contained in lines 1340 to 1360 will only be printed if the correct ending does not correspond to the one given by the student. Before a comparison can be made we shall have to discover how the student ended his/her input. Again, we use LEN and RIGHT$.

Example

R$ = "PORTONS"	R$ is the student's input.
LET H = LEN(H$)	H = 2
LET T$ = RIGHT$(R$,H)	Let T$ = RIGHT$("PORTONS",2);
T$ = "NS"	The value G instead of H could be used.

It is now possible to compare T$("NS") with H$("EZ").

IF T$ = H$ THEN   Conclude that the ending of the student's
input is acceptable. If they are not the
same, print
    REMEMBER,
    THE VOUS ENDING FOR ER
    VERBS IS EZ.

Another message that the student might receive is one to the effect that the stem of the verb that he/she inputs in response to a cue pronoun is not correct.

1250 PRINT TAB(11);"THERE IS AN ERROR IN"
1260 PRINT TAB(11);"THE STEM. ";

A test to see whether or not there is an error in the stem takes place at line 1240.

1240 IF C$ = S$ THEN 1300

The creation of C$ (the stem of the student's input) involves the use of LEFT$ and LEN.

Example

S$ = "PORT"	
LET S = LEN(S$)	
S = 4 because there are four characters in "PORT"	
R$ = "PORREZ"	Student's input.
LET C$ = LEFT$(R$,S)	Let C$ = LEFT$("PORREZ",4).
C$ = "PORR"	

The comparison at line 1240 will reveal an error in the stem.

VAL   A fourth string function has been used in the program. It is called VAL and is used to return the value of a character string. VAL is first used in line 230:

230 ON VAL(B$) GOTO 240,260,280

If we examine a small section of the program we can see how it is used and why. The inessential material has been pruned for the purpose of illustration.

```
70 PRINT "SELECT VERB TYPE"
80 PRINT "1)ER 2)IR 3)RE"
90 PRINT " TYPE 1, 2 OR 3 "
140 INPUT B$
```

The input is treated as alphanumeric even though the desired response is a number. This allows any input to be accepted and handled by the program.

```
170 IF B$<>"1" AND B$<>"2" AND B$<>"3" THEN 190
180 GOTO 230
```

This only applies if B$ equals 1, 2 or 3.

```
190 PRINT "YOUR INPUT"
200 PRINT "IS NOT ACCEPTABLE"
220 GOTO 90
```

In the program the jump is to 50, but with the same effect—the user is invited to input again.

Then comes the point at which VAL is first used. It is necessary to use the instruction RESTORE so that the permissible verbs held in the data statements can be compared with whatever word the student inputs as choice of verb. It is convenient to use ON . . . GOTO for this. Unfortunately, this necessitates the use of a numeric character. The type of verb (1, 2 or 3) has been accepted as alphanumeric, making it unacceptable in the ON . . . GOTO instruction. We can overcome this by working out the value of B$.

Each character has a numeric value within the system. The characters 0 to 9 have the numeric values 0 to 9. This allows us to use the input B$ in one of two ways. We can use:

1) LET B = VAL(B$)
   then use ON B GOTO . . .

or 2) ON VAL(B$) GOTO . . .

VAL is used in the second way.

```
230 ON VAL(B$) GOTO 240,260,280
240 RESTORE 1960
250 GOTO 290
260 RESTORE 1970
270 GOTO 290
280 RESTORE 1980
```

Program Summary

10–290 Selection of type of verb.
300–370 Read verbs of a selected type into a list and print them.
380–590 Student selects verb which is checked to see that it is acceptable.
600–730 Establish P$—root
                S$—stem
                D$—cue pronoun
                L$—First letter of stem. Checked to
                    see that it is not an A, E or O
                Print cue pronoun
740 Student response R$.
760–790 Makes sure that R$ is at least as long as the stem.
800 Directs computer to routine which manufactures the correct answer.
810–1120 Concatenation process.
1130 If G$ is the same as R$ then go to scoring routine.
1150 Increment Q. Number of attempts to input R$.
1180–1260 Compare correct stem against that of R$.
1270–1290 Compare correct ending against ending of R$.
1300–1470 Print Error messages. Take account of il and elle parts of RE verbs.
1480–1580 Routine to check for use of ir endings (nous/vous/ils/elles/) in er and re verbs.
1590–1750 Handles a second input after the error message.
1790 NEXT J sets up next cue pronoun.
1850–1890 Allows another verb to be selected.
1960–1990 Data.

**Program Listing:
Research Machines
380Z 12K BASIC**

```
10 REM VERB. 380Z. 12K BASIC
20 PRINT CHR$(12)
30 LET T=0
40 LET Q=0
50 PRINT TAB(10);"********************"
60 PRINT TAB(10);"*                  *"
70 PRINT TAB(10);"* SELECT VERB TYPE *"
80 PRINT TAB(10);"* 1)ER  2)IR  3)RE *"
90 PRINT TAB(10);"*  TYPE 1, 2 OR 3  *"
100 PRINT TAB(10);"*                  * "
110 PRINT TAB(10);"********************"
120 FOR I=1 TO 6:PRINT:NEXT I
130 PRINT TAB(18);
140 INPUT B$
150 IF B$="AXA" THEN 1940
160 PRINT CHR$(12)
170 IF B$<>"1" AND B$<>"2" AND B$<>"3" THEN 190
180 GOTO 230
190 PRINT TAB(15);"YOUR INPUT"
200 PRINT TAB(11);"IS NOT ACCEPTABLE."
210 PRINT
220 GOTO 50
230 ON VAL(B$) GOTO 240,260,280
240 RESTORE 1960
250 GOTO 290
260 RESTORE 1970
270 GOTO 290
```

```
280 RESTORE 1980
290 PRINT CHR$(12)
300 PRINT TAB(11);"SELECT A VERB FROM"
310 PRINT TAB(11);"THE FOLLOWING LIST"
320 FOR I=1 TO 2500:NEXT I
330 PRINT CHR$(12)
340 FOR M=1 TO 5
350 READ K$(M)
360 PRINT TAB(17);K$(M)
370 NEXT M
380 PRINT
390 PRINT TAB(15);
400 INPUT A$
410 IF A$="AXA" THEN 430
420 GOTO 520
430 FOR I=1 TO 1500:NEXT I:PRINT CHR$(12)
440 PRINT TAB(5);"DO YOU WANT ANOTHER VERB TYPE?"
450 PRINT TAB(13);"TYPE YES OR NO"
460 PRINT TAB(18);
470 INPUT Z$
480 IF Z$="YES" THEN 20
490 IF Z$="NO" THEN 1940
500 IF Z$="AXA" THEN  1940
510 GOTO 450
520 FOR M=1 TO 5
530 IF A$=K$(M) THEN 590
540 NEXT M
550 PRINT CHR$(12)
560 PRINT TAB(12);"NOT A VALID VERB"
570 FOR I=1 TO 2000:NEXT I
580 GOTO 230
590 FOR I=1 TO 1000:NEXT I:PRINT CHR$(12)
600 LET P$=RIGHT$(A$,2)
610 LET X=LEN(A$)-2
620 RESTORE 1990
630 FOR J=1 TO 8
640 PRINT TAB(19);K$(M)
650 PRINT
660 LET S$=LEFT$(K$(M),X)
670 READ D$
680 LET L$=LEFT$(S$,1)
690 IF L$="A" OR L$="E" OR L$="O" THEN710
700 GOTO 730
710 IF D$<>"JE" THEN 730
720 LET D$="J'"
730 PRINT TAB(15);D$;"    ";
740 INPUT R$
750 IF R$="AXA" THEN 1800
760 IF LEN(R$)>=LEN(S$) THEN 800
770 PRINT TAB(5);"THIS IS SHORTER THAN THE STEM."
780 PRINT TAB(14);"THINK AGAIN"
790 GOTO 730
800 ON VAL(B$) GOTO 810,920,1030
810 ON J GOTO 820,840,820,820,860,880,900,900
820 LET G$=S$+"E"
830 GOTO 1130
840 LET G$=S$+"ES"
850 GOTO 1130
860 LET G$=S$+"ONS"
870 GOTO 1130
880 LET G$=S$+"EZ"
890 GOTO 1130
900 LET G$=S$+"ENT"
910 GOTO 1130
920 ON J GOTO 930,930,950,950,970,990,1010,1010
930 LET G$=S$+"IS"
940 GOTO 1130
950 LET G$=S$+"IT"
960 GOTO 1130
```

```
970 LET G$=S$+"ISSONS"
980 GOTO 1130
990 LET G$=S$+"ISSEZ"
1000 GOTO 1130
1010 LET G$=S$+"ISSENT"
1020 GOTO 1130
1030 ON J GOTO 1040,1040,1060,1060,1080,1100,1120,1120
1040 LET G$=S$+"S"
1050 GOTO 1130
1060 LET G$=S$+""
1070 GOTO 1130
1080 LET G$=S$+"ONS"
1090 GOTO 1130
1100 LET G$=S$+"EZ"
1110 GOTO 1130
1120 G$=S$+"ENT"
1130 FOR I=1 TO 750:NEXT I:IF G$=R$ THEN 1760
1140 FOR I=1 TO 500:NEXT I:PRINT CHR$(12)
1150 LET Q=Q+1
1160 PRINT TAB(11);D$;" ";R$;" IS INCORRECT"
1170 IF D$<>"J" THEN 1190
1180 LET D$="JE"
1190 LET S=LEN(S$)
1200 LET G=LEN(G$)
1210 LET G=G-S
1220 LET H$=RIGHT$(G$,G)
1230 LET C$=LEFT$(R$,S)
1240 IF C$=S$ THEN 1300
1250 PRINT TAB(11);"THERE IS AN ERROR IN"
1260 PRINT TAB(11);"THE STEM. ";
1270 LET H=LEN(H$)
1280 LET T$=RIGHT$(R$,H)
1290 IF T$=H$ THEN 1420
1300 IF P$="RE" THEN 1320
1310 GOTO 1340
1320 IF D$="IL" THEN 1380
1330 IF D$="ELLE" THEN 1380
1340 PRINT TAB(18);"REMEMBER,"
1350 PRINT TAB(11);"THE ";D$;" ENDING FOR ";P$
1360 PRINT TAB(11);"VERBS IS ";H$;" .";
1370 GOTO 1590
1380 PRINT TAB(17);"REMEMBER,"
1390 PRINT TAB(11);"THERE IS NO ENDING FOR"
1400 PRINT TAB(11);"THIS PART OF 'RE'VERBS"
1410 GOTO 1590
1420 IF P$<>"RE" THEN 1480
1430 IF D$="IL" THEN 1460
1440 IF D$="ELLE" THEN 1460
1450 GOTO 1480
1460 LET T$=RIGHT$(R$,1)
1470 IF T$<>"D" THEN 1380
1480 IF P$="IR" THEN 1590
1490 IF J<5 THEN 1590
1500 ON J-4 GOTO 1510,1540,1570,1570
1510 LET T$=RIGHT$(R$,6):LET U$=RIGHT$(R$,5)
1520 IF T$="ISSONS" OR U$="ISONS"THEN 1340
1530 GOTO 1590
1540 LET T$=RIGHT$(R$,5):LET U$=RIGHT$(R$,4)
1550 IF T$="ISSEZ" OR U$="ISEZ" THEN 1340
1560 GOTO 1590
1570 LET T$=RIGHT$(R$,6):LET U$=RIGHT$(R$,5)
1580 IF T$="ISSENT" OR U$="ISENT" THEN 1340
1590 PRINT TAB(11);"TRY AGAIN"
1600 PRINT TAB(11);
1610 INPUT R$
1620 IF R$=G$ THEN 1740
1630 IF R$="AXA" THEN 1810
1640 PRINT CHR$(12)
1650 PRINT TAB(13);"INCORRECT. IT"
1660 IF L$="A" OR L$="E" OR L$="O" THEN 1680
```

```
1670 GOTO 1700
1680 IF D$<>"JE" THEN 1700
1690 LET D$="J'"
1700 PRINT TAB(13);"SHOULD BE"
1710 PRINT TAB(13);D$;" ";G$
1720 FOR I=1 TO 2500:NEXT I
1730 GOTO 1770
1740 PRINT TAB(18);"CORRECT"
1750 FOR I=1 TO 1500:NEXT I
1760 LET T=T+1
1770 LET Q=Q+1
1780 PRINT CHR$(12)
1790 NEXT J
1800 IF Q=0 THEN 1850
1810 FOR I=1 TO 2000:NEXT I:PRINT CHR$(12)
1820 PRINT TAB(8);"YOUR SCORE IS";T;"OUT OF";Q
1830 FOR I=1 TO 2000:NEXT I
1840 FOR I=1 TO 4:PRINT:NEXT I
1850 PRINT TAB(13);"ANOTHER  VERB?"
1860 PRINT TAB(13);"TYPE YES OR NO"
1870 PRINT TAB(17);
1880 INPUT A$
1890 IF A$="YES" THEN 20
1900 IF A$="NO" THEN 1940
1910 IF A$="AXA" THEN 1940
1920 PRINT CHR$(12)
1930 GOTO 1860
1940 FOR I=1 TO 1000:NEXT I:PRINT CHR$(12)
1950 PRINT TAB(19);"OK"
1960 DATA FERMER,JOUER,PORTER,RESTER,TOMBER
1970 DATA AGIR,BATIR,CHOISIR,FINIR,OBEIR
1980 DATA ATTENDRE,DESCENDRE,ENTENDRE,PERDRE,VENDRE
1990 DATA JE,TU,IL,ELLE,NOUS,VOUS,ILS,ELLES
```

7 MENU: nutritional analysis

Introduction

It has already been mentioned that the computer can perform a calculating function. The presentation of results for use by the student in table form, and the ability to allow the student to experiment, are also important features. The package MENU was developed for a particular exercise in O-level and A-level Food and Nutrition work, and the design of the layout of the output was important. The feature of Basic programming which enables the required printout to be performed, the PRINT USING statement, is not a standard function of all versions of the language. It is part of Southampton BASIC (SOBS), the language used for the program, and its use is described later.

How the Package is Used

The program enables the student to select a menu from 149 food items. After the weight of each item has been supplied, a breakdown of the menu into its constituent nutritional elements is obtained. Totals for the whole menu and amounts per person are provided, and the output is designed to make analysis easier. Column items and decimal points are lined up with the table headings.

A student booklet explains the operation of the program and details the list of foods available for the chosen menus. Each food has its own code and the booklet is illustrated here for reference.

The Running of the Program

At the start of the program run, a message is printed to the user to read the booklet for instructions. The menu must be typed in, one item at a time, with the weight required. The foods available are identified by a numeric code, and these are listed in the booklet. The beginning of the run looks like this:

```
FOR OPERATING INSTRUCTIONS SEE BOOKLET.
REMEMBER A] TYPE CODE ON ONE LINE AND WEIGHT ON NEXT, WHEN ASKED TO.
         B] TYPE 151 TO SHOW THAT THE MENU IS COMPLETE.
         C] TYPE 152 TO SHOW THAT YOU WISH TO FINISH, PERHAPS
         BECAUSE OF AN ERROR.
```

```
INPUT MENU
ITEM 1   CODE NO. ← 23
         WEIGHT  ← 35
ITEM 2   CODE NO. ← 12
         WEIGHT  ← 100
ITEM 3  CODE NO. ← 151
DO YOU WISH TO CHECK ANY ITEMS ?(YES/NO) ← YES
TYPE ITEM NO. ← 1
ITEM NO. 1     CODE NO. 23    WEIGHT 35
DO YOU WISH TO CHECK ANY ITEMS ?(YES/NO) ← NO
DO YOU WISH TO CHANGE THE MENU ?(YES/NO) ← NO
FOR HOW MANY PERSONS IS THE MEAL ? ← 1
```

When the menu is complete the student uses the code 151 to signal the end of the menu. The items can be checked by answering "yes" to the question

DO YOU WISH TO CHECK ANY ITEMS ?(YES/NO) ←

Instructions are then given:

TYPE ITEM NO. ←

An option to change the menu is then provided with the question

DO YOU WISH TO CHANGE THE MENU ?(YES/NO) ←

If the answer is "yes" then instructions are given:

TYPE IN ITEM NO.,CODE,WEIGHT ←

The item number refers to the order in which the items were originally typed in. When the changes are complete, or there are no changes to the menu, then the computer asks

FOR HOW MANY PERSONS IS THE MEAL ? ←

If the specified menu is for several people then a breakdown is provided of quantities per person. The table is then printed.

CODE	WEIGHT GRAMS	WASTE GRAMS	VIT. C MG	CARB. GRAMS	PROT. GRAMS	FAT GRAMS	KCAL.
77	200.00	0.00	30.00	39.40	2.80	0.00	160.00
24	200.00	0.00	0.00	0.00	46.00	44.20	582.00
73	100.00	0.00	15.00	7.70	5.00	0.00	49.00
TOTAL	500.00	0.00	45.00	47.10	53.80	44.20	791.00
P PERSON	250.00	0.00	22.50	23.55	26.90	22.10	395.50

Student Booklet: MENU

Introduction

This program enables you to examine the nutritional content of a meal.

For any given weight of a particular item of food, it can tell you:

1 The weight of waste   (in grams)
2 The vitamin C content   (in milligrams)
3 The carbohydrate content (in grams)
4 The protein content   (in grams)
5 The fat content   (in grams)
6 The energy content   (in k cals)

If the meal consists of several items, the computer can calculate

a) each item
b) the whole meal
c) each portion.

1-6 above for

It presents this information in the form of a table.

CODE	WEIGHT GRAMS	WASTE GRAMS	VIT.C MG	CARB. GRAMS	PROT. GRAMS	FAT GRAMS	KCAL.
23	40.00	6.80	0.00	0.00	5.28	10.03	111.22
17	50.00	0.00	0.00	0.00	15.45	5.50	111.50
76	40.00	10.80	8.76	5.26	0.61	0.00	22.19
TOTAL	130.00	17.60	8.76	5.26	21.53	15.53	244.91
P.PERSON	65.00	8.80	4.38	2.63	10.67	7.76	122.46

1

Operating Instructions

1 The program is run in SOBS BASIC and can be called up by typing

    MENU

2 The computer will print a short introduction.

3 It will then print INPUT MENU followed by ITEM 1 on the next line. The words CODE NO. and WEIGHT appear on separate lines, each one being followed by a backward facing arrow. This arrow is a signal to type data into the computer. Type in the code number of an item of food (see section headed Codes) and the weight to be used in grams. (An ounces to grams conversion table follows the section headed Codes). For example

    CODE NO. ←23
    WEIGHT ←35

(Remember to press the red accept key after any input).

4 When you have typed in all the ingredients, type the food code 151 to indicate that the menu is complete. The computer will then ask you if you wish to check or change the menu, and you may answer YES or NO. If the answer is YES then you will be asked to supply the ITEM NO. , CODE NO. and WEIGHT.

If you wish to add to the menu, refer to the item by the next number in the item list sequence. For example, a new item added to a list of 4 is referred to as item 5. If you wish to delete an item then change its weight to 0 (zero).

5 In answer to the question, FOR HOW MANY PERSONS IS THE MEAL? type a number (remember to press ACCEPT).

6 The food code 152 allows you to finish immediately, without a table being printed.

2

VEGETABLES

53 Beans, canned in tomato sauce
54 Beans, broad
55 Beans, haricot
56 Beans, runner
57 Beetroot, boiled
58 Brussels sprouts, raw
59 Brussels sprouts, boiled
60 Cabbage, green, raw
61 Cabbage, green, boiled
62 Carrots, old
63 Cauliflower
64 Celery
65 Potato crisps
66 Cucumber
67 Lentils, dry
68 Lettuce
69 Mushrooms
70 Onions
71 Parsnips
72 Peas, fresh or frozen, raw
73 Peas, fresh or frozen, boiled
74 Peas, canned, processed
75 Peppers, green
76 Potatoes, raw
77 Potatoes, boiled
78 Potato chips, fried
79 Potatoes, roast
80 Spinach
81 Sweet corn, canned
82 Tomatoes, fresh
83 Turnips
84 Watercress

FRUIT

85 Apples
86 Apricots, canned including syrup
87 Apricots, dried
88 Bananas
89 Blackcurrants
90 Cherries
91 Dates, dried
92 Figs, dried
93 Gooseberries
94 Grapefruit
95 Lemons
96 Melon
97 Oranges
98 Orange juice canned, unconcentrated
99 Peaches, fresh
100 Peaches, canned including syrup
101 Pears, fresh
102 Pineapple, canned including syrup
103 Plums
104 Prunes, dried
105 Raspberries
106 Rhubarb
107 Strawberries
108 Sultanas

NUTS

109 Almonds
110 Coconut, desiccated
111 Peanuts, roasted

4

Codes

MILK

1 Cream, double
2 Cream, single
3 Milk, liquid, whole
4 Milk, condensed, whole, sweetened
5 Milk, whole, evaporated
6 National dried milk
7 Milk, dried, skimmed
8 Yogurt, low-fat, natural
9 Yogurt, low-fat, fruit

CHEESE

10 Cheese, Cheddar
11 Cheese, cottage

MEAT

12 Bacon, rashers, raw
13 Bacon, rashers, cooked
14 Beef, average
15 Beef, corned
16 Beef, stewing steak, raw
17 Beef, stewing steak, cooked
18 Black pudding
19 Chicken, raw
20 Chicken, roast
21 Ham, cooked
22 Kidney, average
23 Lamb, average, raw
24 Lamb, roast
25 Liver, average, raw
26 Liver, fried
27 Luncheon meat
28 Pork, average
29 Pork chop grilled
30 Sausage, pork
31 Sausage, beef
32 Steak and Kidney pie, cooked
33 Tripe

FISH

34 Cod; Haddock; white fish
35 Cod, fried in batter
36 Fish fingers
37 Herring
38 Kipper
39 Salmon, canned
40 Sardines, canned in oil

EGGS

41 Eggs, fresh

FATS

42 Butter
43 Lard; cooking fat; dripping
44 Low-fat spread
45 Margarine
46 Oils, cooking and salad

PRESERVES ETC

47 Chocolate, milk
48 Honey
49 Jam
50 Marmalade
51 Sugar, white
52 Syrup

3

Conversion Tables

RULE OF THUMB

½ oz =	13g
1 oz =	25g
2 oz =	50g
4 oz =	100g
6 oz =	150g
8 oz =	200g
10 oz =	250g
12 oz =	300g
14 oz =	350g
16 oz =	400g

ACCURATE

½ oz =	14.17g	10 oz =	283.50g
1 oz =	28.35g	11 oz =	311.85g
2 oz =	56.70g	12 oz =	340.20g
3 oz =	85.05g	13 oz =	368.55g
4 oz =	113.40g	14 oz =	396.90g
5 oz =	141.75g	15 oz =	425.25g
6 oz =	170.10g	16 oz =	453.60g
7 oz =	198.45g		
8 oz =	226.80g		
9 oz =	255.15g		

FLUIDS

1 tsp =	5mls,	0.2oz
1 tbsp =	15mls,	0.6oz
¼ pint =	125mls,	5.0oz
½ pint =	250mls,	10.0oz
¾ pint =	375mls,	15.0oz
1 pint =	500mls,	20.0oz

USEFUL WEIGHTS

1 egg 60g
Butter or margarine for
1 slice of bread 10g
Jam for one slice of bread 10g
1 slice of bread, large 25g
1 slice of bread, small 15g
1 medium-sized apple 75g
Coffee, 1 cup 1g
Tea, 1 cup 1g
1 tsp sugar 3g
Milk for 1 cup of tea/coffee 25mls

6

CEREALS

112 Barley, pearl, dry
113 Biscuits, chocolate
114 Biscuits, cream crackers
115 Biscuits, plain semi-sweet
116 Biscuits, rich, sweet
117 Bread, brown
118 Bread, starch reduced
119 Bread, white
120 Bread, wholemeal
121 Cornflakes
122 Custard powder; instant
     pudding; cornflour
123 Crispbread, Ryvita
124 Flour, white
125 Oatmeal
126 Rice
127 Spaghetti

BEVERAGES

128 Chocolate, drinking
129 Cocoa powder
130 Coffee, ground
131 Coffee, instant, dry
132 Cola drink
133 Tea, dry
134 Squash, fruit, undiluted

ALCOHOL PER FL OZ

135 Beer, bitter, draught
136 Spirits, 70° proof
137 Wine, red

PUDDINGS, CAKES ETC

138 Apple pie
139 Bread and butter pudding
140 Buns, currant
141 Custard
142 Fruit cake, rich
143 Jam tarts
144 Plain cake, Madeira
145 Rice pudding
146 Soup, tomato, canned
147 Trifle
148 Yeast extract
149 Ice cream, vanilla

5

Tasks

1 Work out the nutritive content of today's school dinner and compare it with the nutritive value of the following packed lunch.

  2 rounds of corned beef sandwiches
  (100g bread/15g margarine/50g corned beef)

  1 piece of rich fruit cake - 75g

  1 apple - 100g

  1 low fat fruit yogurt - 125g

  1 coffee
  (1g coffee powder/25g milk/5g sugar)

  1 bar of milk chocolate - 50g

What conclusions can you draw from this?

2 Plan a three course midday meal for a secretary who is on a 1200 k/cal diet. Analyse this, then suggest a suitable breakfast and tea.

3 Compare and contrast the following breakfasts.

  a) Fried bacon, egg and mushrooms
    2 slices of bread and butter
    1 cup of coffee with milk and sugar

  b) Cornflakes, milk and sugar
    2 slices of buttered toast with marmalade
    1 cup of coffee with milk and sugar

MENU uses figures taken from **Manual of Nutrition** by the Ministry of Agriculture, Fisheries and Food (H.M.S.O.).

Options to continue, with another menu, or to finish the run are then given,

DO YOU REQUIRE A NEW MENU ?(YES/NO) ← NO
DOES ANYONE ELSE WISH TO USE MENU ?(YES/NO) ← NO
PROJECT FINISHED
STOPPED AT LINE 2700

As the table shows, the layout of the data is important in order to make the output readable. To make this possible the PRINT USING and FORMAT statements are used.

Basic

The PRINT USING and FORMAT Statements

The PRINT USING instruction enables the programmer to specify how the output should be printed, with spacing and special symbols as required. Variations of BASIC handle this instruction differently. The version described here is that of Southampton BASIC (SOBS), but the differences are only slight and the principle involved is the same.

As with the standard PRINT statement, the items to be printed are listed in the PRINT USING statement. For example, the statement looks like:

250 PRINT USING 500: N,A£

The items to be printed are N and A£. The number 500 refers to the line number of the **FORMAT** statement that will be used as a pattern for the printout. For example,

500 FORMAT ###.#,4X,"GROUP",X,###

FORMAT statements can be used to provide a "mask" for various print items

Print item	Symbol	
Spaces	X	
New lines	/	
Strings	e.g. "WORD"	
String variables	#####	(for 5 characters)
Integers	###	(for 3 digits)
Fixed point numbers	e.g. ##.##	
Floating point numbers (i.e. $0.01 = 0.1E-1$)	#.## ↑ ↑ ↑	the exponent is placed in the upward arrows

Groups of expressions, using brackets for multiple patterns, can be formed, greatly increasing the control over the printed line. It is possible to abbreviate some descriptions, e.g.

can be written as 5#
XXX can be written as 3X

In the example already mentioned, the first item in the FORMAT line describes the numeric variable N, and it is to be printed with 3 digits before the point and 1 after. If there are no hundreds or tens digits then spaces would be printed, but if there is no units digit then a zero appears.

The following table indicates the printout expected for various values of N

N	###.#
123.48	123.5
23	23.0
0.23	0.2
−76.9	−76.9

These fixed point expressions can also be abbreviated. For example.

####.###   can be written   4#.3#

Digits after the point are rounded up to fit the description, and zeros are printed if necessary.

The second item in the FORMAT line is 4 spaces, and these are printed directly after the number N.

The third item is the word "GROUP" which is printed immediately after the 4 spaces. This is followed by a single space which is the fourth item in the FORMAT line.

The last FORMAT item describes the string variable A£ and it is expected to consist of 3 characters. If any of the items exceeds its description, then a pattern of asterisks will be printed in place of the number or character string.

How PRINT USING is Incorporated into the Program

The program listing is given at the end of this section.

The headings for the printed table are set out as follows:

CODE	WEIGHT GRAMS	WASTE GRAMS	VIT. C MG	CARB. GRAMS	PROT. GRAMS	FAT GRAMS	KCAL.

The numbers must be printed in columns under these headings, and the lining up of the digits and the decimal points makes reading the data that much easier.

CODE	WEIGHT GRAMS	WASTE GRAMS	VIT. C MG	CARB. GRAMS	PROT. GRAMS	FAT GRAMS	KCAL.
100	400.00	0.00	16.00	91.60	1.60	0.00	352.00

3 spaces / INTE-GER / 3s 1s / fixed point number / 1s1s / f.p.n. 1s / etc.

The row begins with 3 spaces/an integer of up to 3 digits/3 spaces

The integer is printed on line 770.

770 PRINT USING 1190:Q(J,1),

The description is given on line 1190.

1190 FORMAT 3X,###,3X

The printing of the column entries continues on the same line, since there is a trailing comma on line 770. The column entries are printed on line 790.

790 PRINT USING 1200:Q(J,K),

The description is on line 1200.

1200 FORMAT X,####.##,X

The seven column entries are printed in a loop, hence the trailing comma on line 790 to print the items on the same line. The FORMAT descriptions ensure the correct spacing and that the numeric values have up to 4 digits before the point and 2 after. The same pattern

X,####.##,X

is repeated seven times.

The TOTAL and P PERSON lines have the same seven columns but they begin differently. Instead of the 3 digit integer the heading is printed. This is done on lines 830 and 930

830 PRINT "TOTAL   ";
930 PRINT "P PERSON";

The FORMAT on line 1200 is then used for the numbers across the row in each case.

TOTAL	400.00	0.00	16.00	91.60	1.60	0.00	352.00
P PERSON	200.00	0.00	8.00	45.80	0.80	0.00	176.00

**How the
Calculation
is Performed**

The student types in a food code and a weight, and from these the nutritional content is calculated. In the DATA statements a record is kept of the content per 100 grams of waste (grams), vitamin C (mg), carbohydrate (grams), protein (grams), fat (grams), and Kilocalories. All the figures, apart from the first, are based on the net weight, that is when the waste has been removed. An example calculation, for eggs, is given here.

Amounts per 100 grams

Food Code	Waste	Vit.C	Carbo.	Protein	Fat	KCal.
41	12	0	0	12.3	10.9	147

For a weight of 30 grams the waste would be

$$\frac{12 \times 30}{100} = 3.6 \text{ grams}$$

The remaining quantities are calculated from the original weight minus the waste, i.e. $30 - 3.6 = 26.4$ grams

Protein
$$\frac{12.3 \times 26.4}{100} = 3.25 \text{ grams}$$

Fat
$$\frac{10.9 \times 26.4}{100} = 2.88 \text{ grams}$$

KCals.
$$\frac{147 \times 26.4}{100} = 38.81$$

These calculations are performed by the computer program which then totals the amounts for the complete menu, and gives amounts "per person" as well.

Other Facilities

A number of user "traps" and safeguards are built into the program. These make its use easier by allowing errors in the input data to be handled. Discussion of these techniques is left to the chapter on the user/computer interface.

Program Summary

10	Dimension the arrays Q (input menu), V (food details).
20–60	Read food details into array V.
70–140	Print instructions.
150–250	Input menu items and weight.
260–660	Checking and changing the menu.
670–690	Input number of persons.
700–980	Print the menu.
990–1080	Routine for continue or finish.
1090–1180	Subroutine for calculating table values for the menu items as they are typed in.
1190–1200	Formats for table printing.
1210–2690	Data for food items.
2700	End.

The table of values used in this package are taken from *Manual of Nutrition*, Ministry of Agriculture, Fisheries and Food (HMSO, 1976).

**Program Listing:
Southampton
BASIC**

```
10   DIM Q(50,8),V(150,6)
20   FOR J=1 TO 149
30   FOR K=1 TO 6
40   READ V(J,K)
50   NEXT K
60   NEXT J
70   PRINT "FOR OPERATING INSTRUCTIONS SEE BOOKLET."
80   PRINT "REMEMBER A] TYPE CODE ON ONE LINE AND WEIGHT ON NEXT,";
90   PRINT " WHEN ASKED TO."
100  PRINT TAB(9);"B] TYPE 151 TO SHOW THAT THE MENU IS COMPLETE."
110  PRINT TAB(9);"C] TYPE 152 TO SHOW THAT YOU WISH TO FINISH, PERHAPS
120  PRINT TAB(12);"BECAUSE OF AN ERROR."
130  PRINT
140  PRINT
150  PRINT "INPUT MENU"
160  FOR I=1 TO 49
170  PRINT "ITEM ";I;TAB(10);"CODE NO. ";
180  INPUT Q(I,1)
190  IF Q(I,1)=151 THEN 270
200  IF Q(I,1)=152 THEN 990
210  PRINT TAB(12);"WEIGHT    ";
220  INPUT Q(I,2)
230  GOSUB 1090
240  IF X=1 THEN 170
250  NEXT I
260  PRINT "NO MORE ITEMS CAN BE ADDED TO THE MENU"
270  PRINT "DO YOU WISH TO CHECK ANY ITEMS ?(YES/NO)";
280  INPUT C£
290  IF C£<>"YES" AND C£<>"NO" THEN 270
300  IF C£="NO" THEN 380
310  PRINT "TYPE ITEM NO. ";
320  INPUT C
330  IF C>0 AND C<I AND C=INT(C) THEN 360
340  PRINT "NO ITEM ";C;
350  GOTO 270
360  PRINT "ITEM NO. ";C;" CODE NO. ";Q(C,1);" WEIGHT ";Q(C,2)
370  GOTO 270
380  PRINT "DO YOU WISH TO CHANGE THE MENU ?(YES/NO)";
390  INPUT A£
400  IF A£<>"YES" AND A£<>"NO" THEN 380
410  IF A£<>"YES" THEN 670
```

```
420   LET N=I
430   PRINT "TYPE IN ITEM NO. ";
440   INPUT I
450   IF I>0 AND I<N+1 AND I=INT(I) AND I<50 THEN 480
460   PRINT "INCORRECT ITEM NO. ";
470   GOTO 430
480   IF I<N THEN 500
490   LET N=N+1
500   PRINT "          CODE NO. ";
510   INPUT Q(I,1)
520   IF Q(I,1)=151 THEN 270
530   IF Q(I,1)=152 THEN 990
540   PRINT "          WEIGHT";
550   INPUT Q(I,2)
560   GOSUB 1090
570   LET I=N
580   IF X=1 THEN 430
590   PRINT "ANY MORE CHANGES ?(YES/NO)";
600   INPUT B£
610   IF B£<>"YES" AND B£<>"NO" THEN 590
620   IF B£="YES" THEN 420
630   PRINT "ANY MORE CHECKS ?(YES/NO)";
640   INPUT B£
650   IF B£<>"YES" AND B£<>"NO" THEN 630
660   IF B£="YES" THEN 310
670   PRINT "FOR HOW MANY PERSONS IS THE MEAL ?";
680   INPUT W
690   IF W<=0 OR W<>INT(W) THEN 670
700   PRINT
710   PRINT
720   PRINT " CODE     WEIGHT     WASTE     VIT.C     CARB.";
730   PRINT "     PROT.     FAT     KCAL."
740   PRINT TAB(12);"GRAMS     GRAMS     MG      GRAMS     GRAMS     GRAMS"
750   PRINT
760   FOR J=1 TO I-1
770   PRINT USING 1190:Q(J,1),
780   FOR K=2 TO 8
790   PRINT USING 1200:Q(J,K),
800   NEXT K
810   PRINT
820   NEXT J
830   PRINT "TOTAL     ";
840   FOR J=2 TO 8
850   LET Q(50,J)=Q(1,J)
860   FOR K=2 TO I-1
870   LET Q(50,J)=Q(50,J)+Q(K,J)
880   NEXT K
890   PRINT USING 1200:Q(50,J),
900   NEXT J
910   PRINT
920   PRINT
930   PRINT "P PERSON ";
940   FOR J=2 TO 8
950   PRINT USING 1200:Q(50,J)/W,
960   NEXT J
970   PRINT
980   PRINT
990   PRINT "DO YOU REQUIRE A NEW MENU ?(YES/NO)";
1000  INPUT X£
1010  IF X£<>"YES" AND X£<>"NO" THEN 990
1020  IF X£="YES" THEN 150
1030  PRINT "DOES ANYONE ELSE WISH TO USE MENU ?(YES/NO)";
1040  INPUT X£
1050  IF X£<>"YES" AND X£<>"NO" THEN 1030
1060  IF X£="YES" THEN 70
1070  PRINT "PROJECT FINISHED"
1080  GOTO 2700
1090  LET X=0
1100  IF Q(I,1)>0 AND Q(I,1)<150 AND Q(I,1)=INT(Q(I,1)) THEN 1140
1110  PRINT Q(I,1);" IS AN UNKNOWN CODE, TYPE CODE,WEIGHT AGAIN"
```

```
1120    LET X=1
1130    RETURN
1140    LET Q(I,3)=0
1150    FOR J=3 TO 8
1160    LET Q(I,J)=(Q(I,2)-Q(I,3))*V(Q(I,1),J-2)/100
1170    NEXT J
1180    RETURN
1190    FORMAT 3X,###,3X
1200    FORMAT X,####.##,X
1210    DATA  0 ,  0 ,  2.6,  1.8,48.0,449
1220    DATA  0 ,  0 ,  4.2, 2.8,18 ,189
1230    DATA  0 ,  1 ,  4.8, 3.3, 3.8, 65
1240    DATA  0 ,  3 , 55.1, 8.2, 9.2,322
1250    DATA  0 ,  2 , 12.8, 8.5, 9.2,165
1260    DATA  0 , 60 , 37 ,27.6,26.8,490
1270    DATA  0 , 10 , 53.3,36 ,  .9,352
1280    DATA  0 ,  0 ,  6.4, 5 , 1 , 53
1290    DATA  0 ,  1 , 18.2, 4.8, 1 , 96
1300    DATA  0 ,  0 ,  0 ,25.4,34.5,412
1310    DATA  0 ,  0 ,  4.5,15.3, 4 ,114
1320    DATA 13 ,  0 ,  0 ,14.4,40.5,422
1330    DATA  0 ,  0 ,  0 ,24.5,38.8,447
1340    DATA 17 ,  0 ,  0 ,18.1,17.1,226
1350    DATA  0 ,  0 ,  0 ,26.9,12.1,216
1360    DATA  0 ,  0 ,  0 ,20.2,10.6,176
1370    DATA  0 ,  0 ,  0 ,30.9,11 ,223
1380    DATA  0 ,  0 , 15 ,12.9,21.9,305
1390    DATA 31 ,  0 ,  0 ,20.8, 6.7,144
1400    DATA  0 ,  0 ,  0 ,24.8, 5.4,148
1410    DATA  0 ,  0 ,  0 ,24.7,18.9,269
1420    DATA 11 , 12 ,  0 ,16.2, 2.7, 89
1430    DATA 17 ,  0 ,  0 ,15.9,30.2,335
1440    DATA  0 ,  0 ,  0 ,23 ,22.1,291
1450    DATA  0 , 30 ,  2.2,20.7, 8 ,163
1460    DATA  0 , 20 ,  5.6,24.9,13.7,244
1470    DATA  0 ,  0 ,  5.5,12.6,26.9,313
1480    DATA 15 ,  0 ,  0 ,15.8,29.6,330
1490    DATA 40 ,  0 ,  0 ,28.5,24.2,332
1500    DATA  0 ,  0 ,  9.5,10.6,32.1,367
1510    DATA  0 ,  0 , 11.7, 9.6,24.1,299
1520    DATA  0 ,  0 , 14.6,13.3,21.1,304
1530    DATA  0 ,  0 ,  0 , 9.4, 2.5, 60
1540    DATA 40 ,  0 ,  0 ,17.4,  .7, 76
1550    DATA  0 ,  0 ,  7.5,19.6,10.3,199
1560    DATA  0 ,  0 , 16.1,12.6, 7.5,178
1570    DATA 37 ,  0 ,  0 ,16.8,18.5,234
1580    DATA 40 ,  0 ,  0 ,19.8,11.7,184
1590    DATA  2 ,  0 ,  0 ,20.3, 8.2,155
1600    DATA  0 ,  0 ,  0 ,23.7,13.6,217
1610    DATA 12 ,  0 ,  0 ,12.3,10.9,147
1620    DATA  0 ,  0 ,  0 ,  .5,81 ,731
1630    DATA  0 ,  0 ,  0 , 0 ,99.3,894
1640    DATA  0 ,  0 ,  0 , 0 ,40.5,365
1650    DATA  0 ,  0 ,  0 ,  .2,81.5,734
1660    DATA  0 ,  0 ,  0 , 0 ,99.9,899
1670    DATA  0 ,  0 , 54.5, 8.7,37.6,578
1680    DATA  0 ,  0 , 76.4,  .4, 0 ,288
1690    DATA  0 , 10 , 69.2,  .5, 0 ,262
1700    DATA  0 , 10 , 69.5,  .1, 0 ,261
1710    DATA  0 ,  0 ,105 , 0 , 0 ,394
1720    DATA  0 ,  0 , 79 ,  .3, 0 ,298
1730    DATA  0 ,  3 , 10.3, 5.1,  .4, 63
1740    DATA 75 , 30 ,  9.5, 7.2,  .5, 69
1750    DATA  0 ,  0 , 45.5,21.4, 0 ,256
1760    DATA 14 , 20 ,  3.9, 2.2, 0 , 23
1770    DATA 20 ,  5 ,  9.9, 1.8, 0 , 44
1780    DATA 25 , 87 ,  2.7, 4 , 0 , 26
```

```
1790   DATA  0  ,  41  ,   1.7,  2.8,  0   ,  17
1800   DATA 30  ,  53  ,   2.8,  2.8,  0   ,  22
1810   DATA  0  ,  23  ,   2.3,  1.7,  0   ,  15
1820   DATA  4  ,   6  ,   5.4,   .7,  0   ,  23
1830   DATA 30  ,  64  ,   1.5,  1.9,  0   ,  13
1840   DATA 27  ,   7  ,   1.3,  -.9,  0   ,   8
1850   DATA  0  ,  17  ,  49.3,  6.2,35.9,533
1860   DATA 23  ,   8  ,   1.8,   .6,  0   ,   9
1870   DATA  0  ,   0  ,  53.2,23.8,  0   ,295
1880   DATA 20  ,  15  ,   1.2,  1  ,   0   ,   8
1890   DATA 25  ,   3  ,   0  ,  1.8,  0   ,   7
1900   DATA  3  ,  10  ,   5.2,   .9,  0   ,  23
1910   DATA 26  ,  15  ,  11.3,  1.7,  0   ,  49
1920   DATA 63  ,  25  ,  10.6,  5.8,  0   ,  62
1930   DATA  0  ,  15  ,   7.7,  5  ,   0   ,  49
1940   DATA  0  ,   0  ,  13.7,  6.2,  0   ,  76
1950   DATA 16  ,  91  ,   2.2  ,   .9,   .2,  14
1960   DATA 27  ,  30  ,  18  ,  2.1,  0   ,  76
1970   DATA  0  ,  15  ,  19.7,  1.4,  0   ,  80
1980   DATA  0  ,  20  ,  37.3,  3.8,  9   ,236
1990   DATA  0  ,  23  ,  27.3,  2.8,  1   ,111
2000   DATA 25  ,  60  ,   2.8,  2.7,  0   ,  21
2010   DATA  0  ,   4  ,  16.1,  2.9,   .8,  79
2020   DATA  0  ,  21  ,   2.4,   .8,  0   ,  12
2030   DATA 16  ,  25  ,   3.8,   .8,  0   ,  18
2040   DATA 23  ,  60  ,    .7,  2.9,  0   ,  14
2050   DATA 20  ,   5  ,  12  ,   .3,  0   ,  46
2060   DATA  0  ,   5  ,  27.7,   .5,  0   ,106
2070   DATA  0  ,   0  ,  43.4,  4.8,  0   ,182
2080   DATA 40  ,  10  ,  19.2,  1.1,  0   ,  76
2090   DATA  2  ,200  ,   6.6,   .9,  0   ,  28
2100   DATA 15  ,   5  ,  11.8,   .6,  0   ,  47
2110   DATA 14  ,   0  ,  63.9,  2  ,   0   ,248
2120   DATA  0  ,   0  ,  52.9,  3.6,  0   ,213
2130   DATA  1  ,  40  ,   6.3,   .9,  0   ,  27
2140   DATA 50  ,  40  ,   5.3,   .6,  0   ,  22
2150   DATA 60  ,  50  ,   1.6,   .3,  0   ,   7
2160   DATA 40  ,  25  ,   5.2,   .8,  0   ,  23
2170   DATA 30  ,  50  ,   8.5,   .8,  0   ,  35
2180   DATA  0  ,  40  ,  11.7,   .8,  0   ,  47
2190   DATA 13  ,   8  ,   9.1,   .6,  0   ,  36
2200   DATA  0  ,   4  ,  22.9,   .4,  0   ,  88
2210   DATA 25  ,   3  ,  10.6,   .3,  0   ,  41
2220   DATA  0  ,   8  ,  20  ,   .3,  0   ,  76
2230   DATA  8  ,   3  ,   7.9,   .6,  0   ,  32
2240   DATA 17  ,   0  ,  40.3,  2.4,  0   ,161
2250   DATA  0  ,  25  ,   5.6,   .9,  0   ,  25
2260   DATA 33  ,  10  ,   1  ,   .6,  0   ,   6
2270   DATA  3  ,  60  ,   6.2,   .6,  0   ,  26
2280   DATA  0  ,   0  ,  64.7,  1.7,  0   ,249
2290   DATA 63  ,   0  ,   4.3,20.5,53.5,580
2300   DATA  0  ,   0  ,   6.4,  6.6,62  ,608
2310   DATA  0  ,   0  ,   8.6,28.1,49  ,586
2320   DATA  0  ,   0  ,  83.6,  7.7,  1.7,360
2330   DATA  0  ,   0  ,  65.3,  7.1,24.9,497
2340   DATA  0  ,   0  ,  78  ,   8.1,16.2,471
2350   DATA  0  ,   0  ,  75.3,  7.4,13.2,431
2360   DATA  0  ,   0  ,  72.7,  5.6,22.3,496
2370   DATA  0  ,   0  ,  48.3,  9.2,  1.4,230
2380   DATA  0  ,   0  ,  47.6,10.5,  1.5,234
2390   DATA  0  ,   0  ,  54.3,  8  ,   1.7,251
2400   DATA  0  ,   0  ,  46.7,  9.6,  3.1,241
2410   DATA  0  ,   0  ,  85.4,  7.4,   .4,354
2420   DATA  0  ,   0  ,  92  ,   .5,   .7,353
2430   DATA  0  ,   0  ,  69  ,  10  ,   2.1,318
2440   DATA  0  ,   0  ,  80  ,  10  ,    .9,348
2450   DATA  0  ,   0  ,  72.8,12.1,  8.7,400
2460   DATA  0  ,   0  ,  86.8,  6.2,  1  ,359
```

```
2470  DATA  0 ,   0 ,  84  ,  9.9,  1  ,364
2480  DATA  0 ,   0 ,  84.8,  5.5,  6.3,397
2490  DATA  0 ,   0 ,  45.4,19  ,21.9,443
2500  DATA  0 ,   0 ,   0  ,  0 ,  0  ,   0
2510  DATA  0 ,   0 ,  35.5,  4  ,  .7,155
2520  DATA  0 ,   0 ,  12.2,  0  ,  0  ,  46
2530  DATA  0 ,   0 ,   0  ,  0 ,  0  ,   0
2540  DATA  0 ,   1 ,  32.2,  .1,  .1,122
2550  DATA  0 ,   0 ,   2.3,  0 ,  0  ,  30
2560  DATA  0 ,   0 ,   0  ,  0 ,  0  ,221
2570  DATA  0 ,   0 ,   .3,  0 ,  0  ,  67
2580  DATA  0 ,   2 ,  40.4,  3.2,14.4,281
2590  DATA  0 ,   0 ,  18.3,  5.6,  7 ,154
2600  DATA  0 ,   0 ,  58.6,  7.8,  8.5,328
2610  DATA  0 ,   0 ,  12.9,  3.0,  3.5,  92
2620  DATA  0 ,   0 ,  55  ,  4.6,15.9,368
2630  DATA  0 ,   0 ,  67.7,  3.2,13.8,391
2640  DATA  0 ,   0 ,  49.7,  6 ,24 ,426
2650  DATA  0 ,   1 ,  15.7,  3.6,  7.6,142
2660  DATA  0 ,   6 ,   5.9,  .8,  3.3,  55
2670  DATA  0 ,   2 ,  26.5,  3.1,  5.6,162
2680  DATA  0 ,   0 ,   0  ,  1.4,  0  ,   6
2690  DATA  0 ,   1 ,  19.8,  4.1,11.3 ,192
2700  END
```

8 VILLAGE: a geography simulation

Introduction

VILLAGE is a simulation* but, unlike the others described, it incorporates a new concept, that of **Computer-Aided Instruction** (C.A.I.) The possibility of using the computer for the purpose of instruction will be considered in greater depth later; it is sufficient at this stage to comment only briefly on its purpose in this package.

It is possible to program the computer so that it can fulfil the role of the teacher in some aspects of work which require instruction. In VILLAGE the student receives instruction by example, using both the computer and printed material, on a method for calculating the best site for a village in about 600 A.D.—this being a period in which such an activity would have been undertaken and when the variables to be considered would necessarily be limited. Having established the method, the computer directs the student to exercises in the accompanying booklet which are designed to test his understanding of the principles involved.

Aims

The basic aim of the project is to establish for the student the concept of efficiency (in this case expressed in terms of the efficient use of the resource time) and its relationship to the factors that influenced the early sitings of settlements; namely, the availability of water, grazing and arable land, fuel and building materials. In addition, it attempts to show that these factors vary in importance and that some attempt should be made to "weight" them. Finally, it encourages the student to consider the effect that the need for choosing a good defence site would have on the location of the village, and thus introduce the notion of a "trade-off" (in this case between economic efficiency and defence).

The Magic Formula

Consider the situation in which a village is to be sited in an area which provides water, arable land and a fuel supply. Suppose that water has to be collected three times each day, the arable land visited and worked once each day, and fuel collected once each day.

---

* This simulation was developed from an exercise in *European Patterns*, the Oxford Geography Project (Oxford University Press, 1976 Edition).

The formula involved is also discussed in *Settlement Patterns*, J. A. Everson and B. P. Fitzgerald (Longman, 1969).

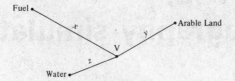

Fig 8.1

If these resources were distributed as suggested in the map (Fig 8.1), and a site for the village proposed (V), the method for establishing its efficiency rating would be as follows.

a)   Measure the distance from each resource to the proposed site.
b)   Double the distance to allow for the return journey.
c)   Multiply the distance in each case by the number of visits.
d)   Add the results to give the total travelling involved.

This can then be converted into an efficiency rating by the computer in order to make a comparison between different sites easier.

Resource	Distance from V	Number of visits per day
Fuel	x units	1
Arable land	y	1
Water	z	3

Total travelling distance $= (2x$ times $1) + (2y$ times $1) + (2z$ times $3)$

THE "BEST" SITE CAN BE FOUND BY COMPARING TOTAL DISTANCES FOR SEVERAL SITES. IT CANNOT BE DETERMINED BY CALCULATING THE TOTAL DISTANCE FOR ONLY ONE SITE.

It should be clear that the smaller the distance walked each day, the less time will be wasted in travelling.

An extended version of this formula forms the basis of the simulation and the subject of the C.A.I.

Why use a computer?

1   To establish that some sites are better than others before introducing the formula, and hopefully arouse interest at this point.
2   Students can experiment in order to establish the quality of their intuitive guesses, and perhaps identify with the problems of early settlers. This is something which could be done without the aid of the computer but without the immediate feedback that the computer can provide. (The calculations take time and make demands on the accuracy of the student, lack of which may come between the student and the idea.)
3   In developing the map for VILLAGE, the program was adapted slightly to print out a table of all the efficiency ratings. The table was then used to assess how good the map was in terms of there being several efficient areas

to site the village. If the table did not show this and there was only one very obvious location for the village, then the map was redrawn and a further table of efficiency ratings produced.

Repeating this process enabled a map to be produced which was reasonably complex and offered many reasonable possibilities for the siting of the village. (As you can imagine, the time required to develop a map using the above method, but calculating the distances by hand, would be prohibitive.)

4 A small program was also written to produce a check table for the Geography teacher to accompany the exercise in the back of the booklet. This produced a table of all the "total distances" for all the possible sites on the simple map.

5 Finally, the use of the computer provides the opportunity for group work.

The Scheme of Work and General Procedure

The student is given a booklet and invited to study the first page which is an introduction explaining the purpose of the simulation and the procedures to be observed; a map is given on page 3.

Having read through the introduction, the student begins using the computer program. The student is invited to select three separate sites for a village. After each selection the computer responds with an efficiency rating for the selected site.

After three attempts to site the village the student is instructed by the computer to read page 2 in the booklet. It describes the factors which contribute to the calculation of the Efficiency Rating.

Having read this information, the student activates the computer which has waited for the signal to continue. Two further attempts are allowed to improve the location of the village. For these two attempts the computer demonstrates the formula used to calculate the Efficiency Rating.

The simulation then moves into its final phase in which the defence of the village is considered. No guidance is given as to what determines a good defensive location for the village. Five attempts are made by the student to find a good defensive position and it is hoped that by comparing the Defence Ratings the student will obtain an insight into what constitutes a good defensive location. The student is also instructed to try and maintain a good Efficiency Rating for the village if at all possible.

Obviously, students working together in a small group would discuss defensive strategies and may select better defensive locations as a result.

The Defence Rating scale reads from 1 to 100 and the lower the rating the better the defence position. For each location selected, the computer prints out an Efficiency Rating and a Defence Rating. This shows the student how efficiency may have to be sacrificed in order to defend the village.

The computer has now finished its part in the simulation and ends by listing the tasks to be completed in the booklet.

Last part of the printout

YOU SHOULD NOW BE ABLÉ TO COMPLETE THE REMAINING
PARTS OF YOUR BOOKLET BACK IN THE CLASSROOM.

THE TASKS ARE:–
(1)
CUT OUT THE WORKED EXAMPLE ON FINDING THE EFFICIENCY
RATING FROM YOUR PRINT-OUT AND STICK IN THE
PLACE PROVIDED ON PAGE 4 (OR COPY IT INTO THE SPACE).

(2)
CARRY OUT THE TASK DESCRIBED ON PAGE 5

(3)
CARRY OUT THE TASK DESCRIBED ON PAGE 7

PROJECT FINISHED

The remaining parts of the booklet include the following:

Page 4   Space for an example printout to be inserted.
Pages 5 and 6   The student is asked to select three sites on a simplified
map and to work out the travelling distances involved in each
case. The results are entered in the appropriate positions on
page 5.
Page 7   A table for entering the results of the last five chosen locations
so that the trade-off between Defence and Efficient Siting can
be examined.
Page 8   A set of questions.

Student Booklet: VILLAGE

The program is run in JBAS and is named VILL.

The Aim

This is a simulation concerned with the siting of a new village. You must imagine that you are living in about 600 A.D. The village in which you live at present is becoming overcrowded so you and some others have decided to establish a settlement of your own. On page 3 is a map showing an area in which you can site your new village. The members of your group are relying upon you, and perhaps a small group of advisers, to choose the best place.

It is important that you remember that you are farmers. You need to farm in order to survive. At this stage of the simulation it is not important that you choose a good defensive position. These are peaceful times.

How to play

You must select a site where two lines cross, See A, B and C in the example.

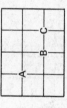

The computer will ask you where you want to site the village. You must respond by typing in the co-ordinates of the position you have chosen by using the letters and the numbers, e.g. D/8 or N/9. You must then press the ACCEPT key. Separate the letter and number by /. Do not leave spaces between the letter, /, and number.

1

When you have made your choice the computer will tell you how good it was by printing a number described as an efficiency rating (ER). The lower the number, the better the position.

Note.
1. FOLLOW THE COMPUTER'S INSTRUCTIONS.
2. DO NOT READ THE REST OF THE BOOKLET UNTIL INSTRUCTED TO.
3. DO NOT SITE THE VILLAGE ON MARSH.

Calculating the Best Site

There is a method which can be used to determine the best location for the village. It involves calculating the amount of time wasted in walking from the village to each of the available resources (water, grazing land, arable land, the wood — for fuel and building materials). The smaller the distance which has to be walked, the less time that is wasted, and so the better the position.

The following table suggests the number of visits to each of the above-mentioned resources in a two-week period.

RESOURCE	NUMBER OF VISITS
WATER	30
GRAZING LAND	15
ARABLE LAND	10
FUEL	7
BUILDING MATERIALS	2

TYPE CON TO CONTINUE

(NOTE TO TEACHER: it should be clear from the context that the section Calculating the Best Site should not be seen by the student until 3 attempts have been made to site the village.)

2

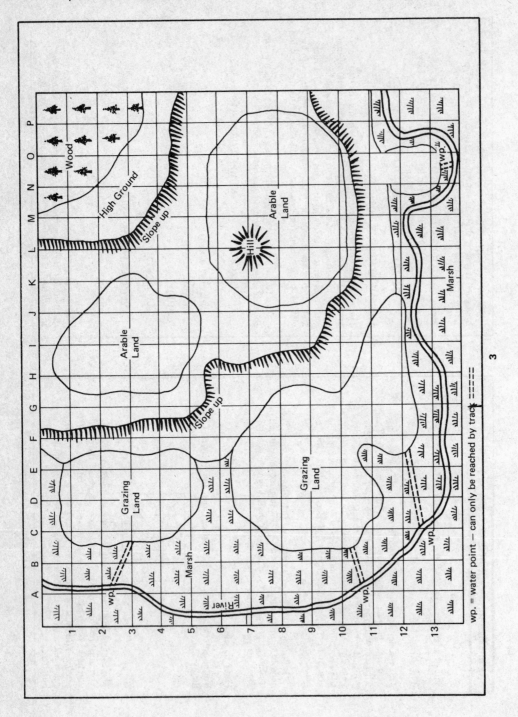

wp. = water point – can only be reached by track ======

3

Task Using the map on page 6, work out the distance travelled for three sites. Mark each one on the map by a cross. Your site must be a place where two lines cross. Do the calculations in the space provided below. When you have finished, draw a circle round the best site on the map, and then show your teacher.

	DISTANCE TRAVELLED ON A RETURN JOURNEY FROM VILLAGE TO:	NUMBER OF VISITS IN A TWO WEEK PERIOD	
SITE ☐	WATER	mm x 30 =	mm
	GRAZING LAND	mm x 15 =	mm
	ARABLE LAND	mm x 10 =	mm
	FUEL	mm x 7 =	mm
	BUILDING MATERIAL	mm x 2 =	mm
		TOTAL	mm

	DISTANCE TRAVELLED ON A RETURN JOURNEY FROM VILLAGE TO:	NUMBER OF VISITS IN A TWO WEEK PERIOD	
SITE ☐	WATER	mm x 30 =	mm
	GRAZING LAND	mm x 15 =	mm
	ARABLE LAND	mm x 10 =	mm
	FUEL	mm x 7 =	mm
	BUILDING MATERIAL	mm x 2 =	mm
		TOTAL	mm

	DISTANCE TRAVELLED ON A RETURN JOURNEY FROM VILLAGE TO:	NUMBER OF VISITS IN A TWO WEEK PERIOD	
SITE ☐	WATER	mm x 30 =	mm
	GRAZING LAND	mm x 15 =	mm
	ARABLE LAND	mm x 10 =	mm
	FUEL	mm x 7 =	mm
	BUILDING MATERIAL	mm x 2 =	mm
		TOTAL	mm

5

COMPUTER EXAMPLE

4

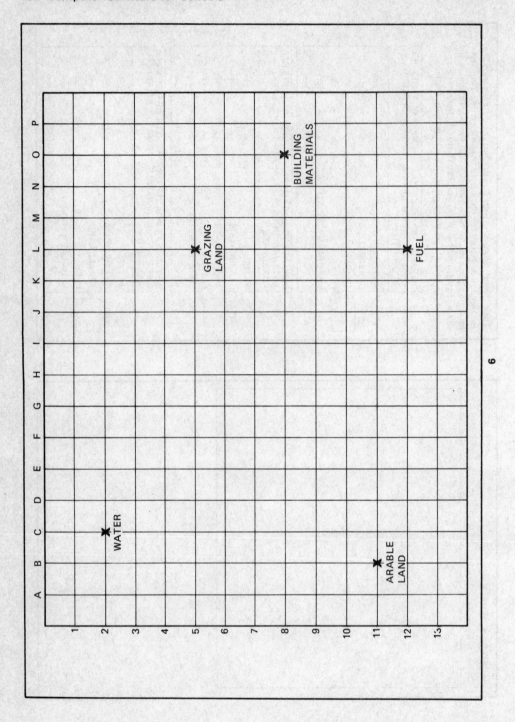

6

Defence

Record the Defence Ratings (DR) and the Efficiency Ratings (ER) which appeared on the printout in the spaces provided below.

	DR	ER
Defence Site 1	☐	☐
Defence Site 2	☐	☐
Defence Site 3	☐	☐
Defence Site 4	☐	☐
Defence Site 5	☐	☐

7

Questions

Answer the following questions on a separate piece of paper and then place it in the back of your booklet.

1 What sort of places make good defensive positions for a village. Try to give a reason for each type of place.

2 Why might the total distance travelled be shorter in a real situation? (Consider the case where the water point is directly beyond your arable land).

3 Does the ER value vary even though the DR value may be repeated? If so, in troubled times, when defence is important what should be your aim regarding Defence and Efficient Siting? How should you try to achieve a sensible balance?

8

Sample Run

VILLAGE LOCATION PROJECT
=========================

I HOPE YOU HAVE THE MAP OF THE AREA IN FRONT OF YOU.
WHERE HAVE YOU DECIDED TO ESTABLISH YOUR VILLAGE?
TYPE IN YOUR CHOICE NOW AS IN THE EXAMPLE. (EG. A/2)
←C/3

THIS SITE HAS AN EFFICIENCY RATING OF 35
NOTE. THE LOWER THE EFFICIENCY RATING, THE BETTER THE SITE.
THE RANGE IS BETWEEN 1 AND 100
TRY TO CHOOSE A BETTER POSITION.
TYPE IN YOUR NEW CHOICE NOW.
←H/11

THIS SITE HAS AN EFFICIENCY RATING OF 48
TRY TO CHOOSE A BETTER POSITION.
TYPE IN YOUR NEW CHOICE NOW.
←N/10

THIS SITE HAS AN EFFICIENCY RATING OF 43

CLEARLY SOME SITES ARE BETTER THAN OTHERS. LIKE YOU EARLY
SETTLERS WOULD HAVE NO WAY OF KNOWING WHICH WAS THE BEST
POSSIBLE SITE. THEY WOULD HAVE MADE A RATIONAL/SENSIBLE
CHOICE BUT ONE CAN IMAGINE THAT A GOOD DEAL OF TRIAL AND
ERROR WOULD HAVE BEEN INVOLVED. TURN TO PAGE 2 OF YOUR
BOOKLET AND READ WHAT IT SAYS THERE.

WHEN YOU ARE READY TYPE CON TO CONTINUE.

←CON
NOW TRY TO CHOOSE A BETTER SITE FOR YOUR VILLAGE.
TYPE IN YOUR CHOICE NOW.
←N/12

THIS SITE HAS AN EFFICIENCY RATING OF 37

THERE NOW FOLLOWS A DESCRIPTION OF HOW THE COMPUTER
WORKED OUT THE EFFICIENCY RATING FOR THE LAST SITE.

DISTANCE FROM VILLAGE TO RESOURCE AND BACK AGAIN	NUMBER OF VISITS IN A TWO WEEK PERIOD
WATER	$38\,MM \times 30 = 1140\,MM$
GRAZING	$80\,MM \times 15 = 1200\,MM$
ARABLE	$44\,MM \times 10 = 440\,MM$
FUEL	$184\,MM \times 7 = 1288\,MM$
BUILDING MATERIAL	$184\,MM \times 2 = 368\,MM$

TOTAL   4436 (EFF.RAT. 37)

IT MEASURES THE DISTANCES IN MILLIMETRES (MM)
ON THE MAP FROM THE POINT CHOSEN TO THE
NEAREST POINT OF EACH RESOURCE AND THEN DOUBLES
THESE DISTANCES TO ALLOW FOR THE RETURN JOURNEY.
IT THEN MULTIPLIES THE NEW DISTANCES
BY THE NUMBER OF VISITS IN EACH
CASE.IT CONSIDERS ONLY THE NEAREST WATER,GRAZING LAND,ETC.
IT THEN ADDS UP THESE DISTANCES TO OBTAIN A TOTAL.
THE TOTAL IS THEN CONVERTED INTO AN EFFICIENCY RATING
FOR SIMPLICITY.

IF YOU FOLLOW THIS PROCEDURE WITH A NUMBER OF SITES YOU WILL
BE ABLE TO WORK OUT WHICH WILL INVOLVE THE LEAST WALKING
DISTANCE.THE SHORTER THE DISTANCE,THE BETTER THE POSITION.

BEARING IN MIND THIS METHOD,SELECT ANOTHER SITE.
HOWEVER,DO NOT TRY TO MEASURE DISTANCES AT THIS STAGE.
TYPE IN YOUR CHOICE.
←L/11

DISTANCE FROM VILLAGE TO RESOURCE AND BACK AGAIN	NUMBER OF VISITS IN A TWO WEEK PERIOD

WATER	80 MM × 30 =	2400 MM
GRAZING	44 MM × 15 =	660 MM
ARABLE	20 MM × 10 =	200 MM
FUEL	178 MM × 7 =	1246 MM
BUILDING MATERIAL	178 MM × 2 =	356 MM

= = =
TOTAL   4862 (EFF.RAT. 40)
= = =

NOW IMAGINE THAT YOU ARE HAVING TO ESTABLISH YOUR VILLAGE
IN TROUBLED TIMES. YOU MUST CONSIDER THE PROBLEM OF DEFENCE.
WHERE WOULD YOU SITE YOUR VILLAGE NOW?
TYPE IN YOUR CHOICE.
←O/9

THE DEFENCE RATING IS 90
AGAIN THE LOWER THE RATING THE BETTER THE POSITION.
THE RANGE IS AGAIN BETWEEN 1 AND 100

THE EFFICIENCY RATING IS 47

YOU MAY NOW HAVE FOUR FURTHER ATTEMPTS TO IMPROVE
THE DEFENCE RATING OR TO FIND AN EQUALLY GOOD POSITION.
REMEMBER YOU WANT TO KEEP THE EFFICIENCY RATING
AS LOW AS POSSIBLE STILL.
WHERE WOULD YOU SITE YOUR VILLAGE NOW?
TYPE IN YOUR CHOICE.
←N/3

THE DEFENCE RATING IS 90

THE EFFICIENCY RATING IS 82

WHERE WOULD YOU SITE YOUR VILLAGE NOW?
TYPE IN YOUR CHOICE.
←C/3

THE DEFENCE RATING IS 20

THE EFFICIENCY RATING IS 35

WHERE WOULD YOU SITE YOUR VILLAGE NOW?
TYPE IN YOUR CHOICE.
←C/10

THE DEFENCE RATING IS 20

THE EFFICIENCY RATING IS 44

WHERE WOULD YOU SITE YOUR VILLAGE NOW?
TYPE IN YOUR CHOICE.
←L/7

THE DEFENCE RATING IS 5

THE EFFICIENCY RATING IS 57

YOU SHOULD NOW BE ABLE TO COMPLETE THE REMAINING
PARTS OF YOUR BOOKLET BACK IN THE CLASSROOM.

THE TASKS ARE:–

(1)
CUT OUT THE WORKED EXAMPLE ON FINDING THE EFFICIENCY
RATING FROM YOUR PRINT-OUT AND STICK IN THE
PLACE PROVIDED ON PAGE 4 (OR COPY IT INTO THE SPACE).

(2)
CARRY OUT THE TASK DESCRIBED ON PAGE 5

(3)
CARRY OUT THE TASK DESCRIBED ON PAGE 7

PROJECT FINISHED

Program Summary

If we now turn to the program, without going into too great a depth, we can see that there are certain procedures which are repeated throughout the course of a run. There are also blocks of letters and numbers with each line headed by the word DATA. Let us begin by separating the program into two areas.

1 Lines 10 ↕ 1080   Main program. Mostly PRINT statements giving information to the student and INPUT statements, where the student types in his choice of location.

2 Lines 8000 ↕ 9900   This section of the program is divided into two parts, dealing on the one hand with Subroutines and on the other with DATA statements.

Subroutines		*DATA Statements*		
8200 ↕ 8265	Fills the "type of ground" array M$.	8000	Water	This block of data contains the coordinates of the boundary points of all the resources.
8270 ↕ 8850	Calculates the Efficiency Rating.	8010 } 8020 } 8030 }	Grazing	
8900 ↕ 9070	Calculates the values for the printed calculations.	8040 } 8050 }	Arable	
9230 ↕ 9300	Fills the Defence Rating array S$.	8060	Forest	
		8070 ↕ 8190	Type of ground of each intersection point on the map.	
9400 ↕ 9560	Checks the input format of a chosen site.	9100 ↕ 9225	Defence Rating of each intersection point.	

Explanation and Examples of DATA Statements

When the computer calculates distances, it requires the coordinates for the student's choice of site to be in numeric form. In order to avoid confusion for the student it was decided to use letters for one axis and numbers for the other. This necessitated converting the letter into numeric form for calculating purposes. Part of the grid is shown in Fig 8.2 with its numeric values in brackets accompanying the map references.

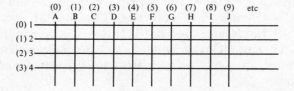

Fig 8.2

Boundary Points

Example

8060 DATA 0,13,1,14,2,15   (Wood, Fig 8.3)

When the distance to a resource is calculated, the computer only compares the distances to the points just inside the boundary of the resource.

In this example the computer would only compare the distances from (3, 12), the selected site, to (0, 13), (1, 14) and (2, 15) because the distances of the other points in the wood, such as (0, 15), would obviously be greater.

Fig 8.3

Fig 8.4

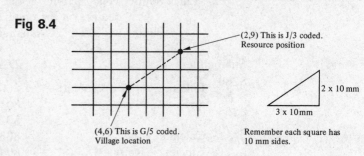

Type of Ground and Defence Value Data

The DATA line 8070 contains 16 letters representing the type of ground for the top line of the map. The coordinates of these points would be (0, 0), (0, 1), (0, 2) across to (0, 15).

8070 DATA M,M,G,G,G,P,P,A,A,P,P,P,P,F,F,F

M—Marsh, G—Grazing land, P—Poor soil, A—Arable land, F—Wood (Fuel).

Similarly, DATA line 9100 contains the 16 Defence Rating values for the top line of the map.

9100 DATA 100,100,20,20,20,40,10,90,90,90,90,40,10,90,90,90

The Subroutines

1st Subroutine   When the program commences running, the first subroutine reads the "type of ground" data into the array M$. Each intersection point on the map is allocated a letter e.g. A for Arable, etc.

2nd Subroutine   When the student selects a site, the computer moves to the second subroutine which calculates the Efficiency Rating of the site. The array M$ is consulted and the type of ground on which the village has been sited is determined. This is necessary because the village could be located on one of the resources and so the journey distance to that particular resource will be zero. (Obviously there will be some walking involved within a resource area, but to take this into account would not be particularly helpful.)

Let us consider an example. If the student selected D/3 which places the village on grazing land, then the distance to the resources Arable land, Wood and Water alone need to be calculated. The subroutine begins by calculating the distance to each of the four water points from the selected site and determining which is the nearest. The positions of the four water points are held on line 8000 in the program. The subroutine then calculates the distances to all the boundary points of the Grazing land from the chosen site. The boundary points appear on lines 8010, 8020, 8030 in the data block. The computer would again select the shortest distance. However, in the example we are considering, the village is located on grazing land and so the distance would be zero. The subroutine continues and now checks the distances to all the boundary points of the Arable land and selects the shortest distance. The coordinates of the Arable land appear on lines 8040, 8050 in the data block. Finally, the subroutine checks the distances to the boundary points of the Forest and selects the shortest distance. The co-ordinates of the Forest are found on line 8060 of the program.

This subroutine is repeated each time the student selects a site for the village.

3rd Subroutine   The third subroutine is an extension of the second and is used when the example calculations are printed out. It is necessary in order to obtain the individual distances and the results of multiplying them by the number of visits for each. The second subroutine calculates only the total distance without establishing values for each individual resource.

4th Subroutine   When the program reaches the stage where the defence of the site has to be considered, the program uses a fourth subroutine to load into an array S$ the values of the defence rating of each site. Thereafter, each time the student selects a site, the computer finds the relevant defence rating from the array S$. The defence rating values are contained in the block of data 9100 to 9225.

5th Subroutine   The fifth subroutine is used each time a student selects a site for the village. It is a check to see that a letter A–P inclusive and a number 1–13 inclusive have been used and that they are separated by an oblique. If the selected site is acceptable it changes the input into numeric form to suit the calculations. If it is incorrect it gives an example input, i.e. A/12, and then invites the student to type in a selection again, using the correct format.

Calculating Distances

For those who may be interested, the subroutine which calculates distances makes use of Pythagoras's theorem. Referring to Fig 8.4,

$$\text{Distance} = \sqrt{[30^2 + 20^2]} = \sqrt{[900 + 400]} = \sqrt{1300} \approx 36 \text{ mm}$$

Program Listing:
ICL-CES
BASIC

```
10 REM              VILLAGE LOCATION
15 GOSUB 8200
16 LET I=0
17 LET K9=0
20 PRINT "VILLAGE LOCATION PROJECT"
30 PRINT "========================="
40 PRINT LIN$(3)
50 PRINT "I HOPE YOU HAVE THE MAP OF THE AREA IN FRONT OF YOU."
60 PRINT "WHERE HAVE YOU DECIDED TO ESTABLISH YOUR VILLAGE?"
70 PRINT "TYPE IN YOUR CHOICE NOW AS IN THE EXAMPLE. (EG. A/2 )"
80 INPUT A$
90 GOSUB 9400
100 IF J7=1 THEN 110
105 GOTO 80
110 GOSUB 8270
120 PRINT
125 IF K=1 THEN 60
130 PRINT "THIS SITE HAS AN EFFICIENCY RATING OF ";INT(T/120.46+0.5)
140 IF I>0 THEN 190
145 PRINT "NOTE. THE LOWER THE EFFICIENCY RATING,THE BETTER THE SITE."
146 PRINT "THE RANGE IS BETWEEN 1 AND 100"
150 FOR I=1 TO 2
160 PRINT "TRY TO CHOOSE A BETTER POSITION."
170 PRINT "TYPE IN YOUR NEW CHOICE NOW."
180 GOTO 80
190 NEXT I
200 PRINT LIN$(2)
210 PRINT "CLEARLY SOME SITES ARE BETTER THAN OTHERS.LIKE YOU ,EARLY"
220 PRINT "SETTLERS WOULD HAVE NO WAY OF KNOWING WHICH WAS THE BEST"
230 PRINT "POSSIBLE SITE. THEY WOULD HAVE MADE A RATIONAL/SENSIBLE"
240 PRINT "CHOICE BUT ONE CAN IMAGINE THAT A GOOD DEAL OF TRIAL AND"
250 PRINT "ERROR WOULD HAVE BEEN INVOLVED. TURN TO PAGE 2 OF YOUR"
260 PRINT "BOOKLET AND READ WHAT IT SAYS THERE."
270 PRINT
271 PRINT "WHEN YOU ARE READY TYPE CON TO CONTINUE."
272 PRINT "                         ===  "
280 INPUT A$
298 IF A$="CON" THEN 310
300 GOTO 270
310 PRINT "NOW TRY TO CHOOSE A BETTER SITE FOR YOUR VMLLAGE."
320 PRINT "TYPE IN YOUR CHOICE NOW."
330 INPUT A$
340 GOSUB 9400
350 IF J7=1 THEN 360
355 GOTO 330
360 GOSUB 8270
370 PRINT
375 IF K=1 THEN 310
380 PRINT "THIS SITE HAS AN EFFICIENCY RATING OF ";INT(T/120.46+0.5)
390 PRINT
400 PRINT "THERE NOW FOLLOWS A DESCRIPTION OF HOW THE COMPUTER"
410 PRINT "WORKED OUT THE EFFICIENCY RATING FOR THE LAST SITE."
420 PRINT
430 PRINT "DISTANCE FROM VILLAGE TO     NUMBER OF VISITS IN"
440 PRINT "RESOURCE AND BACK AGAIN      A TWO WEEK PERIOD"
450 PRINT
455 GOSUB 8900
460 LET X1=LEN(STR$(Z1))
461 LET X2=LEN(STR$(Y1))
462 PRINT "WATER";TAB(23-X1);Z1;" MM   X   30 =";TAB(43-X2);Y1;" MM"
470 LET X1=LEN(STR$(Z2))
471 LET X2=LEN(STR$(Y2))
472 PRINT "GRAZING";TAB(23-X1);Z2;" MM   X   15 =";TAB(43-X2);Y2;" MM"
480 LET X1=LEN(STR$(Z3))
481 LET X2=LEN(STR$(Y3))
482 PRINT "ARABLE";TAB(23-X1);Z3;" MM   X   10 =";TAB(43-X2);Y3;" MM"
490 LET X1=LEN(STR$(Z4))
491 LET X2=LEN(STR$(Y4))
```

```
492 PRINT "FUEL"; TAB(23-X1); Z4; " MM   X   7 ="; TAB(43-X2); Y4; " MM"
500 LET X2=LEN(STR$(Y5))
501 PRINT "BUILDING MATERIAL"; TAB(23-X1); Z4;
502 PRINT " MM   X   2 ="; TAB(43-X2); Y5; " MM"
505 PRINT TAB(40); "===="
506 LET X1=LEN(STR$(T))
510 PRINT
    TAB(33); "TOTAL"; TAB(43-X1); T; "(EFF.RAT."; INT(T/120.46+0.5); ")"
520 PRINT TAB(40); "===="
530 PRINT
535 IF K9=1 THEN 720
540 PRINT "IT MEASURES THE DISTANCES IN MILLIMETRES(MM)"
545 PRINT "ON THE MAP FROM THE POINT CHOSEN TO THE"
550 PRINT "NEAREST POINT OF EACH RESOURCE AND THEN DOUBLES"
554 PRINT "THESE DISTANCES TO ALLOW FOR THE RETURN JOURNEY."
558 PRINT "IT THEN MULTIPLIES THE NEW DISTANCES"
560 PRINT "BY THE NUMBER OF VISITS IN EACH"
570 PRINT "CASE.IT CONSIDERS ONLY THE NEAREST WATER,GRAZING LAND, ETC."
580 PRINT "IT THEN ADDS UP THESE DISTANCES TO OBTAIN A TOTAL."
585 PRINT "THE TOTAL IS THEN CONVERTED INTO AN EFFICIENCY RATING"
586 PRINT "FOR SIMPLICITY."
590 PRINT
600 PRINT
    "IF YOU FOLLOW THIS PROCEDURE WITH A NUMBER OF SITES YOU WILL"
610 PRINT "BE ABLE TO WORK OUT WHICH WILL INVOLVE THE LEAST WALKING"
620 PRINT "DISTANCE.THE SHORTER THE DISTANCE,THE BETTER THE POSITION."
630 PRINT
640 PRINT "BEARING IN MIND THIS METHOD,SELECT ANOTHER SITE."
645 PRINT "HOWEVER,DO NOT TRY TO MEASURE DISTANCES AT THIS STAGE."
650 PRINT "TYPE IN YOUR CHOICE."
655 LET K9=1
660 INPUT A$
670 GOSUB 9400
680 IF J7=1 THEN 690
685 GOTO 660
690 GOSUB 8270
700 PRINT
705 IF K=1 THEN 650
708 GOTO 420
710 PRINT "THE EFFICIENCY RATING IS "; INT(T/120.46+0.5)
720 PRINT
725 LET E2=1
728 GOSUB 9100
730 PRINT "NOW IMAGINE THAT YOU ARE HAVING TO ESTABLISH YOUR VILLAGE"
740 PRINT
    "IN TROUBLED TIMES. YOU MUST CONSIDER THE PROBLEM OF DEFENCE."
745 LET F=0
750 PRINT "WHERE WOULD YOU SITE YOUR VILLAGE NOW?"
760 PRINT "TYPE IN YOUR CHOICE."
770 INPUT A$
780 GOSUB 9400
790 IF J7=1 THEN 800
795 GOTO 770
800 GOSUB 8270
810
820 PRINT
825 IF K=1 THEN 750
830 PRINT "THE DEFENCE RATING IS "; S$(C1,C2)
835 IF F=1 THEN 850
840 PRINT "AGAIN THE LOWER THE RATING THE BETTER THE POSITION."
845 PRINT "THE RANGE IS AGAIN BETWEEN 1 AND 100"
850 PRINT
851 PRINT "THE EFFICIENCY RATING IS "; INT(T/120.46+0.5)
860 PRINT
863 IF F=1 THEN 920
865 LET F=1
870 PRINT "YOU MAY NOW HAVE FOUR FURTHER ATTEMPTS TO IMPROVE"
880 PRINT "THE DEFENCE RATING OR TO FIND AN EQUALLY GOOD POSITION."
```

```
890 PRINT "REMEMBER YOU WANT TO KEEP THE EFFICIENCY RATING"
895 PRINT "AS LOW AS POSSIBLE STILL."
900 FOR I=1 TO 4
910 GOTO 750
920 PRINT
930 NEXT I
940 PRINT "YOU SHOULD NOW BE ABLE TO COMPLETE THE REMAINING"
950 PRINT "PARTS OF YOUR BOOKLET BACK IN THE CLASSROOM."
960 PRINT
970 PRINT "THE TASKS ARE:-"
975 PRINT
976 PRINT "(1)"
980 PRINT "CUT OUT THE WORKED EXAMPLE ON FINDING THE EFFICIENCY"
990 PRINT "RATING FROM YOUR PRINT-OUT AND STICK IN THE"
1000 PRINT "PLACE PROVIDED ON PAGE 4 (OR COPY IT INTO THE SPACE)."
1010 PRINT
1020 PRINT "(2)"
1030 PRINT "CARRY OUT THE TASK DESCRIBED ON PAGE 5"
1040 PRINT
1050 PRINT "(3)"
1060 PRINT "CARRY OUT THE TASK DESCRIBED ON PAGE 7"
1070 PRINT LIN$(3);"PROJECT FINISHED";LIN$(1)
1080 GOTO 9900
8000 DATA 2,1.6,9.4,1.4,11.3,4.6,12.3,13.6
8010 DATA 6,3,6,4,6,5,7,6,8,6,9,6,10,7,10,8,11,9,11,8,11,7,11,6,11,5
8020 DATA 10,5,9,5,9,4,10,3,9,2,8,2,7,2,0,2,0,3,0,4,1,4,2,4,3,4,4,4
8030 DATA 4,3,3,2,2,2,1,2
8040 DATA 5,11,5,12,5,13,5,14,6,15,7,15,8,15,9,14,9,13,9,12,9,11
8050 DATA 8,10,7,10,6,10,0,7,0,8,1,9,2,10,3,9,4,9,4,8,3,7,2,7,1,7
8060 DATA 0,13,1,14,2,15
8070 DATA M,M,G,G,G,P,P,P,A,A,P,P,P,P,F,F,F
8080 DATA M,M,G,G,G,P,P,A,A,A,P,P,P,P,F,F
8090 DATA M,M,G,G,G,P,P,A,A,A,A,P,P,P,P,F
8100 DATA M,M,G,G,G,P,P,A,A,A,A,P,P,P,P,P
8110 DATA M,M,M,G,G,P,P,P,A,A,P,P,P,P,P,P
8120 DATA M,M,M,M,M,P,P,P,P,P,P,A,A,A,A,P
8130 DATA M,M,M,G,G,G,P,P,P,P,A,A,A,A,A,A
8140 DATA M,M,G,G,G,G,G,P,P,P,A,A,A,A,A,A
8150 DATA M,M,G,G,G,G,G,P,P,P,A,A,A,A,A,A
8160 DATA M,M,G,G,G,G,G,P,P,P,A,A,A,A,A,P
8170 DATA M,M,M,G,M,G,G,G,P,P,P,P,P,P,P,P
8180 DATA M,M,M,M,M,G,G,G,G,G,M,M,M,P,P,M
8190 DATA M,M,M,M,M,M,M,M,M,M,M,M,M,P,P,M
8200 RESTORE 8070
8210 DIM M$(12,15)
8220 FOR R1=0 TO 12
8230 FOR R2=0 TO 15
8240 READ M$(R1,R2)
8250 NEXT R2
8260 NEXT R1
8265 RETURN
8270 RESTORE
8275 LET K=0
8280 LET P$=M$(C1,C2)
8290 IF P$<>"M" THEN 8320
8295 IF E2=1 THEN 8303
8299 LET K=1
8300 PRINT "IT WOULD BE UNWISE TO BUILD ON THE MARSH."
8301 PRINT "MARSH = SOFT GROUND/WET/UNABLE TO SUPPORT STRUCTURES."
8302 GOTO 8310
8303 PRINT " A PIECE OF DRY GROUND IN THE MIDDLE OF THE MARSH AREA"
8304 PRINT " WOULD BE A VERY GOOD DEFENCE SITE.HOWEVER YOU CANNOT"
8305 LET K=1
8306 PRINT " DEDUCE THIS FROM THE MAP.YOU WILL HAVE TO DO A THOROUGH"
8307 PRINT " GROUND SURVEY.SELECT ANOTHER DEFENSIVE POSITION."
8310 RETURN
8320 LET S=100
```

```
8330 FOR N=1 TO 4
8340 READ C8,C9
8350 LET S1=SQR((C1-C8)↑2+(C2-C9)↑2)
8360 ON N GOTO 8370,8390,8410,8430
8370 LET S1=S1+1.5
8380 GOTO 8440
8390 LET S1=S1+1.2
8400 GOTO 8440
8410 LET S1=S1+2.4
8420 GOTO 8440
8430 LET S1=S1+0.5
8440 IF S<=S1 THEN 8460
8450 LET S=S1
8460 NEXT N
8470 LET Z1=INT(S*10+0.5)*2
8480 LET T=Z1*30
8490 IF P$<>"G" THEN 8520
8500 RESTORE 8040
8505 LET Z2=0
8510 GOTO 8610
8520 LET S=100
8530 FOR R3=1 TO 31
8540 READ K1,K2
8550 LET S1=SQR((C1-K1)↑2+(C2-K2)↑2)
8560 IF S<=S1 THEN 8580
8570 LET S=S1
8580 NEXT R3
8590 LET Z2=INT(S*10+0.5)*2
8600 LET T=T+(Z2*15)
8610 IF P$<>"A" THEN 8640
8620 RESTORE 8060
8625 LET Z3=0
8630 GOTO 8730
8640 LET S=100
8650 FOR R3=1 TO 24
8660 READ K1,K2
8670 LET S1=SQR((C1-K1)↑2+(C2-K2)↑2)
8680 IF S<=S1 THEN 8700
8690 LET S=S1
8700 NEXT R3
8710 LET Z3=INT(S*10+0.5)*2
8720 LET T=T+(Z3*10)
8730 IF P$="F" THEN 8840
8740 LET S=100
8750 FOR R3=1 TO 3
8760 READ K1,K2
8770 LET S1=SQR((C1-K1)↑2+(C2-K2)↑2)
8?8 IF S<=S1 THEN 8800
8790 LET S=S1
8800 NEXT R3
8810 LET Z4=INT(S*10+0.5)*2
8820 LET T=T+(Z4*9)
8830 GOTO 8850
8840 LET Z4=0
8850 RETURN
8900 IF Z1=0 THEN 8930
8910 LET Y1=Z1*30
8920 GOTO 8940
8930 LET Y1=0
8940 IF Z2=0 THEN 8970
8950 LET Y2=Z2*15
8960 GOTO 8980
8970 LET Y2=0
8980 IF Z3=0 THEN 9010
8990 LET Y3=Z3*10
9000 GOTO 9020
9010 LET Y3=0
9020 IF Z4=0 THEN 9060
9030 LET Y4=Z4*7
```

```
9040 LET Y5=Z4*2
9050 GOTO 9070
9060 LET Y4=Y5=0
9070 RETURN
9100 DATA 100,100,20,20,20,40,10,90,90,90,90,40,10,90,90,90
9110 DATA 100,100,20,90,90,40,10,90,90,90,90,40,10,90,90,90
9120 DATA 100,100,20,90,90,40,10,90,90,90,90,40,10,90,90,90
9130 DATA 100,100,20,90,90,40,10,90,90,90,90,40,40,10,10,10
9140 DATA 100,100,100,20,20,40,10,10,10,90,90,90,40,40,40,40
9150 DATA 100,100,100,100,100,30,40,40,10,90,90,90,90,90,90,90
9160 DATA 100,100,100,20,20,90,90,40,10,90,90,5,90,90,90,90
9170 DATA 100,100,20,90,90,90,90,40,10,90,90,90,90,90,90,90
9180 DATA 100,100,20,90,90,90,90,40,10,90,90,90,90,90,90,10
9190 DATA 100,100,20,90,90,90,90,90,40,40,10,10,10,10,10,40
9200 DATA 100,100,100,20,100,20,90,90,90,40,40,40,40,40,40,40
9210 DATA 100,100,100,100,100,20,20,20,20,20,100,100,100,10,10,100
9220 DATA 100,100,100,100,100,100,100,100,100,100,100,100,100
9225 DATA 5,5,100
9230 RESTORE 9100
9240 DIM S$(12,15)
9250 FOR R4=0 TO 12
9260 FOR R5=0 TO 15
9270 READ S$(R4,R5)
9280 NEXT R5
9290 NEXT R4
9300 RETURN
9400 LET J7=0
9410 IF (CHR(A$)-32)*(49-CHR(A$))<=0 THEN 9550
9430 IF (LEN(A$)-2)*(5-LEN(A$))<=0 THEN 9550
9450 IF POS(A$,"/")<>2 THEN 9550
9470 IF SUB$(A$,3)>"9" THEN 9550
9480 IF SEG$(A$,4)="" THEN 9500
9490 IF SEG$(A$,4)>"3" THEN 9550
9500 LET C1=VAL(SEG$(A$,3))-1
9510 LET C2=CHR(A$)-33
9530 LET J7=1
9540 GOTO 9560
9550 PRINT "PLEASE TYPE IN YOUR SITE IN THE FORM A/12."
9560 RETURN
9900 END
```

Computer-aided Instruction (C.A.I.)

This is an aspect of computer-assisted learning which has provoked considerable comment by educationalists and, perhaps for different reasons, by the media which has to some extent popularised this image of the computer in the classroom. At one extreme it can be regarded as a potential usurper of the teacher's traditional role as instructor, while another view is that it will merely complement that role. The hardware and technical and educational expertise which makes both possibilities feasible is already available, and in the United States large-scale experiments are being carried out in this field. One can envisage a time when computers servicing a large number of students engaged on a variety of exercises is a common feature in schools and other educational institutions, should there be a concensus supporting such a development. As well as allowing audio, visual and written communication between itself and the student, the computer could be expected to utilise a bank of resources which includes tape recordings, video cassettes, slides and the like. But not yet. The microprocessors being acquired by schools are not in this league and those contemplating the use or development of C.A.I. programs will have to content themselves with a rather more modest, less adventurous approach to the subject.

At present, many C.A.I. programs are limited to "this is what you do" followed by a series of exercises which become progressively more difficult. These often rely upon the use of multiple choice answers to overcome the problems associated with correct responses which the computer has not been programmed to accept. This relatively low-key approach is within the capacity of the hardware currently available to schools, if one accepts that for the time being at least these exercises will have to be undertaken with a one-to-one student/microprocessor ratio, and a teacher might reasonably consider establishing a library of programs which suits the needs of his or her syllabus.

One might seek to improve on the "example/increasingly more difficult exercise" routine by including a facility in the program whereby exercises of equal difficulty or of a simpler nature can be presented to the student if the computer determines that the student is experiencing difficulties. It would be an advantage if the program included a routine to show the student how to derive the answers to the problems that prove difficult. A further degree of sophistication can be incorporated into the program by taking a student back to an earlier stage when it becomes evident that a principle has not been fully grasped. Simply repeating the example may be adequate but it is possible that an entirely new presentation of an idea might be more effective.

The measure of a student's success, or lack of it, may not in itself demonstrate the cause, and returning to an earlier part of the exercise may not help the student to overcome the difficulty. The student may well be aware of what this is and would benefit from the availability of a HELP signal. It might work like this. In response to any invitation to input data, the student can type HELP. This causes, always supposing there is provision for it in the program, the computer to abandon the exercise which is currently being worked upon, perhaps permanently, perhaps temporarily. It prints

WHAT KIND OF HELP DO YOU WANT?
DO YOU I) WANT TO GO BACK TO AN EARLIER STAGE
       2) WANT TO HAVE A DEFINITION EXPANDED
       3) HAVE A VOCABULARY PROBLEM
       4) WANT TO BEGIN THIS EXPLANATION AGAIN
TYPE I,2,3 OR 4

Depending upon the request, the computer can then provide the required assistance, although before doing so it may be necessary to ask another series of questions.

OK. YOU WANT TO GO BACK TO AN EARLIER STAGE
WHICH ONE?
STAGE I (WHICH WAS.....)
STAGE 2 (WHICH WAS.....)
STAGE 3 (WHICH WAS.....)
TYPE I,2 OR 3

Obviously the more help that is available to the student, either at the student's request or based on the computer's analysis of the situation, the more complex, and certainly longer, the program will be. Many people may feel that the effort involved in producing such packages, especially until whole classes can be accommodated at the same time, means that C.A.I. programs are not a cost effective proposition, unless they are the result of work carried out by a team with the time and a brief to create them. Others may immediately feel that they are particularly valuable in the context of small group or individual learning and strive to achieve a satisfactory compromise with regard to the possible levels of sophistication in such programs.

A Flowchart to Illustrate a C.A.I. Program

The flowchart (Fig 8.5) has been included to show a possible way of giving a student instruction in a method for calculating the areas of plane figures. The flowchart is not intended to indicate the correct way to teach area calculations, but is given to illustrate the way in which a computer can lead a student along a path particular to the student's needs. It can allow the student to practise a stage many times, backtrack to an earlier stage, provide example solutions, and always allow withdrawal for consultation with the teacher. The use of graphics on a V.D.U. would be a most suitable medium for this type of program.

Fig 8.5

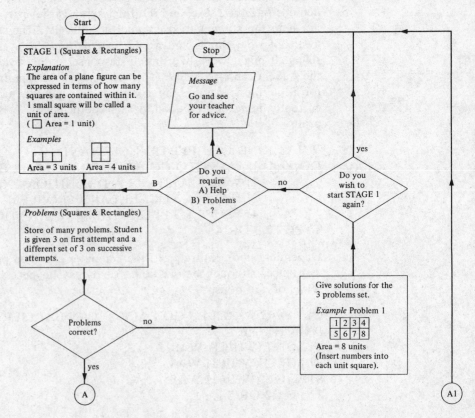

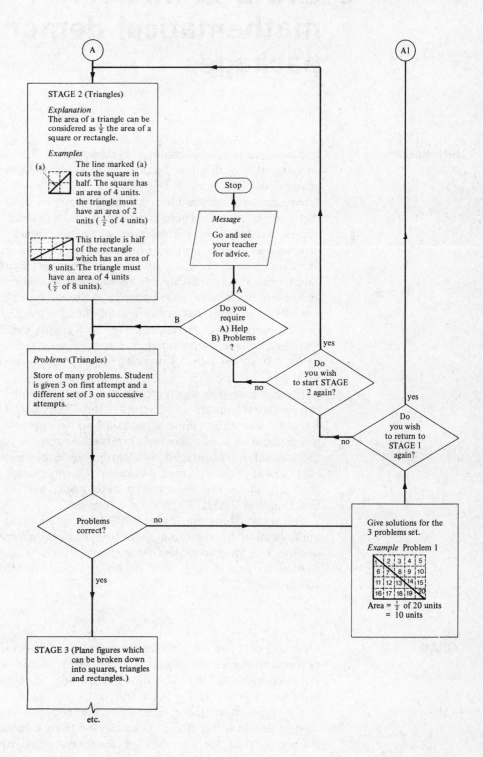

A

A1

STAGE 2 (Triangles)

Explanation
The area of a triangle can be considered as ½ the area of a square or rectangle.

Examples

(a)
The line marked (a) cuts the square in half. The square has an area of 4 units. the triangle must have an area of 2 units (½ of 4 units)

This triangle is half of the rectangle which has an area of 8 units. The triangle must have an area of 4 units (½ of 8 units).

Stop

Message

Go and see your teacher for advice.

A

Do you require
A) Help
B) Problems
?

B

Problems (Triangles)

Store of many problems. Student is given 3 on first attempt and a different set of 3 on successive attempts.

no

yes

Do you wish to start STAGE 2 again?

no

yes

Do you wish to return to STAGE 1 again?

Problems correct?

no

Give solutions for the 3 problems set.

Example Problem 1

1	2	3	4	5
6	7	8	9	10
11	12	13	14	15
16	17	18	19	20

Area = ½ of 20 units
= 10 units

yes

STAGE 3 (Plane figures which can be broken down into squares, triangles and rectangles.)

etc.

9 GRAD & MATRIX: mathematical demonstration packages

It is possible to use a computer to demonstrate a technique or a principle, and, together with some tasks for the student, to compile a package of instruction.

Mathematical applications on a computer seem obvious, at first sight, but there are difficulties. There is a range of mathematical symbols which may not be available on the teletype or microcomputer keyboard, and the programmer is left with an arithmetic facility that cannot be illustrated. Simulations and exercises which have been programmed can be varied almost indefinitely, making use of the random number generator. Graphs and charts can be drawn on paper or a screen, and they can be constructed speedily. This does not make use of the computer's facility for decision making, controlling or randomising, and graphs can be drawn manually. Similarly, computer-generated exercises are no improvement on a textbook, unless instruction, help, or marking is provided by the computer program as well.

The two programs which are discussed in this chapter attempt to illustrate two different aspects of demonstration. The first, GRAD, enables the student to use the arithmetic capability to perform awkward calculations of the gradient of a succession of chords to a curve. A pattern emerges which the student is encouraged to identify, the package providing a practical background to the differential calculus. The program is intended to produce printout, which the student can take away, and is designed to run in Southampton BASIC (SOBS) on a teletype.

The second program, called MATRIX, attempts to demonstrate matrix multiplication by performing, for the student, a repeating animated sequence. The program makes use of graphics on a visual display screen, and is written to run in 12K BASIC on a Research Machines 380Z microcomputer.

GRAD

One approach to the differential calculus is to consider the gradient of tangents to curves. A *tangent* is a line which touches a curve at one point. Gradient measures the slope of a straight line, for example, the gradient of the line illustrated in Fig 9.1 is 1.5.

The gradient of the tangent to a curve keeps changing as you move along the curve, but it can be calculated from a formula which is directly connected with the equation of the curve. This formula is called the

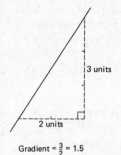

Gradient = $\frac{3}{2}$ = 1.5

Fig 9.1

"derivative" of the equation of the curve. For example, the curve given by the equation $y = x^2$ is a parabola (Fig 9.2).

The gradient of a tangent at any point on the curve can be calculated from the formula

$$\text{gradient} = 2x$$

where x is the x-coordinate of the point of contact of the tangent with the curve. The derivative of x^2 is $2x$.

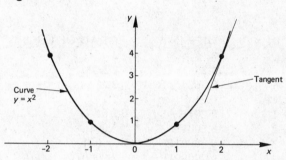

Fig 9.2

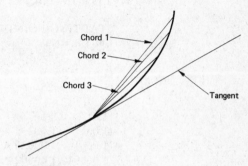

Fig 9.3

The package starts by asking the student to draw the curve $y = x^2$ and to draw a tangent and measure its gradient. This is difficult to do because it is not easy to be precise with the drawing of the tangent, and so accurate answers are not likely. Another approach is to measure the gradient of a succession of chords. A *chord* is a line joining two points on the curve, and since the coordinates of the points are known the gradient can be calculated precisely. The technique is to let the chords get closer and closer to the tangent (see Fig 9.3). The gradient of the chords is found to approach the gradient of the tangent.

STARTING POINT (2 ,4)

END POINT	DIFF IN X	DIFF IN Y	GRAD OF CHORD
(3 ,9)	1	5	5
(2.5 ,6.25)	0.5	2.25	4.5
(2.25 ,5.0625)	0.25	1.0625	4.25
(2.1 ,4.41)	0.1	0.41	4.1
(2.01 ,4.0401)	0.1E−1	0.401E−1	4.01
(2.001 ,4.004)	0.1E−2	0.4001E−2	4.001
(2.0001 ,4.0004)	0.1E−3	0.40001E−3	4.0001
(2.00001 ,4.00004)	0.999999E−5	0.400001E−4	4.00001

At first the student performs the calculations, but they become tedious and so the computer program then calculates, quickly, producing a table of the results. Options are provided in the program for choosing a different point on the curve by giving its x-coordinate. A series of eight chords is then used and the gradient of each is calculated. Although the initial curve used is $y = x^2$ others can be requested during the program run. They are $y = x^3$, $y = x^4$, $y = x^5$.

The student is provided with a booklet giving the details of the package, and it is included here for reference (page 170).

Sample Run

THIS PROGRAM CALCULATES GRADIENTS OF CHORDS WHICH ARE TENDING TO TANGENTS. YOU HAVE DRAWN THE CURVE Y = X↑2 AND CALCULATED THE GRADIENT AT X = 1. NOW TRY SOME OTHER POINTS USING THIS PROGRAM
TYPE IN YOUR X VALUE ← 1

STARTING POINT (1 ,1)

END POINT	DIFF IN X	DIFF IN Y	GRAD OF CHORD
(2 ,4)	1	3	3
(1.5 ,2.25)	0.5	1.25	2.5
(1.25 ,1.5625)	0.25	0.5625	2.25
(1.1 ,1.21)	0.1	0.21	2.1
(1.01 ,1.0201)	0.1E−1	0.201E−1	2.01
(1.001 ,1.002)	0.1E−2	0.2001E−2	2.001
(1.0001 ,1.0002)	0.1E−3	0.20001E−3	2.0001
(1.00001 ,1.00002)	0.1E−4	0.200001E−4	2.00001

WOULD YOU LIKE TO TRY ANOTHER VALUE FOR X?(YES/NO) ← NO
WOULD YOU LIKE TO TRY Y = X↑3   ? (YES/NO) ← NO
WOULD YOU LIKE TO TRY Y = X↑4   ? (YES/NO) ← YES
TYPE IN YOUR X VALUE ← 3

STARTING POINT (3 ,81   )

END POINT	DIFF IN X	DIFF IN Y	GRAD OF CHORD
(4 ,256)	1	175	175
(3.5 ,150.062)	0.5	69.0625	138.125
(3.25 ,111.566)	0.25	30.5664	122.266
(3.1 ,92.3521)	0.1	11.3521	113.521
(3.01 ,82.0854)	0.1E−1	1.08541	108.541
(3.001 ,81.1081)	0.1E−2	0.108054	108.054
(3.0001 ,81.0108)	0.1E−3	0.108005E−1	108.005
(3.00001 ,81.0011)	0.999999E−5	0.108E−2	108

WOULD YOU LIKE TO TRY ANOTHER VALUE FOR X?(YES/NO) ← YES
TYPE IN YOUR X VALUE ← 4

STARTING POINT (4 ,256)

END POINT	DIFF IN X	DIFF IN Y	GRAD OF CHORD
(5 ,625)	1	369	369
(4.5 ,410.062)	0.5	154.062	308.125
(4.25 ,326.254)	0.25	70.2539	281.016
(4.1 ,282.576)	0.1	26.5761	265.761
(4.01 ,258.57)	0.1E−1	2.56962	256.962
(4.001 ,256.256)	0.1E−2	0.256096	256.096
(4.0001 ,256.026)	0.1E−3	0.25601E−1	256.01
(4.00001 ,256.003)	0.1E−4	0.256001E−2	256.001

WOULD YOU LIKE TO TRY ANOTHER VALUE FOR X?(YES/NO) ← NO
WOULD YOU LIKE TO TRY Y = X ↑ 5   ? (YES/NO) ← NO
YOU MAY BE ABLE TO SEE A PATTERN IN THE RESULTS YOU
HAVE OBTAINED. RETURN TO THE BOOKLET NOW AND DRAW
YOUR CONCLUSIONS.
STOPPED AT LINE 420

Program Flowchart

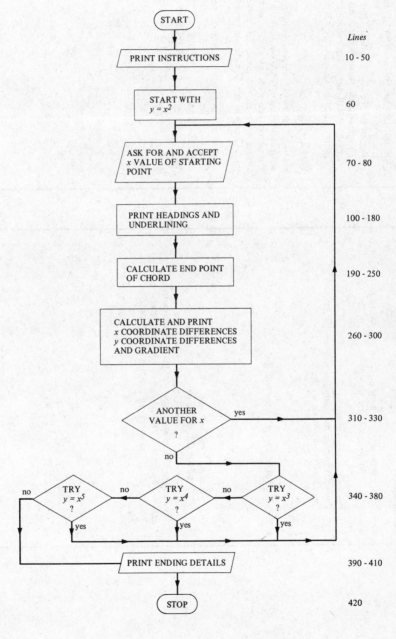

Fig 9.4

Student Booklet: GRAD

Introduction

This package is intended to show how the gradient of the tangent to a curve can be found. There are three parts:

1. Drawing and measuring.
2. Calculating using the computer program GRAD.
3. Drawing a conclusion from the results.

Part 1

a) Carefully draw a graph of the equation

$y = x^2$

with axes

x : 0 to 5, 2 cm. as 1 unit
y : 0 to 25, 1 cm. as 2 units

Try to draw a tangent at the point (1,1). Measure its gradient by dividing the increase in y by the increase in x. You should get an answer of 2, but it is difficult to be accurate.

1

b) Now draw the chord starting at the point (1,1) and ending at the point (2,4).
Measure the gradient of this chord (you should get an exact answer of 3).
Again, draw the chord from (1,1) to (1½ 2¼) and measure its gradient.
Repeat for the chord from (1,1) to (1¼, 1⁹⁄₁₆).
The gradient decreases as the chord approaches the tangent at (1, 1). Will the gradient continue to decrease indefinitely as the points get closer, or does it approach a fixed value?

Part 2

For small values the calculations become awkward. The computer program GRAD will calculate for you. You may choose any values for the starting point of the chord, but integer values are recommended. Initially the curve used is $y = x^2$ but you may also choose $y = x^3$, $y = x^4$, $y = x^5$ later on.

Now try the program, it is called up by

SOBS GRAD   or   SOBS
OLD GRAD
RUN

2

An Example Run of the Program GRAD

TYPE IN YOUR X VALUE   1

STARTING POINT (1,1)

END POINT	DIFF IN X	DIFF IN Y	GRAD OF CHORD
(2 ,4)	1	3	3
(1.5 ,2.25)	0.5	1.25	2.5
(1.25 ,1.5625)	0.25	0.5625	2.25
(1.1 ,1.21)	0.1	0.21	2.1
(1.01 ,1.0201)	0.1E-1	0.201E-1	2.01
(1.001 ,1.002)	0.1E-2	0.2001E-2	2.001
(1.0001 ,1.0002)	0.1E-3	0.20001E-3	2.0001
(1.00001 ,1.00002)	0.1E-4	0.200001E-4	2.00001

WOULD YOU LIKE TO TRY ANOTHER VALUE FOR X? (YES/NO)→NO

WOULD YOU LIKE TO TRY Y = X↓3 ?   (YES/NO)→ON

WOULD YOU LIKE TO TRY Y = X↓4 ?   (YES/NO)→ON

WOULD YOU LIKE TO TRY Y = X↓5 ?   (YES/NO)→ON

YOU MAY BE ABLE TO SEE A PATTERN IN THE RESULTS YOU
HAVE OBTAINED. RETURN TO THE BOOKLET NOW AND DRAW
YOUR CONCLUSIONS.

4

Part 3

Study the results that you have obtained. See if you can identify the pattern. For each equation can you find a formula which will predict the gradient of the tangent at any point, given its x-coordinate? Start with the curve $y = x^2$ and work up through the powers trying to apply the same rule each time.

You should try to confirm your findings. Your teacher or a textbook on Calculus will be able to do this for you.

Notes

1 When you are running the computer program you must press the red ACCEPT key after each reply.

2 Some small numbers will appear as, for example,

0.4E-5

This means

$0.4 \times 10^{-5} = 0.000004$

3 It is helpful to choose starting points with whole number coordinates.

3

GRAD:
Program Listing:
Southampton
BASIC

```
10   REM DIFFERENTIATION FROM 1ST PRINCIPLES
20   PRINT "THIS PROGRAM CALCULATES GRADIENTS OF CHORDS WHICH ARE"
30   PRINT "TENDING TO TANGENTS. YOU HAVE DRAWN THE CURVE Y=X↑2"
40   PRINT "AND CALCULATED THE GRADIENT AT X=1. NOW TRY SOME OTHER"
50   PRINT "POINTS USING THIS PROGRAM."
60   LET N=2
70   PRINT "TYPE IN YOUR X VALUE";
80   INPUT X
90   LET Y=X**N
100  PRINT
110  PRINT
120  PRINT "STARTING POINT","(";X;",";Y;")"
130  PRINT TAB(3);"END POINT";TAB(19);"DIFF IN X";TAB(34);"DIFF IN Y";
140  PRINT "        GRAD OF CHORD"
150  FOR I=1 TO 72
160  PRINT "=";
170  NEXT I
180  PRINT
190  FOR I=1 TO 8
200  IF I>3 THEN 240
210  LET X1=X+2**(-I+1)
220  LET Y1=X1**N
230  GOTO 260
240  LET X1=X+10**(-I+3)
250  LET Y1=X1**N
260  PRINT "(";X1;",";Y1;")";TAB(21);(X1-X);TAB(36);(Y1-Y);TAB(50);
270  PRINT (Y1-Y)/(X1-X)
280  NEXT I
290  PRINT
300  PRINT
310  PRINT "WOULD YOU LIKE TO TRY ANOTHER VALUE FOR X?(YES/NO)";
320  INPUT A£
330  IF A£="YES" THEN 70
340  LET N=N+1
350  PRINT "WOULD YOU LIKE TO TRY Y=X↑";N;"? (YES/NO)";
360  INPUT A£
370  IF A£="YES" THEN 70
380  IF N<5 THEN 340
390  PRINT "YOU MAY BE ABLE TO SEE A PATTERN IN THE RESULTS YOU"
400  PRINT "HAVE OBTAINED. RETURN TO THE BOOKLET NOW AND DRAW"
410  PRINT "YOUR CONCLUSIONS."
420  END
```

MATRIX

Most secondary school mathematics courses include the use of matrices. The multiplication of two matrices is an involved process and it is important in a number of related topics, such as simultaneous equations and transformations.

A matrix is simply an array of numbers, for example

$$\begin{pmatrix} 1 & 2 & 3 \\ -2 & \frac{1}{2} & 0.33 \end{pmatrix}$$

The process of multiplying two matrices can be illustrated using a row and a column matrix.

$$(1 \quad 2 \quad 3)\begin{pmatrix}4\\5\\6\end{pmatrix} = (1\times4+2\times5+3\times6)$$
$$= (4+10+18)$$
$$= (32)$$

The method used is "rows into columns". Each number in a row combines with a corresponding number in a column, and these individual multiplications are totalled. There must be the same number of numbers in the row as there are in the column, otherwise multiplication is impossible. The same process can be performed with more complicated matrices.

$$(1 \quad 2 \quad 3)\begin{pmatrix}4 & 7\\5 & 8\\6 & 9\end{pmatrix} = (32 \quad 50)$$

and

$$\begin{pmatrix}1 & 2 & 3\\1 & 0 & 2\end{pmatrix}\begin{pmatrix}4 & 7\\5 & 8\\6 & 9\end{pmatrix} = \begin{pmatrix}32 & 50\\16 & 25\end{pmatrix}$$

These processes are demonstrated by the program MATRIX. This is done by an animated sequence in which the row numbers are seen to move alongside their respective column numbers. The individual multiplications are then carried out, totalled and the total positioned in the answer matrix. The three stages illustrated above are the three stages of the program, and each can be repeated as often as required, each time with different numbers.

How the Demonstration Operates

To begin with a message is printed to the student.

THIS IS AN INTRODUCTION TO
MATRIX MULTIPLICATION.

Then

WE START AT STAGE 1.
YOU MAY MOVE TO STAGES 2,3
WHEN YOU FEEL YOU ARE READY.

Stage 1 multiplies a row of three numbers into a column of three numbers. Copies of the row numbers move until they are positioned next to their respective column numbers.

```
(1  2  3) .4  :·
            · 5  ↓ ·
            :.6  3 .
```

and

```
(1  2  3) :4  ↓:
            · 5  2 ·
            :.6  3 :
```

and

```
(1  2  3) .4  1:
            · 5  2 ·
            :.6  3.:
```

The brackets of the right-hand matrix have been constructed from "dots" because the character set does not include large brackets. The use of "high resolution" graphics, enabling the dots to be plotted much closer together, would improve the appearance of the brackets.

Multiplication signs and equals signs are placed in position and the multiplications are performed.

```
(1  2  3) :4×1 =  4:
            · 5×2 = 10  ·= (32)
            :.6×3 = 18.:
                    32
```

At the end of this sequence another message is printed.

TYPE 1,2 OR 3
FOR STAGES 1,2 OR 3, AND PRESS RETURN,
OR 0 (ZERO) TO FINISH.

The response 1 causes a re-run of stage 1. Stage 2 multiplies one row into two columns, and it finishes as

```
(1  2  3) :4×1 =  4   7×1 =  7:
            · 5×2 = 10   8×2 = 16  ·= (32   50)
            :.6×3 = 18   9×3 = 27.:
                    32           50
```

The animated sequence is performed twice, once for each column of the right-hand matrix. The third stage multiplies two rows into two columns. This is a longer sequence, in fact as above, but with two rows. The first row multiplications are wiped out before the second row begins, and the process finishes as

$$\begin{pmatrix} 1 & 2 & 3 \\ 1 & 0 & 2 \end{pmatrix} \begin{matrix} 4\times1= & 4 & 7\times1= & 7 \\ 5\times0= & 0 & 8\times0= & 0 \\ 6\times2=\underline{12} & & 9\times2=\underline{18} \\ \underline{16} & & \underline{25} \end{matrix} = \begin{pmatrix} 32 & 50 \\ 16 & 25 \end{pmatrix}$$

Any of the stages may be repeated, with different numbers each time. The numbers occur randomly and are whole numbers in the range 0 to 9. This range has been chosen to keep the arithmetic simple.

Description of the Program

The program listing is provided at the end of this chapter, but there are some features that have not arisen before in this book. The program runs on a RM 380Z microcomputer, and 9K and 12K BASIC enable graphics to be used, and displayed on a screen. Also, multiple statement lines may be used, and other small changes such as dropping the LET in arithmetical statements.

Basic

Plotting Graphics

Graphics symbols are placed on the screen using the PLOT instruction. It is used in the following way:

150 PLOT 4,39,40

The first and second numbers following the PLOT refer to the coordinates of the location of the symbol. The first number, the x-coordinate, determines the position across the screen. The second number, the y-coordinate, determines the position up the screen. The third number is the code number for the symbol to be used.

The Coordinates

When using graphics, the screen can be split into two areas. Normally the screen allows for 24 lines of 40 characters, but the instruction

110 GRAPH 1

gives four lines for printing at the bottom of the screen, and an area above for graphics. This graphics area is referenced by coordinates, 0–79 across the page and 0–59 upwards (Fig 9.5).

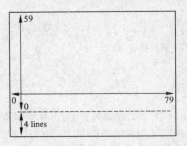

Fig 9.5

Fig 9.6

Characters are printed in blocks of 2×3 positions, as shown in Fig 9.6. This means that "effective" coordinates count in twos across the page and threes upwards. If a character is positioned in location 20, 30 (i.e. 20 across the screen and 30 up), then the next location across will be 22, 30 and the next upwards will be 20, 33.

To return to a normal screen the following instruction is used

1570 GRAPH 0

The Graphics

A whole range of symbols is available. Some systems have others, or more symbols. The program only uses some of them and they are listed here with their code numbers.

Symbol	Code number
(	40
)	41
.	46
=	61
×	120
■	204
blank screen	12
single space	32

The large matrix brackets are formed from full stops (.). This is not entirely satisfactory, other systems may be able to cope better. Each bracket is formed from five dots i.e.

The code number for each symbol can be found using the Basic function

$$ASC(".") = 46$$

ASC is derived from ASCII, the name for the standardising body for electronic character recognition. This function enables the programmer to recognise a symbol in the program listing, for example,

```
870 PLOT 14+14*N,39-3*I,ASC("×")
880 PLOT 18+14*N,39-3*I,ASC(" = ")
```

The character codes for digits 0 to 9 start at 48 for 0, hence the code for 5 is

$$5 + 48 = 53$$

At several points in the program digits are printed,

```
980 PLOT 20+14*N,39-3*I,T+48
```

plots the digit T.

The complicated nature of the coordinate expressions results from the need to print the digits at varying places on the screen according to the stage that the program is at. This is particularly true in the subroutine at 1590 to 1770. Here the matrix numbers are made to "walk" in the animated sequence. The technique used is to plot the digit one space at a time and to replace the preceding one by a blank space.

Multiple Statements

Several statements on one line are allowed, each one being separated from the next by a colon. In the program this has been used when a delay loop has been inserted to slow the animation down to a watchable pace, e.g.

```
40 FOR J = 1 TO 2000:NEXT J
```

Since there is nothing inside the loop it is convenient to keep it on one line.
    Another example occurs where the start and end positions of the walk sequence are set:

```
810 LET X1 = 20-4*L:Y1 = 45-6*M:X2 = 16+14*N:Y2 = 27+3*1:K = R(M,4-L)+48
```

Here, also, the LET has been dropped on all but the first statement, to make the line more concise. The variable K holds the code of the character to be walked in the subroutine.

Student Booklet: MATRIX

The program MATRIX shows you how two matrices can be multiplied together. The process is described by three stages of the program:

1 One row multiplies one column
2 One row multiplies two columns
3 Two rows multiply two columns

How to Run the Program

The program runs on the RM 380Z microcomputer. It runs in 12K BASIC and is called up by typing

LOAD "MATRIX"

To run the program type

RUN

Each stage can be used as often as you like, and you can return to previous stages if you wish. After each stage you will be asked

TYPE 1, 2 OR 3
FOR STAGES 1, 2 OR 3

Watch what happens carefully, try to predict the answers. Every time a stage is performed different numbers will be used. This enables you to practice if you wish.

1

Try some matrix multiplications for yourself to see whether you have understood the process. Some questions are given below. Ask for answers to be checked.

Questions

1 $\begin{pmatrix} 3 & 2 & 1 \end{pmatrix} \begin{pmatrix} 2 \\ 0 \\ 3 \end{pmatrix}$
2 $\begin{pmatrix} 1 & 0 & -1 \end{pmatrix} \begin{pmatrix} 5 \\ 7 \\ 9 \end{pmatrix}$

3 $\begin{pmatrix} 1 & 1 & 1 \end{pmatrix} \begin{pmatrix} 2 & 4 \\ 0 & 7 \\ -1 & 2 \end{pmatrix}$
4 $\begin{pmatrix} \frac{1}{2} & 0 & 1 \end{pmatrix} \begin{pmatrix} 6 & 10 \\ 1 & 0 \\ 1 & -2 \end{pmatrix}$

5 $\begin{pmatrix} 3 & 0 & 2 \\ 1 & 2 & 1 \end{pmatrix} \begin{pmatrix} 7 & 0 \\ 7 & 2 \\ 7 & 1 \end{pmatrix}$
6 $\begin{pmatrix} 2 & 0 \\ 1 & 1 \end{pmatrix} \begin{pmatrix} 5 & -1 \\ 2 & 0 \end{pmatrix}$

7 $\begin{pmatrix} 1 & 1 & 0 \\ 2 & 7 & 1 \\ 4 & 2 & 2 \end{pmatrix} \begin{pmatrix} 1 & 1 & 1 \\ 0 & 1 & 0 \\ 0 & 0 & 1 \end{pmatrix}$

2

Program Summary

10	Clear the screen.
20–90	Print student information —with delays.
100	1st. stage, set G = 1.
110	Create plotting area on the screen.
120–130	Set constants.
140–250	Plot brackets for the left-hand matrix.
260	Initiate the random number generator.
270–320	Generate the numbers for the matrices.
330–390	Plot numbers in left-hand matrix.
400	Delay.
410–450	Plot left-hand bracket of right-hand matrix.
460–530	Plot numbers in right-hand matrix.
540–660	Plot right-hand bracket of right-hand matrix.
670–730	Move numbers in 2nd. column of right-hand matrix.
740–1470	Loops to:
	plot ×, =
	perform multiplications
	total
	separate totals into single digits
	plot answers
1480–1580	Print end instructions and act on student response.
1590–1770	Subroutine to "walk" the numbers.
1780	End.

MATRIX:
Program Listing:
Research Machines
380Z 12K BASIC

```
10 PRINT CHR$(12)
20 PRINT "THIS IS AN INTRODUCTION TO"
30 PRINT "MATRIX MULTIPLICATION."
40 FOR J=1 TO 2000:NEXT J
50 PRINT CHR$(12)
60 PRINT "WE START AT STAGE 1."
70 PRINT "YOU MAY MOVE TO STAGES 2,3"
80 PRINT "WHEN YOU FEEL YOU ARE READY."
90 FOR J=1 TO 2000:NEXT J
100 LET G=1
110 GRAPH 1
120 LET D=0
130 LET E=0
140 IF G=3 THEN 180
150 PLOT 4,39,40
160 PLOT 20,39,41
170 GOTO 260
180 PLOT 6,42,46
190 PLOT 18,42,46
200 FOR I=1 TO 3
210 PLOT 4,42-3*I,46
220 PLOT 20,42-3*I,46
230 NEXT I
240 PLOT 6,30,46
250 PLOT 18,30,46
260 RANDOMIZE
270 FOR I=1 TO 3
280 FOR J=1 TO 2
290 LET R(J,I)=INT(RND(1)*10)
300 LET C(I,J)=INT(RND(1)*10)
310 NEXT J
320 NEXT I
330 IF G=1 OR G=2 THEN 370
```

```
340 FOR I=1 TO 3
350 PLOT 4+4*I,33,R(2,I)+48
360 NEXT I
370 FOR I=1 TO 3
380 PLOT 4+4*I,39,R(1,I)+48
390 NEXT I
400 FOR J=1 TO 500:NEXT J
410 PLOT 24,39,46
420 FOR I=1 TO 3
430 PLOT 22,39-3*I,46
440 NEXT I
450 PLOT 24,27,46
460 IF G=1 THEN 510
470 FOR I=1 TO 3
480 PLOT 30,39-3*I,C(I,2)+48
490 NEXT I
500 LET D=4
510 FOR I=1 TO 3
520 PLOT 26,39-3*I,C(I,1)+48
530 NEXT I
540 PLOT 28+D,39,46+E
550 FOR I=1 TO 3
560 PLOT 30+D,39-3*I,46+E
570 NEXT I
580 PLOT 28+D,27,46+E
590 IF D=10 OR D=24 THEN 670
600 IF E<>0 THEN 640
610 FOR J=1 TO 500:NEXT J
620 LET E=ASC(" ")-46
630 GOTO 540
640 LET D=D+10+(D/4)*10
650 LET E=0
660 GOTO 540
670 IF G=1 THEN 740
680 FOR I=1 TO 3
690 PLOT 30,39-3*I,32
700 NEXT I
710 FOR I=1 TO 3
720 PLOT 40,39-3*I,C(I,2)+48
730 NEXT I
740 LET R=1
750 IF G=3 THEN R=2
760 LET C=2
770 IF G=1 THEN C=1
780 FOR M=1 TO R
790 FOR N=1 TO C
800 FOR L=1 TO 3
810 LET X1=20-4*L:Y1=45-6*M:X2=16+14*N:Y2=27+3*L:K=R(M,4-L)+48
820 FOR J=1 TO 500:NEXT J
830 GOSUB 1590
840 NEXT L
850 FOR I=1 TO 3
860 LET A=0
870 PLOT 14+14*N,39-3*I,ASC("X")
880 PLOT 18+14*N,39-3*I,ASC("=")
890 NEXT I
900 LET B=0
910 FOR I=1 TO 3
920 FOR J=1 TO 500:NEXT J
930 LET A=R(M,I)*C(I,N)
940 LET T=INT(A/10)
950 LET U=A-T*10
960 LET B=B+A
970 IF T=0 THEN 990
980 PLOT 20+14*N,39-3*I,T+48
990 PLOT 22+14*N,39-3*I,U+48
1000 NEXT I
1010 FOR J=1 TO 500: NEXT J
1020 FOR I=1 TO 3
1030 PLOT 16+2*I+14*N,27,204
1040 PLOT 16+2*I+14*N,21,204
1050 NEXT I
```

```
1060 FOR J=1 TO 500:NEXT J
1070 LET H=INT(B/100)
1080 LET T=INT((B-H*100)/10)
1090 LET U=B-H*100-T*10
1100 IF H=0 THEN 1120
1110 PLOT 18+14*N,24,H+48
1120 IF H=0 AND T=0 THEN 1140
1130 PLOT 20+14*N,24,T+48
1140 PLOT 22+14*N,24,U+48
1150 FOR J=1 TO 500:NEXT J
1160 PLOT 32+12*C,33,61
1170 IF G<>3 THEN 1240
1180 PLOT 62,42,46
1190 FOR I=1 TO 3
1200 PLOT 60,42-3*I,46
1210 NEXT I
1220 PLOT 62,30,46
1230 GOTO 1250
1240 PLOT 36+12*C,39,40
1250 IF H=0 THEN 1270
1260 PLOT 30+12*C+8*N,45-6*M,H+48
1270 IF H=0 AND T=0 THEN 1290
1280 PLOT 32+12*C+8*N,45-6*M,T+48
1290 PLOT 34+12*C+8*N,45-6*M,U+48
1300 IF G<>3 THEN1370
1310 PLOT 76,42,46
1320 FOR I=1 TO 3
1330 PLOT 78,42-3*I,46
1340 NEXT I
1350 PLOT 76,30,46
1360 GOTO 1380
1370 PLOT 34+22*C,39,41
1380 NEXT N
1390 IF G<>3 OR M=2 THEN 1470
1400 FOR H=1 TO 2
1410 FOR I=1 TO 5
1420 FOR J=1 TO 6
1430 PLOT 12+14*H+2*I,18+3*J,32
1440 NEXT J
1450 NEXT I
1460 NEXT H
1470 NEXT M
1480 PRINT "TYPE 1,2 OR 3"
1490 PRINT "FOR STAGES 1,2 OR 3, AND PRESS RETURN."
1500 PRINT "OR 0 (ZERO) TO FINISH."
1510 INPUT G
1520 IF G=0 OR G=1 OR G=2 OR G=3 THEN 1540
1530 GOTO 1480
1540 IF G=0 THEN 1570
1550 PRINT CHR$(12)
1560 GOTO 110
1570 GRAPH 0
1580 GOTO 1780
1590 PLOT X1,Y1+3,K
1600 IF M=1 THEN 1650
1610 PLOT X1,Y1+9,K
1620 PLOT X1,Y1+3,32
1630 LET Y1=Y1+6
1640 FOR J=1 TO 200:NEXT J
1650 PLOT X1,Y1+6,K
1660 PLOT X1,Y1+3,32
1670 FOR SI=X1 TO X2 STEP 2*SGN(X2-X1)
1680 PLOT SI,Y1+6,K
1690 PLOT SI-2,Y1+6,32
1700 FOR J=1 TO 100:NEXT J
1710 NEXT SI
1720 FOR SI=Y1+3 TO Y2 STEP 3*SGN(Y2-Y1)
1730 PLOT X2,SI,K
1740 PLOT X2,SI+3,32
1750 FOR J=1 TO 100:NEXT J
1760 NEXT SI
1770 RETURN
1780 END
```

10 JOEL: information retrieval

Files

A **file** is used for storing large quantities of data which is arranged in such a way that it can be analysed and manipulated by a program. Files are created independently of a program and, having an identity of their own, will be given an individual name. There are two things that one can do with a file: the first is to read its contents with a view to printing some of the data contained there or using some of that data during the course of actions taken by the program; the second is to create a new file, which is an update of one already stored, by a process known as writing to a file.

There are certain conventions to be observed when using a file and these will vary in their particulars depending upon the system in question, but the principles will remain the same. We have chosen to demonstrate these principles by reference to file handling using Southampton BASIC run in MAXIMOP on an ICL 1903A mainframe computer and in 12K BASIC run on a Research Machines 380Z.

Reading from a File

An obvious use for files in school is in the context of information retrieval. Two applications in this area which come readily to mind are the library catalogue system and student records. It is these which we have chosen to illustrate the process of reading from a file. To simplify matters the examination of the library catalogue will be restricted to works of fiction.

The Library Fiction Catalogue

A file representing an author and fiction catalogue might usefully be thought of as a list of names and titles written on a sheet of paper; the bigger the file, the longer the sheet of paper.

Example
ADAMS R   , WATERSHIP DOWN
BUCHAN J , THIRTY NINE STEPS
CONRAD J , THE ROVER
DICKENS C , BLEAK HOUSE
DICKENS C , OLIVER TWIST
ELIOT G   , THE MILL ON THE FLOSS
GREENE G , BRIGHTON ROCK

If we had such a list and someone wanted to know whether there were any books by Dickens in stock, we would read down the left-hand side of the list and attempt to match the requested name against those we found there. As soon as we found Dickens' name in the left-hand column we would read the title in the right-hand column and pass the information on to the enquirer. A sensible search would not terminate at this point but would continue in case there were any other books by Dickens. We would abandon the search only when we were sure that there were no more books by that author.

It is often the case that a borrower can remember a title but not the author and is therefore unable to find the book on the shelves. A search in this case would be conducted by focusing attention on the data in the right-hand column, effectively reversing the process. In order to be sure that a book was not in stock it would be necessary to read all of the titles in the list, but once the book had been found the search could be abandoned immediately—unless one was not confident that there were not two books with the same title but by different authors.

The computer can be programmed to undertake this search for us, the program being constructed so that it reflects the nature of the manual search just described. However, unlike a human, the computer cannot ignore items in a file. Each item of data must be accounted for in some way. This means that the computer cannot literally read down the left-hand column, only consulting the data in the right-hand column once a match has been made. One way to overcome this is to program it to "read" an author's name *and* a related title. This combination of name and title is known as a **RECORD.** A record may be composed of one or several items of data and will represent a "whole" or complete unit. When a record contains several distinct pieces of data it is sometimes convenient to separate them into what are called **FIELDS**. In our example the author's name is in the first field and the title is in the second. The comma is the device used to separate fields within a record and, where necessary, to separate records. This does not apply to the end of a line, hence no comma in this position in the example.

The file need not be constructed with the authors listed in alphabetical order, but this will make it impossible to abandon a search for books by a particular author until the end of the file is reached. This will mean that in some instances a search of the file will take longer than would have been the case had a strict alphabetical order been adhered to. Some people would feel that this loss of time would be more than compensated for by the fact that the names of authors and the titles of new books can be added to the file as they are acquired, no time being wasted in sorting them or inserting them into the correct positions in the file. (Inevitably, there is a computer solution to this problem too, in the form of a process known as sorting.)

The fact that data can be separated into fields is the key to the problem of having to read two things at once. This is demonstrated in the set of program "instructions" which follow and which relate to the file described as a FICTION FILE.

Example   FICTION FILE

	Field 1	,	Field 2
Record 1	TOLKIEN R	,	THE HOBBIT
Record 2	ADAMS R	,	WATERSHIP DOWN
Record 3	ORWELL G	,	ANIMAL FARM
Record 4	ZINDEL P	,	MY DARLING MY HAMBURGER
Record 5	BAWDEN N	,	CARRIE'S WAR
Record 6	GARNER A	,	THE RED SHIFT

**Program to Search
for Author and to
Print Titles**

1 Ask the user to type in the author's name.
2 Write the name in a box and call the box X$.
(Writing a word in a box is considered to be a useful metaphor to describe what actually happens.)

BOX   AUTHOR REQUESTED

X$	BAWDEN N

3 Read a record. (The computer reads from the first record when a run is initiated.)
4 If the end of the file has been reached, stop. If the end of the file has not been reached, carry out instruction 5.
5 Write the name in the first field in a box called A$

BOX   AUTHOR'S NAME

A$	TOLKIEN R

and write the title which is in the second field in a box called B$

BOX   TITLE

B$	THE HOBBIT

6 Compare the contents of box X$ with the contents of box A$.
7 If the contents of the boxes X$ and A$ are identical, print the contents of box B$ and then read the next record (i.e. return to instruction 3).
8 If the contents of boxes X$ and A$ are not identical, read the next record (i.e. return to instruction 3).

The contents of the boxes A$ and B$ will change each time the computer is instructed to read a new record. This process obliges the computer to read both the author's name and the title at the same time but focuses attention on the data in the first field. In this way it might be said to be imitating the human activity of reading one column only and referring to the other as it becomes necessary.

Those readers who have studied the programming section of the book which deals with the simulation DRAKE will be familiar with the use of symbols like X$, A$ and B$. For other readers, the explanation for using such symbols is simple. The computer can be instructed to give names to data items. Those data items that are composed of letters, a combination of numbers and letters or numbers and symbolic characters, and numbers which will not be used in calculations are given a letter of the alphabet as the name, and this letter is followed by a dollar or pound sign. Numbers which will be used in calculations are given a letter as the name, and this is not accompanied by a dollar or pound sign. The choice of X$, A$ and B$ in the example is arbitrary; it could have been F$, P$ and Y$.

To write a program which will allow the name of an author to be discovered when the title is known, only minor adjustments have to be made to the previous set of program instructions.

Program to Search for a Title and to Print Author's Name

1 Ask the user to type in the title.
2 Write the title in a box and call the box X$.

BOX	TITLE
X$	CARRIE'S WAR

3 Read a record.
4 If the end of the file has been reached, stop. If the end of the file has not been reached, carry out instruction 5.
5 Write the name in the first field in a box called A$

BOX	AUTHOR'S NAME
A$	TOLKIEN

and write the title which is in field two in a box called B$

BOX	TITLE
B$	THE HOBBIT

6 Compare the contents of box X$ with the contents of box B$.
7 If the contents of the two boxes are identical, print the contents of box A$ and then stop.
8 If the contents of box X$ and the contents of box A$ are not identical, read the next record (i.e. return to instruction 3).

It would be sensible to combine these two small programs. Having done so, it is necessary to include a few lines of program instructing the computer to print an invitation to the user to nominate the kind of search that is required. Finally, because the program does not contain the data which is to be examined, it must name the file to be referenced. The relationship of the key program and file elements are described in Fig 10.1.

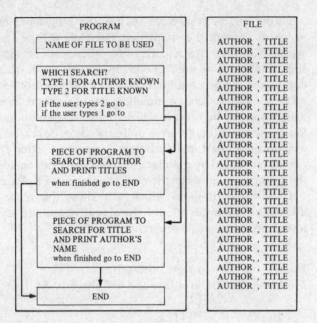

Fig 10.1

The Shape of the File

In the FICTION FILE, a record corresponds to data contained in a single line. When given the instruction to read, not all systems automatically move to the next line of the file. Some will tolerate a file which is constructed with more than one record on a line.

Example
AUTHOR 1 , TITLE 1 , AUTHOR 2 , TITLE 2
AUTHOR 3 , TITLE 3 , AUTHOR 4 , TITLE 4

That is to say, when the instruction to read a record is encountered for the second time, and the boxes A$ and B$ are already filled with AUTHOR 1 and TITLE 1, they will be replaced by AUTHOR 2 and TITLE 2. This is the case with Southampton BASIC run in MAXIMOP on an ICL 1903A mainframe. The Research Machines 380Z, using 12K BASIC and disks, does not behave like this but would, on the second invitation to read, put AUTHOR 3 and TITLE 3 in boxes A$ and B$.

More than Two Fields in a Record

If a record is to contain more than two fields, these will have to be taken into account in the program. (The system of naming by letter and dollar sign, or by letter alone, allows at least fifty-two separate entities to be named in a program at any one time. The qualification "at least" is added because there are ways to extend this generous allowance.) An extension to the library catalogue which includes data which will probably only be useful to the librarian allows us to examine this situation.

Example

```
            Field 1 ,       Field 2 , Field 3
Record 1   AUTHOR 1 , TITLE , PUBLISHER AND PRICE
Record 2   AUTHOR 2 , TITLE , PUBLISHER AND PRICE
Record 3   AUTHOR 3 , TITLE , PUBLISHER AND PRICE
Record 4   AUTHOR 4 , TITLE , PUBLISHER AND PRICE
Record 5   AUTHOR 5 , TITLE , PUBLISHER AND PRICE
```

In order to allow a request for titles of books in stock by a particular author or the name of the author who wrote a particular book, the program instructions given previously will have to be modified slightly. Instruction 5 will have to read:

Write the name in the first field in a box called A$

BOX	AUTHOR'S NAME
A$	TOLKIEN

Write the title which is in field two in a box called B$

BOX	TITLE
B$	THE HOBBIT

Write the publisher's name and the price of the book in a box called C$

BOX	PUBLISHER/PRICE
C$	UNWIN/.60

On making a positive comparison the required information can be printed.

Miss, are there any Stories about Horses?

"Yes," said Miss Jones as she looked up from the book that she was issuing, "certainly." She spoke with confidence. There are always stories about horses in children's libraries; it's almost a fact of life. Another hurdle in this morning's assault course successfully negotiated.

"Miss?"

Apprehension. "Yes, what is it?"

"How many?"

"How many what?"

"Books on horses, Miss."

"Several." Said in the same light tone but with less inner confidence this time. The sun shone outside the classroom.

"Where are they? On the shelves, I mean," said the dwarfish inquisitor who had moved a step or two closer.

Check. But not mate. "Try the T's. There's an author called Thomson, try her." Or was it Pullein–Thomson she wondered, or was she thinking of a man called Thomas something.

"Not there, Miss."

"Probably out. Perhaps if you try again next week." She smiled; her eyes twinkled. And he was gone.

There was no reason why Miss Jones should have been able to put her finger, or in this case her hand, on the right book at the right time. She made three sorties into the library each week with different classes, certainly hadn't read more than a handful of children's books, and had no idea how many or what books the teacher in charge of the library had smuggled into that room. She supposed that the other members of the department experienced similar difficulties. The day continued.

The inexpensive answer to Miss Jones's problem is to provide a file of three inch by five inch cards which are arranged by theme and which contain the names of authors and titles of books. This file of cards can stand alongside the one dedicated to authors, and that alongside the one containing cards arranged by title.

Or a further field could be included in the computer record which holds one letter. That letter will be a code for a theme. (M for mystery, H for horses, W for war stories.) A program can be written to search the file for a theme and, after every successful comparison, to print the name of the author and the title of the book. Such a program would make it possible to produce periodically updated theme lists which are compiled and printed by the computer, and these could be displayed in the library. The prospect of analytical indexing, something which is discussed later, makes this an even more attractive proposition.

Student Records

It should be apparent that a student record file can be constructed and interrogated in the same way as the library file. To begin with we might consider including the student's name, form, date of birth and address in one record, and dividing the record into two fields.

Example

Field 1   , Field 2
NAME   , FORM / DATE OF BIRTH / ADDRESS
ADAMS R , 1F   / 10.4.69   / 15 ST MARY'S CLOSE GORLESTON

Before accepting this arrangement it would be worth considering whether two fields might not prove rather limiting. Are there likely to be occasions when the person making the enquiry knows the surname of the student but not his or her christian name and so cannot supply the initial? As the file stands, a search for ADAMS will prove negative because the computer, quite rightly, will regard ADAMS as something very different to ADAMS blank R, and so fail to make a match. It would seem sensible to put the initial in a field of its own, providing an option in the program to make a request by surname only (which might produce details about several students) or by surname and initial.

Example

Field 1 , Field 2 , Field 3
NAME , INITIAL , FORM / DATE OF BIRTH / ADDRESS
ADAMS , R , 1F / 10.4.69 / 15 ST MARY'S CLOSE GORLESTON

Because a request for ADAMS might draw the records of several students it might be advisable to write the program so that the request can be made by surname and form. Even this might make it desirable to separate the year group (1) from the name of the form (F).

Would it sometimes be useful to contact one student through another who lives nearby? The only way that we can offer this option is to put the name of the street, road, avenue or close in a field of its own. Clearly the more fields we have the greater become the possibilities for the retrieval of information. With the two-field record there is some information which cannot be obtained, but at the same time we can expect to get all of the information that is available once a positive comparison has been made. Both are probably unsatisfactory. It may become necessary to run the data held on each student over several lines of the file if extensive records are to be maintained.

Example

Line 1 SURNAME,INITIAL,FORM,DATE OF BIRTH,NUMBER/HOUSE,STREET,TOWN
Line 2 DOCTOR'S NAME AND ADDRESS,ALLERGIES,WHO TO CONTACT IN AN EMERGENCY
Line 3 SURNAME,INITIAL,FORM,DATE OF BIRTH,NUMBER/HOUSE,STREET,TOWN
Line 4 DOCTOR'S NAME AND ADDRESS,ALLERGIES,WHO TO CONTACT IN AN EMERGENCY

Here there are two records, each containing ten fields spread over two lines of the file. The first line of each record contains seven fields and the second line three fields. Where a piece of data is unknown there must be an entry in the appropriate field. A zero could be used to indicate that an item of data is not known and NA or * to stand for "not applicable". Any otherwise insignificant letter, character or number would do.

Example

Line 5 SURNAME,INITIAL,FORM,DATE OF BIRTH,NUMBER/HOUSE,STREET,TOWN
Line 6 DOCTOR'S NAME AND ADDRESS,*,0

It is a simple matter to cope with this new situation and a solution is demonstrated in the following set of program instructions.

**Program to Find a
Student's Address**

1 Ask the user to type in the student's surname.
2 Write the name in a box and call the box X$.

BOX	STUDENT'S SURNAME
X$	SMITH

3 Ask the user to type in the student's first initial.
4 Write the initial in a box called Y$.

BOX	INITIAL
Y$	T

5 Read the first seven fields of a record.
6 If the end of the file has been reached, stop. If the end of the file has not been reached, carry out instruction 7.
7 Put the data in fields 1 to 7 in boxes A$, B$, C$, D$, E$, F$, G$

BOX	DATA
A$	SURNAME
B$	INITIAL
C$	FORM
D$	DATE OF BIRTH
E$	NUMBER/HOUSE
F$	STREET
G$	TOWN

8 Read the remaining three fields of the record.
9 Put the data in boxes H$, I$, J$ respectively.

BOX	DATA
H$	DOCTOR'S NAME AND ADDRESS
I$	ALLERGIES
J$	WHO TO CONTACT IN AN EMERGENCY

10 Compare the contents of X$ with the contents of A$.
11 If X$ doesn't match A$, return to instruction 5.
12 If X$ is the same as A$, see if Y$ is the same as B$.

13 If Y$ doesn't match B$, return to instruction 5.
14 If Y$ does match B$, print E$, F$, G$ and then stop.

As with the fiction file, a number of small programs can be combined to allow a variety of requests to be made and the information to be printed.

Narrowing the Search

To conduct a search on a file will take time, but it is in the interests of the user that the time lapse between making a request and receiving an answer should be as brief as possible. One way that we can make a radical difference in this respect is by the use of multiple files, where this facility is available. Southampton BASIC will allow any one program to reference up to seven files; the Research Machine 12K BASIC with disks will allow more. Instead of running a program against one mammoth file it is possible to organise the data in a number of smaller files. Assuming the seven files to be available in Southampton BASIC, they could be named FIC1, FIC2, FIC3, FIC4, FIC5, FIC6, FIC7 for the library catalogue and REC1 through to REC7 for the student records. They could contain the following information.

FIC1	author's surnames	A to C	REC1	year 1	records
FIC2	"	" D to G	REC2	" 2	"
FIC3	"	" H to K	REC3	" 3	"
FIC4	"	" L to N	REC4	" 4	"
FIC5	"	" O to R	REC5	" 5	"
FIC6	"	" S to U	REC6	" LVI	"
FIC7	"	" V to Z	REC7	" UVI	"

It is a simple matter to include a few lines of program which enables one of the seven files to be examined. One approach uses a menu which is presented to the enquirer either as part of the printout or in accompanying documentation.

Example: menu printout
DO YOU REQUIRE A) CHECK FOR BOOKS BY AN AUTHOR
                        B) CHECK FOR THE AUTHOR OF A BOOK
TYPE A OR B
←A
THE FOLLOWING FILES ARE AVAILABLE:
1. AUTHOR'S SURNAME A–C
2.   ,,   ,,   D–G
3.   ,,   ,,   H–K
4.   ,,   ,,   L–N
5.   ,,   ,,   O–R
6.   ,,   ,,   S–U
7.   ,,   ,,   V–Z
WHICH FILE DO YOU REQUIRE?
TYPE A NUMBER
←1

A second approach is to write the program in such a way that the correct file is selected within the program. Having invited the user to type in the author's name, the first letter is examined by using a string function. (String functions are considered in detail in the chapter titled VERB.) The results of this examination are used to determine the appropriate file. This alternative is possibly easier for the user because it eliminates a decision, and requires only a marginally more complicated piece of programming.

By using several files it is possible to dispense with the time-wasting effort of a search through authors A to K when the required author's name begins with, for example, an L. A provision can be made for a search on all of the files should the object be to find the author of a particular book.

Basic

Comments on the Basic used in file handling are related to Southampton BASIC run on an ICL 1903A machine, with the corresponding lines for the Research Machines 380Z using disk files included in the program example to demonstrate the broad similarity between the systems.

Creating a File

A file can be created using a statement like those already considered. In the ICL 1903A system this is the word INPUT followed by the name to be given to the file. Although it should not give cause for concern, it might be noted that this is done in what is known as the command language of the system, not in Basic. For a file named FIC1 the instruction would look like this: INPUT FIC1. The data is then typed in one line at a time.

Example
←INPUT FIC1
←ADAMS R,WATERSHIP DOWN
←ADAMS R,SHARDICK
←CLARKE A,CHILDHOOD'S END
←AMIS K,LUCKY JIM
←BAWDEN N,CARRIE'S WAR
←CONRAD J,THE ROVER

We proceed in this manner until the file is complete. The signal to terminate the construction of the file is four asterisks.

←ASIMOV I,FOUNDATION
←****

There are certain conventions to be observed when creating the file.

1 There are no line numbers.
2 Fields must be separated by a comma.
3 No comma is required at the end of a line.
4 Data items which include commas must be surrounded by quotation marks.

Referencing the File

The data in the file is referenced in a similar way to data contained in data statements. It is necessary to use a READ statement (or its equivalent, depending upon the system in question) in the program.

Example
20 READ#1,A$,B$

A$ refers to the first field and B$ to the second.

Line 20 gives the instruction to read a record, names the file to be read from, and defines the number and names of the fields to be read.

The variables A$ and B$ must be separated by a comma and separated from #1 by another comma.

The hash symbol # indicates that it is a file which is to be read from and not data statements. The number 1 is significant because it nominates the file to be read, the first. 2 would be used if the second of a series of files was to be read.

Program to Analyse a File Named FIC1

It will search the file for a title and, if it is found, print the name of the author. As it stands the program is of little practical value and is included merely to show the key program statements at work, and to emphasize the basically simple nature of such a program.

```
SOUTHAMPTON BASIC −ICL 1903A
  10 FILES FIC1
  20 IF END#1 THEN 100
  30 PRINT "TYPE TITLE"
  40 INPUT X$
  50 READ#1,A$,B$
  60 IF X$ = B$ THEN 80
  70 GOTO 50
  80 PRINT A$
  90 GOTO 110
 100 PRINT "THIS BOOK IS NOT IN STOCK"
 110 END
```

```
RESEARCH MACHINE 380Z
FILES 1,"B:FIC1"
ON EOF GOTO 100   (on end of file go
                   to 100)

INPUT#;A$,B$
```

FILES and IF END#1 THEN ...

All files used in a program must be declared in a FILES statement.

Line 10 FILES FIC1

Had all seven files been made available line 10 would have read:

10 FILES FIC1,FIC2,FIC3,FIC4,FIC5,FIC6,FIC7

The numbers after FIC are coincidentally the same as the number which would follow the hash symbol in line 50. The number used in line 50 refers to the position of the file name in the FILES statement.

Example

     #1 #2 #3 #4 #5 #6 #7
10 FILES FIC1,FIC4,FIC3,FIC7,FIC2,FIC6,FIC5

Without an indication of what to do should the end of the file be reached, the program will, should this happen, terminate with an error message to the effect that it has run out of data. This is taken care of in line 20 by the IF END OF FILE statement, which must be executed before an end of file condition is reached.

RESET

If we want to introduce the possibility of several searches during one run of the program, we need to make sure that the search will begin at the first record in the file. This is done in Southampton BASIC by using the statement RESET which must be placed on a line which will be read by the computer before the statement READ is acted upon again. By adding a few more lines to the above program we can introduce this feature.

```
110 RESET#1 (replaces END)        FILES 1,"B:FIC1::
120 PRINT "ANOTHER TITLE?"
130 PRINT "TYPE YES OR NO"
140 INPUT X$
150 IF X$ = "YES" THEN 30
160 IF X$ = "NO" THEN 180
170 GOTO 140
180 PRINT "OK"
190 END
```

Unlike RESTORE which fulfils a similar function with regard to data statements, RESET cannot take a line number—because there are none in the file. It will always return the pointer to the beginning of the file.

Using Several Files in One Program

This can be done by making four minor changes.

1 Change line 10

10 FILES FIC1,FIC2,FIC3,FIC4,FIC5,FIC6,FIC7 . . . . FILES 1,"B:FIC"+STR$(Y)

                ↑   ↑

               disk B. give FIC1,FIC2
                    etc. depending
                    upon value of
                    Y

2 Introduce 25 PRINT "WHICH FILE?"
The question presupposes that the user has been informed of the significance of each file.
3 Introduce 26 INPUT Y
One might consider including 27 IF Y>7 THEN 25.
4 Change line 50

  50 READ#Y,A$,B$ INPUT#;A$,B$

JOEL

JOEL is a program which was written for the Research Machines 380Z, using 12K BASIC and discs. It functions as a multi-media resource information retrieval system and includes an analytical indexing feature.

A Hypothetical Problem Defined

The Biology, English and Geography departments have collected and are sharing a wide range of materials to be used in the study of pollution. These include magazine articles, newspaper cuttings, tapes, slides, filmstrips, television programs, and wall charts. The number of items has increased to such an extent that no one is sure what is contained in each item, nor where all the items are located. Some form of retrieval system is considered to be desirable. It has been decided that as well as being simple to use, it must be capable of focusing attention on a particular aspect of a topic, declaring the location of an item, and describing its format as tape, slide, etc. Because a student will almost invariably be interested in only one aspect of the subject at any one time, it must be possible to retrieve references to information on, for example, the causes of river pollution in the United Kingdom without also being given references to items containing information on all forms of water pollution, both within and outside the United Kingdom. A teacher must be able to request references to information which is presented in a specified format, perhaps a television program about air pollution.

Accessioning

The first steps towards solving the problem and meeting the requirements can be taken by organising the material. Each item can be given an accession number as it is acquired. The first will be referred to as AC.1 (Accession number 1), the second as AC.2, and so on. They can hereafter be referred to by this number, irrespective of the manner in which they are stored. This process gives all the different media items a common characteristic and allows us to dispense with cumbersome titles or, as will sometimes be the case, to overcome the absence of titles.

Featuring

The next move is to analyse the items to see what information is contained in each. This can be done by what is termed "featuring", which is the result of using a "feature list". Such a list, when applied to the subject in question, might be expected to contain the following features—each of which is given a numerical code:

CODE	FEATURE	CODE	FEATURE	CODE	FEATURE	CODE	FEATURE
50	pollution	67	U.K.	71	Pacific	75	19th C
51	air	68	U.S.A.	72	Atlantic	76	20th C
52	water	69	Japan	73	Mediterranean	77	1950–60
53	river	70	Italy	74	Baltic	78	1961–70
54	lake					79	1971–80
55	sea						
56	noise						
57	radio-activity						
58	oil						
59	chemicals						
60	industry						
61	cars						
62	cause						
63	effect						
64	birds						
65	animals						
66	fish						

The choice of code numbers in this example is arbitrary, but it is important that no code should be used twice. The list itself is intended to be representative rather than definitive.

Each item can now be examined to see which of the features it contains. Reference is made to these by using the code number. These numbers will also be used in a computer file. Because a number will almost certainly be shorter than a word, time can be saved in both featuring, which involves recording the code on a data collection sheet, and when establishing the file. Feature numbers will also constitute the user's input. In this way we can expect to reduce the incidence of error at this stage since, on the whole, there will be fewer digits in a number than characters in a word. At the same time, a numerical code rules out problems arising from variations in input such as THE UNITED STATES OF AMERICA, AMERICA, U.S.A., THE U.S.A., THE USA, etc.

By including the feature pollution (50) the system will allow us to extract a complete list of references so that we can gain an overview of the state of information collection. This is more significant when other subject areas are being handled as well.

The Coding Sheet

The information obtained as a result of featuring will need to be recorded on a coding sheet prior to establishing or adding to the file. It can be set out to resemble the structure of the file that we intend to create. Each record will relate to one item and will be divided into a number of fields.* The first field is to be used for the accession number and the fifth and subsequent fields for feature codes. The number of fields available for the latter must be flexible which is why the fourth holds the number of features included in the record. This number will be used in the program to identify fields which contain feature codes.

In the example coding sheet (Fig 10.2) the item with accession number 1 contains information on the cause (62) of air pollution (51) in the United Kingdom (67) and makes specific reference to factories (60) and cars (61). The second item is about river pollution (53) in the United States (68), making special references to the period 1950 to 1960 (77). Both include the code number (50), and the latter the codes (52) and (76), ensuring that the item will not be overlooked if a request is made for information on water pollution in general or for items pertaining to the twentieth century as a whole.

If the number of feature codes exceeds 10 we can continue to enter features on the next line, as long as we remember to record the appropriate number of features in field four. Alternatively, we can construct a coding sheet with more space for features. The order in which the features are entered is not significant, and this should save time when featuring.

CODING SHEET

RECORD	AC. No.	LOCATION ROOM	FORMAT	NUMBER OF FEATURES	FEATURES									
					F1	F2	F3	F4	F5	F6	F7	F8	F9	F10
1	1	20	6	6	62	51	67	60	61	50				
2	2	19	10	6	53	68	77	52	76	50				
3														

Fig 10.2

---

* In the program JOEL the first four fields described in Fig 10.2 appear on one line of the file. Feature codes are handled separately, each appearing on a new line.

Location and Format Codes

Although departments are sharing, the material might not be located centrally. As well as obtaining accession numbers from the computer we need to know where an item is located in the school (if it is within the school) and also the format because this will affect the location within any given area. The knowledge that an item is a tape as opposed to a magazine will narrow the physical search since one will be kept in a tape rack and the other in a filing cabinet. It may also be the case that, given references to a number of items pertinent to the enquiry, the enquirer may have a preference for one format and so locate and examine that item first. This data, a room number and a format code, occupies fields two and three of each record.

FORMAT CODES USED IN JOEL

CODE	FORMAT
1	Book or material stored outside school
2	Booklet
3	Computer program
4	Document
5	Experiment
6	Filmstrip
7	Magazine
8	Map
9	Newspaper
10	News/Mag cutting
11	Offprint
12	Pamphlet
13	Picture
14	Poster
15	Slides
16	Slide/Tape
17	Tape
18	Television

The format codes can serve a dual purpose. They must be used in the format field of a record, but they may be used in the feature field. The latter will make possible requests for information presented in a specially desired format.

A User's Guide

A student wishing to interrogate the file that has been established will need to know how to refer to each item when making a request, as well as being familiarised with the general operating procedures. It will be necessary to produce a booklet which

1 Outlines the operating procedures.
2 Lists features and their codes.
3 Lists format codes and describes each one.

The Program

The program used to interrogate the file will have to read each record in turn and apply a test to it to see whether it contains the enquirer's desired combination of features. It is by specifying these features by their numerical code that the required information can be obtained. If it does, the accession number, room number and format description must be printed. If not, the next record must be analysed.

A part-run of JOEL
(On the 380Z a question mark replaces the backward facing arrow.)

```
HOW MANY CHARACTERISTICS TO MATCH?
        TYPE A NUMBER.
?3
INPUT ONE CODE NUMBER AFTER EACH
        QUESTION MARK
ITEM 1?62
ITEM 2?51
ITEM 3?68
DO YOU WISH TO MAKE ANY CORRECTIONS?
YOU MAY ADD, DELETE OR CHANGE ITEMS.
        PLEASE TYPE YES OR NO.
?NO


        ************************
        * SEARCH IN PROGRESS *
        ************************
```

In this example the user has made a request for references to material which includes information on the causes (62) of air pollution (51) in the United States (68).

Note The word ITEM followed by a number in the printout is used as a cue and to aid correction should that be necessary. It should not be confused with the previous use of the word as a single resource item.

The codes that are typed in during a run are stored by the computer in what is called a List, just as if it had written the numbers 62, 51 and 68 on a piece of paper for future reference. So that it can distinguish the numbers in this List from any other that it might make, the computer gives it a name. It calls the user's List Z, and labels the first item $Z(1)$, the second $Z(2)$, and the third $Z(3)$ (see Fig 10.3). Subsequent items would have been $Z(4)$, $Z(5)$, etc.

Fig 10.3

LIST Z	$Z(1)$	$Z(2)$	$Z(3)$
FEATURES	62	51	68

AC. No.	LOCATION ROOM	FORMAT	NUMBER OF FEATURES	FEATURES									
				F1	F2	F3	F4	F5	F6	F7	F8	F9	F10
1	20	6	6	62	51	67	60	61	50				

DATA HELD READY TO PRINT

LIST P	P(1)	P(2)	P(3)	P(4)	P(5)	P(6)
FEATURES	62	51	67	60	61	50

Fig 10.4

At a later point in the program, after a routine which allows corrections to be made to List Z, it begins the search through the file. It takes the first record and reads the first four fields, holding the contents ready to print what is in the first three should that become necessary. The number in the fourth field is then used to count the appropriate number of feature codes into a List called P (Fig 10.4).

The computer then commences to compare the first number in the Z List against each of the numbers in the P List in turn. If a positive comparison is made it ignores the numbers remaining in the P List and proceeds to compare the second number in the Z List $Z(2)$ against each of the numbers in the P List. This process will continue until either all of the numbers in the Z List are found in the P List—in which case the accession number, location number and format description are printed—or until an item in the Z List fails to match any of the numbers in the P List. When this happens the computer abandons the search on the record, moving on to the next, and so on through the file. In the example, the search will move to the next record as soon as $Z(3)$ fails to match $P(6)$. Had 68 been typed in by the user as ITEM 1, making it $Z(1)$ in the List, the search on the record would have been abandoned as soon as $Z(1)$ failed to match $P(6)$.

The False Drop

This is the name given to a situation in which the results of the process of featuring implies a link between features where none exists. If a magazine contained one article on the causes (62) of air pollution (51) and another on the effects (63) of water pollution (52), a request for information on the effects (63) of air pollution (51) would lead to the accession number of the given magazine being printed, with the result that the computer would appear to have made an error.

Example of normal featuring

AC. No.	LOCATION ROOM	FORMAT	NUMBER OF FEATURES	FEATURES									
				F1	F2	F3	F4	F5	F6	F7	F8	F9	F10
300	19	7	5	51	62	52	63	50					

Fig 10.5

This problem can be overcome by a process of double entry. The magazine is credited with one accession number but is entered in two consecutive records in the file. The first contains the codes of one set of features that are related and the second the other set of related codes. This method can be used to handle unrelated features within a single article.

Example of double entry

AC. No.	LOCATION ROOM	FORMAT	NUMBER OF FEATURES	FEATURES									
				F1	F2	F3	F4	F5	F6	F7	F8	F9	F10
300	19	7	3	51	62	50							
300	19	7	3	52	63	50							

Fig 10.6

Sample Run

```
                        JOEL

        ****************************
        * FILE NUMBER AND SUBJECT  *
        *  1     ART               *
        *  2     BIOLOGY           *
        *  3     COMPUTER STUDIES  *
        *  4     ENGLISH LANGUAGE  *
        *  5     ENGLISH LITERATURE *
        *  6     GEOGRAPHY         *
        *  7     HISTORY           *
        *  8     INTERNATIONAL     *
        *        RELATIONS         *
        *  9     RELIGIOUS EDUCATION *
        *  10    TECHNICAL STUDIES *
        ****************************

              WHICH FILE?
        TYPE A NUMBER BETWEEN 1 AND 10
?  7


              *****************


        HOW MANY CHARACTERISTICS TO MATCH?
               TYPE A NUMBER.
?  1
     INPUT ONE CODE NUMBER AFTER EACH ' ? '
               ITEM  1 ? 381
        DO YOU WISH TO MAKE ANY CORRECTIONS?
        YOU MAY ADD, DELETE OR CHANGE ITEMS.
             PLEASE TYPE YES OR NO.
?  YES
     HOW MANY CHANGES DO YOU WISH TO MAKE?
               TYPE A NUMBER.
?  1
        DO YOU REQUIRE INSTRUCTIONS?
             TYPE YES OR NO
?  YES
        AFTER EACH ' ? ', TYPE IN THE
        ITEM NUMBER THEN A COMMA THEN
        THE NEW FEATURE NUMBER. IF YOU
        WISH TO ADD TO THE LIST, TYPE
        THE NEW ITEM NUMBERS IN ORDER.
        THE NEXT NEW ITEM NUMBER WILL
        BE  2 .
        OTHER CHANGES CAN BE MADE IN
        ANY ORDER.
        TO DELETE AN ITEM, TYPE ITEM
        NUMBER COMMA ZERO.
?  2,611
```

```
***********************
*                     *
* SEARCH IN PROGRESS  *
*                     *
***********************

AC•302•ROOM 19•    OFF-PRINT
AC•303•ROOM 19•    OFF-PRINT
AC•304•ROOM 19•    OFF-PRINT
AC•305•ROOM 19•    OFF-PRINT
AC•319•ROOM 19•    OFF-PRINT
AC•320•ROOM 19•    OFF-PRINT
AC•323•ROOM 19•    MAGAZINE
AC•359•ROOM 19•    OFF-PRINT

        FINISHED

    *****************

DO YOU REQUIRE MORE INFORMATION?
        TYPE YES OR NO•? NO
              OK
    *****************
```

Notes

1 The structure of the file must be as follows.

A record
accession number, room number, format number, number of features
feature code
feature code
feature code

Example
300,19,9,3
62
51
50

2 The program allows reference to up to 10 files. This number can be increased. If the number of files is increased attention should be given to lines 220 and 280.

220 PRINT "TYPE A NUMBER BETWEEN 1 AND 10"
280 IF Y > 10 THEN 220

3 The range of format descriptions can be increased. Simply extend the data statements which appear on lines 1470 to 1500. Any additions to or subtractions from these data items must be accompanied by a change to line 240. This begins the loop which reads the format descriptions into the list M$. This loop runs from 2 to 18. The feature BOOK is coded 1 and this is handled differently to the others.

4 *Books* When constructing the file replace the accession number by the title of the book, and replace the room number by the author's name and a suitable location description.

5 The dimension statement on line 20 sets limits on the lists M$, Z and P.

M$ is the format list; Z allows a user's feature list to contain 20 items; P sets a limit of 20 feature codes which can be read from a record. This last constraint must be remembered when constructing the file. Any change to DIM Z(20) should be accompanied by a change to lines 380 and 780.

This program uses common BASIC statements. To make it suitable for systems other than the 380Z attention must be given to:

1 Line 290   the FILES statement
2 Line 1000   the ON END OF FILE statement
3 Line 1320   which reopens the file
4 Line 30   which clears the screen

JOEL:
Program Listing:
Research Machines
380Z 12K BASIC

```
10 REM INFORMATION RETRIEVAL.   JOEL
20 DIM M$(18),Z(20),P(20)
30 PRINT CHR$(12)
40 PRINT TAB(18);"JOEL"
50 PRINT
60 PRINT TAB(6);"*****************************"
70 PRINT TAB(6);"* FILE NUMBER AND SUBJECT  *"
80 PRINT TAB(6);"* 1      ART                *"
90 PRINT TAB(6);"* 2      BIOLOGY            *"
100 PRINT TAB(6);"* 3      COMPUTER STUDIES   *"
110 PRINT TAB(6);"* 4      ENGLISH LANGUAGE   *"
120 PRINT TAB(6);"* 5      ENGLISH LITERATURE *"
130 PRINT TAB(6);"* 6      GEOGRAPHY          *"
140 PRINT TAB(6);"* 7      HISTORY            *"
150 PRINT TAB(6);"* 8      INTERNATIONAL      *"
160 PRINT TAB(6);"*        RELATIONS          *"
170 PRINT TAB(6);"* 9      RELIGIOUS EDUCATION *"
180 PRINT TAB(6);"* 10     TECHNICAL STUDIES  *"
190 PRINT TAB(6);"*****************************"
200 PRINT
210 PRINT TAB(14);"WHICH FILE?"
220 PRINT TAB(5);"TYPE A NUMBER BETWEEN 1 AND 10"
230 RESTORE
240 FOR L=2 TO 18
250 READ M$(L)
260 NEXT L
270 INPUT Y
280 IF Y>10 THEN 220
290 FILES 1,"B:BEN"+STR$(Y)
300 PRINT
310 PRINT
320 PRINT TAB(11)"******************"
330 PRINT
340 PRINT
350 PRINT TAB(3);"HOW MANY CHARACTERISTICS TO MATCH?"
360 PRINT TAB(13);"TYPE A NUMBER."
370 INPUT N
380 IF N<=20 THEN 420
390 PRINT TAB(8);"THE NUMBER IS TOO LARGE."
400 PRINT TAB(15);"TRY AGAIN."
410 GOTO 350
420 PRINT TAB(1);"INPUT ONE CODE NUMBER AFTER EACH ' ? '."
430 FOR J=1 TO N
440 PRINT TAB(13);"ITEM ";J;
450 INPUT Z(J)
```

```
460   NEXT J
470   PRINT TAB(2);"DO YOU WISH TO MAKE ANY CORRECTIONS?"
480   PRINT TAB(3);"YOU MAY ADD, DELETE OR CHANGE ITEMS."
490 PRINT TAB(9);"PLEASE TYPE YES OR NO."
500   INPUT D$
510   IF D$="NO" THEN 920
520   IF D$="YES" THEN 540
530   GOTO 490
540   PRINT TAB(1);"HOW MANY CHANGES DO YOU WISH TO MAKE?"
550 PRINT TAB(13);"TYPE A NUMBER."
560   INPUT C
570 PRINT TAB(6);"DO YOU REQUIRE INSTRUCTIONS?"
580 PRINT TAB(13);"TYPE YES OR NO"
590   INPUT W$
600   IF W$="YES" THEN 630
610   IF W$="NO" THEN 750
620   GOTO 580
630 PRINT TAB(6);"AFTER EACH ' ? ', TYPE IN THE"
640   PRINT TAB(6);"ITEM NUMBER THEN A COMMA THEN"
650 PRINT TAB(6);"THE NEW FEATURE NUMBER.IF YOU"
660 PRINT TAB(6);"WISH TO ADD TO THE LIST, TYPE"
670   PRINT TAB(6);"THE NEW ITEM NUMBERS IN ORDER."
680   PRINT TAB(6);"THE NEXT NEW ITEM NUMBER WILL"
690   PRINT TAB(6);"BE ";N+1;"."
700   PRINT TAB(6);"OTHER CHANGES CAN BE MADE IN"
710 PRINT TAB(6);"ANY ORDER."
720   PRINT TAB(6);"TO DELETE AN ITEM, TYPE ITEM"
730   PRINT TAB(6);"NUMBER COMMA ZERO."
740   GOTO 760
750 PRINT TAB(13);"OK. INPUT NOW."
760   FOR E=1 TO C
770 INPUT F,G:IF F<=20 THEN 790
780 PRINT "INPUT AGAIN. ITEM NUMBER 1-20 ONLY":GOTO 770
790 IF F<=N THEN 900
800   LET Z=F-N
810   IF Z>1 THEN 840
820   LET N=N+1
830   GOTO 900
840   PRINT TAB(9);"PLEASE INPUT NEW ITEMS"
850   PRINT TAB(9);"IN ORDER. THE LAST ITEM"
860 PRINT TAB(9);"NUMBER SHOULD HAVE BEEN"
870 PRINT TAB(8);N+1;". INPUT THE LAST ITEM"
880 PRINT TAB(9);"AGAIN."
890   GOTO 770
900   LET Z(F)=G
910   NEXT E
920   PRINT
930 PRINT TAB(9);"**********************"
940 PRINT TAB(9);"*";TAB(30);"*"
950 PRINT TAB(9);"* SEARCH IN PROGRESS *"
960 PRINT TAB(9);"*";TAB(30);"*"
970 PRINT TAB(9);"**********************"
980   PRINT
990   LET Q=0
1000 ON EOF GOTO 1220
1010   LET T=1
1020 INPUT #;H$,K$,M,B
1030   FOR I=1 TO B
1040 INPUT#;A
1050   LET P(I)=A
1060   NEXT I
1070   FOR S=1 TO B
1080   IF P(S)=Z(T) THEN 1120
1090   NEXT S
1100   IF Z(T)=0 THEN 1120
1110   GOTO 1180
1120   LET T=T+1
1130   IF T=N+1 THEN 1150
1140   GOTO 1070
1150 IF M=1 THEN 1190
```

```
1160   PRINT TAB(7)"AC.";H$;".";TAB(14);"ROOM ";K$;".";TAB(24);M$(M)
1170   LET Q=Q+1
1180   GOTO 1010
1190   PRINT TAB(7);H$;"."
1200   PRINT TAB(7);K$;"."
1210   GOTO 1170
1220   IF Q=0 THEN 1290
1230   PRINT
1240   PRINT TAB(16);"FINISHED"
1250   PRINT
1260   PRINT TAB(11);"*****************"
1270   PRINT
1280   GOTO 1320
1290   PRINT TAB(8);"NO INFORMATION AVAILABLE."
1300   PRINT TAB(3);"CONSIDER ALTERING YOUR REQUIREMENTS"
1310   PRINT TAB(10);"BY ONE OR MORE ITEMS."
1320   FILES 1,"B:BEN"+STR$(Y)
1330   PRINT TAB(4);"DO YOU REQUIRE MORE INFORMATION?"
1340   PRINT TAB(10);"TYPE YES OR NO.";
1350   INPUT X$
1360   IF X$="YES" THEN 1390
1370   IF X$="NO" THEN 1450
1380   GOTO 1340
1390   PRINT TAB(12);"FROM THIS FILE?"
1400   PRINT TAB(12);"TYPE YES OR NO."
1410   INPUT X$
1420   IF X$="YES" THEN 300
1430   IF X$="NO" THEN 30
1440   GOTO 1400
1450   PRINT TAB(19);"OK"
1460   PRINT TAB(11);"*****************"
1470   DATA BOOKLET,COMPUTER PROGRAM,DOCUMENT,EXPERIMENT,FILMSTRIP
1480   DATA MAGAZINE,NEWSPAPER,MAP,OFF-PRINT,PAMPHLET
1490   DATA PICTURE,POSTER,NEWS/MAG CUTTING,SLIDES
1500   DATA SLIDE/TAPE,TAPE,TELEVISION
1510   END
```

SORT

The program SORT is used to sort features into alphabetical order and so assist with the preparation of a feature list. It uses common Basic statements and the user instructions are included in the program.

The user is invited to type in each feature and its code. The format for this is FEATURE COMMA CODE, e.g. LAW, 600. When the list is complete the input *,* terminates this routine. There is an opportunity to check items that have been typed in. One can request a complete list or a particular item. Items may also be changed. When satisfied that the list is complete and accurate, the instruction to sort can be given. The features will then be sorted into alphabetical order, the appropriate code being printed alongside each one.

Notes

1 Lines 450, 460 and 470 each hold two statements. These are separated by a colon. For use in systems which do not allow this, a new line must be created for each statement which follows the colon.

2 Line 20—which clears the screen—can safely be deleted.

3 The DIM statement in line 30 sets a limit on the number of features that can be sorted. This is an arbitrary limit. It may be considered insufficient in which case the numbers inside the brackets can be increased.

SORT:
Program Listing:
Research Machines
380Z 12K BASIC

```
10 REM SORTING
20 PRINT CHR$(12)
30 DIM F$(100),C$(100)
40 PRINT "THIS PROGRAM WILL SORT"
50 PRINT "UP TO 100 FEATURES AND"
60 PRINT "CODES INTO ALPHABETICAL ORDER"
70 PRINT
80 PRINT "TYPE IN 'FEATURE','CODE'"
90 PRINT "ONE SET PER LINE"
100 PRINT "TYPE *,* TO FINISH"
110 LET N=1
120 PRINT "ITEM";N;
130 INPUT F$(N),C$(N)
140 IF F$(N)="*" AND C$(N)="*" THEN N=N-1:GOTO 170
150 LET N=N+1
160 GOTO 120
170 PRINT "CHECK/CHANGE/LIST/SORT ?"
180 INPUT  A$
190 IF A$="CHECK" THEN 240
200 IF A$="CHANGE" THEN 290
210 IF A$="LIST" THEN 370
220 IF A$="SORT" THEN 410
230 GOTO 170
240 PRINT "TYPE ITEM NUMBER (0 TO STOP)"
250 INPUT M
260 IF M=0 THEN 170
270 PRINT F$(M),C$(M)
280 GOTO 240
290 PRINT "TYPE 'ITEM NUMBER','FEATURE','CODE'"
300 PRINT " ( 0,*,* TO STOP )"
310 INPUT I,F$(I),C$(I)
320 IF I>N+1 THEN 290
330 IF M=0 AND  F$(I)="*" AND C$(I)="*" THEN 170
340 IF I<=N THEN 360
350 LET N=N+1
360 GOTO 290
370 FOR I=1 TO N
380 PRINT I;TAB(5);C$(I),F$(I)
390 NEXT I
400 GOTO 170
410 PRINT "SORT IN PROGRESS"
420 FOR I=1 TO N
430 FOR J=1 TO N-1
440 IF F$(J)<F$(J+1) THEN 480
450 LET G$=F$(J):D$=C$(J)
460 LET F$(J)=F$(J+1):C$(J)=C$(J+1)
470 LET F$(J+1)=G$:C$(J+1)=D$
480 NEXT J
490 NEXT I
500 PRINT "THE SORTED LIST IS"
510 PRINT
520 FOR I=1 TO N
530 PRINT C$(I),F$(I)
540 NEXT I
550 PRINT
560 END
```

11 Testing

The ability of the computer to "score" was taken advantage of in DRAKE and VERB, but in neither case was it intended that the mark obtained should be of any significance to the teacher. The feature was included solely for the benefit and satisfaction of the student. It should be clear that, if it can assess responses in a relatively friendly way, it can be programmed to administer a genuine test. In this capacity it can set the test, mark it, store the results, and, if desired, analyse the results.

The chapter dealing with the decision-making facility showed how the computer handled multiple choice questions, crediting the user with a mark and keeping a running total of the score. Computer-marked multiple choice examination papers are commonplace and, in theory, there is no reason why this form of testing should not be extended to become part of the normal assessment procedure in secondary schools. In practice there are, of course, limitations to the development of this sphere of computer activity, not the least of which is the availability of hardware. The second problem is that they depend upon test formulation skills which many teachers do not possess and are time-consuming in terms of preparation. Finally, there is the problem of secrecy. This will arise if tests are being conducted where an adequate number of microcomputers or terminals do not exist. By the time that the 3rd, 4th or 5th student has taken the test, one might expect the questions to have been passed on to the rest of the group. To some extent this problem, if it exists, can be overcome by programming the computer to hold a large number of questions on a topic but to generate only some of them during a test and then at random. This, however, produces its own problems because the results cannot be used for direct comparison. In the interests of secrecy, with or without randomly generated questions, the use of a visual display unit and the absence of a hard copy is probably desirable.

Testing need not be restricted to multiple choice questions. Two other possibilities are the use of a true-false test and the type of test which requires a one-word answer. The one-word answer brings with it the problem of correct answers which the computer does not recognise because the spelling is incorrect. Measures which can be taken to deal with this are considered in the chapter on the student/computer interface in the context of a French vocabulary test. It is possible that the computer will reject an essentially correct answer for reasons other than incorrect spelling. For example, the required answer is amber and the student offers yellow as his answer. There are three ways of handling this type of situation. The first is to avoid questions of this sort. The second is to make sure that there is only one correct answer. The third is to anticipate a number of correct answers.

Very low scores are unlikely to be acceptable and one might argue that this manner of testing lends itself to a student's poor progress going undetected for some time. The onus is clearly on the teacher to ensure that this does not happen. To diminish the time between the student achieving a low score and the teacher being made aware of it, the computer can easily be programmed to print something along the following lines at the end of the test.

YOUR SCORE ON THIS TEST WAS RATHER LOW. PLEASE CONSULT YOUR TEACHER BEFORE CONTINUING WITH THE NEXT TASK.

Such a message could be printed if the score is less than that which is considered acceptable by the teacher constructing the test.

Whether the teacher adopts computer-assisted testing or accepts the described tests as desirable or valid will be a matter for his or her own judgement. Our principal concern is to show that questions can be posed by the computer, answers marked, and the sum of the marks stored for future reference. Multiple choice, true-false and one-word answer tests are referred to in order to show that there can be a variety of approaches and at the same time suggest some of the difficulties associated with testing.

A Computer Assessment System

Many questions have been raised in the discussion of the assessment function of the computer and the reader may feel that many have been left unanswered. The main reason for this is that the authors believe that each teacher will view the possibility of computer testing from a different position and the points raised will have a different significance for each one. It was therefore decided to prepare a suite of programs to enable the teacher to experiment with computer assessment and thereby decide the answers to the questions raised. Obviously, the number of possible formats for the suite of programs prevents them from being all encompassing, but they do allow the teacher to observe one possibility for computer testing.

What is Possible

Items marked with an asterisk (*) are included in the system described later.

TYPE OF TEST

a)   * Test held on computer storage device and student completes the test using a terminal or V.D.U. keyboard.

b)   Test held on written document. Student completes the test by marking answers on computer cards to be mark sensed or on specially prepared documents to be read by a document reader. (Similar to those used for O-level multiple choice examinations.) This format would require the appropriate device for reading answers to be capable of being linked to the computer used for holding the results obtained by the students.

c) Test held on written document. Answers input at the keyboard. It may be more valid for a remote terminal using a slow speed printer.

FORMAT OF TEST

a) * Multiple choice.
b) True/False/Don't Know.
c) Actual answers typed by the student. This, of course, entails careful consideration of the wide range of student responses, including any spelling difficulties.

SCORING OF TEST

a) * 1 for correct and 0 for incorrect.
b) Other forms of scoring, perhaps a weighting for each possible answer.

TEST DETAILS

a) * Same test for everybody with fixed number of questions.
b) Fixed number of questions but drawn randomly from a larger collection of questions.

COMPUTER RESPONSE TO ANSWERS GIVEN BY STUDENT

a) * Print correct or incorrect.
b) Correct answer given to each incorrectly answered question.
c) * Opportunity to write down the question if the answer given is incorrect. (This may be useful for revision-based tests or for encouraging students to consult resource material which may have been neglected in initial researching of a particular topic.) This does, however, negate the idea of eliminating hard copy.
d) No response.

SCORING

a) * Score for test given to student.
b) Score not given, but a message printed giving details of further actions to be taken by the student. These could include the following:
"Consult your teacher before moving on to the next piece of work as your test result was rather low."
"Your test result was quite satisfactory, continue with the next piece of work."

The system for computer assessment, which will now be described, was designed to illustrate some of the possibilities mentioned above. The authors do not present it as a desirable system but merely include it to enable teachers to have something tangible to help them decide whether computer assessment has a useful role to play in schools.

The Hardware for the System

The system has been designed to be run on the Research Machines 380Z microcomputer incorporating a visual display screen and floppy disk storage. The use of the screen means there will be no hard copy of the test to be circulated amongst the students. The need to hold 5 test files and a student record file available while students are using the test monitoring program does rule out the possibility of using tape cassette storage unless there is going to be a person continually available to organise the cassette system. Using a floppy disk system enables the teacher to call up the test monitoring program and then students need only type RUN on arrival at the keyboard and then go on to complete the test.

The Computer Assessment System

The system consists of four programs, SETSTUD, QUEST, STUDTEST and INTERROG. The SETSTUD is used by the teacher to set up the student record file. QUEST, the second program, is also used by the teacher, to prepare the question files (5 in this system). They must be called TEST1, TEST2, TEST3, TEST4 and TEST5 as these will be the file names that the third program STUDTEST will be searching the disk to locate. This third program actually administers the tests and on completion of a test it updates the student record file. The final program INTERROG is again used by the teacher to obtain information about results gained by students using the tests.

Each of the programs will be explained from the point of view of their use and any deviations from the Basic instructions already encountered will be explained at the end of the chapter.

SETSTUD

This program is designed to set up the student record file which will contain names and scores obtained by students using the tests. Initially the file will contain only names followed by a set of asterisks, the number of which will be determined by the number of tests to be taken by the students. The asterisk will inform the teacher on examining the file that a student has not completed a particular test. The record file can contain any number of pupils, the maximum number being determined by the space available on the floppy disk, but it is probably best to experiment initially with the number of students within one class. The system is designed to handle a maximum of 5 tests. With numbers in excess of 5, problems arise in relation to printing out the record file in tabular form. If more than 5 tests are required, the names of the record file and question files can be changed and by altering references to them in the program, another system of 5 tests can be set up.

Example of using the program

HOW MANY TESTS ARE THERE TO BE?
? 5
HOW MANY STUDENTS IN THE FILE?
? 10
TYPE IN NAMES OF STUDENTS.
EXAMPLE JOHN SMITH WITH ONE SPACE
BETWEEN CHRISTIAN NAME AND SURNAME.
NAME 1
? ALAN LADD
NAME 2
? RICHARD BURTON
NAME 3

‖
‖
‖
‖
‖

NAME 10
? DUSTIN HOFFMAN
STUDENT FILE NOW COMPLETE.

QUEST   This program is used to set up the question files. For 5 tests it would be used five times and each time the program is used a new name must be given to the respective question file, starting with TEST1 through to TEST5. Of course, the user does not have to set up 5 question files, only one need be used if so wished. Once the name of the question file has been defined the user can then type in as many questions as he likes, within reason. He has to specify for each question the position number of the correct choice, the number of choices and the actual choices themselves. The number of choices of answer for each question can vary from question to question. In the example, five choices are given, but this should not be taken as a recommended number. For example, the word question can take the form of a statement and the teacher may wish to use the test in the following ways.

QUESTION 1
? MEN ARE THE DOMINANT SEX.
ANSWER
?   (Reply to be inserted by the user)
NUMBER OF CHOICES
? 2
CHOICE 1
? TRUE
CHOICE 2
? FALSE

QUESTION 2
? WHEN IT RAINS THERE IS A RAINBOW.
ANSWER
? 2
NUMBER OF CHOICES
? 3
CHOICE 1
? ALWAYS
CHOICE 2
? OCCASIONALLY
CHOICE 3
? NEVER

The length of the question is restricted to 130 characters, which is approximately 3 lines of print on a 40 character width visual display screen. The same applies to each answer choice.

Example of using the program

```
TYPE NAME OF QUESTION FILE.
START WITH TEST1 AND THEN
TEST2 AND SO ON.
? TEST1

NOW TYPE IN YOUR QUESTION
                ANSWER NUMBER
                NUMBER OF CHOICES
AND THE CHOICES TO SELECT FROM.
WHEN ALL QUESTIONS ARE ENTERED
TYPE NONE IN RESPONSE TO QUESTION
QUESTION 1
? WHO WROTE 'JACK SHEPPERD'
ANSWER
? 3
NUMBER OF CHOICES
? 5
CHOICE 1
? DICKENS
CHOICE 2
? BAILEY
CHOICE 3
? AINSWORTH
CHOICE 4
? LOCKHART
CHOICE 5
? SURTEES
QUESTION 2
? WHO WROTE 'THE CRICKET ON THE HEARTH'
ANSWER
? 1
NUMBER OF CHOICES
? 5
CHOICE 1
? DICKENS
CHOICE 2
? FLEMING
CHOICE 3
? GOLDING
CHOICE 4
? HARDY
CHOICE 5
? AUSTEN
```

etc.
.
.
.

QUESTION 21
? NONE
QUESTION FILE TEST1 IS
NOW SET UP.

STUDTEST

The administration of the tests is carried out by this program and therefore a little more attention has been paid to the "traps" required to enable the student to use the program without experiencing too many problems. It is all too easy for a student to type a response incorrectly and therefore the student must be allowed to correct or have a change of mind about a response. The student must be told beforehand the number of the test to complete and must also be instructed to type his/her name as it would appear in a register. If, for example, his name was TIMOTHY EFORANOTHER, he must not type TIM EFORANOTHER.

When the student has completed the test, the program locates the student's name in the student record file and replaces the asterisk in the position of that particular test with the mark obtained. The program will allow a student to retake any test, if the teacher so wishes, the mark scored first time round simply being replaced by the new score.

The program does contain the facility to enable the student to copy down on paper any question to which the answer is not known. If, however, this facility is not required then it would only mean removing a few program instructions to cancel it.

Traps in Action

YOU WILL NEED A PEN AND
A PIECE OF PAPER

PLEASE TYPE IN YOUR NAME
WITH A SPACE BETWEEN YOUR
CHRISTIAN NAME AND SURNAME.
EXAMPLE: JOHN SMITH

? SUE GEORGE

YOUR NAME DOES NOT APPEAR
TO BE ON RECORD.PLEASE
TYPE IT IN AGAIN.DON'T
FORGET THE SPACE.
? SUSAN GEORGE

SORRY ABOUT THAT

WHICH TEST,SUSAN?
TYPE THE NUMBER PLEASE.

YOU WILL NEED A PEN AND
A PIECE OF PAPER

PLEASE TYPE IN YOUR NAME
WITH A SPACE BETWEEN YOUR
CHRISTIAN NAME AND SURNAME.
EXAMPLE: JOHN SMITH

? LYNNE REDGRAVE

YOUR NAME DOES NOT APPEAR
TO BE ON RECORD.PLEASE
TYPE IT IN AGAIN.DON'T
FORGET THE SPACE.
? LYNNE REDGRAVE
YOU HAD BETTER CHECK
WITH YOUR TEACHER
AS THERE SEEMS TO BE
A PROBLEM.

BYE

Sample of a
STUDTEST run

YOU WILL NEED A PEN AND
A PIECE OF PAPER.

PLEASE TYPE IN YOUR NAME
WITH A SPACE BETWEEN YOUR
CHRISTIAN NAME AND SURNAME.
EXAMPLE: JOHN SMITH

? JAMES MASON

WHICH TEST, JAMES?
TYPE IN THE NUMBER PLEASE
? 1

QUESTION 1

WHO WROTE 'JACK SHEPPERD'?

1) DICKENS
2) BAILEY
3) AINSWORTH
4) LOCKART
5) SURTEES

TYPE NUMBER OF YOUR CHOICE.
? 3

DO YOU WISH TO CHANGE YOUR ANSWER?
TYPE N FOR NO OR RETYPE YOUR
SELECTION IF YOU WISH TO CHANGE.
? N

CORRECT

QUESTION 2

WHO WROTE 'THE CRICKET ON THE HEARTH'?

1) DICKENS
2) FLEMING
3) GOLDING
4) HARDY
5) AUSTEN

TYPE NUMBER OF YOUR CHOICE.
? 2

DO YOU WISH TO CHANGE YOUR ANSWER?
TYPE N FOR NO OR RETYPE YOUR
SELECTION IF YOU WISH TO CHANGE.
? 1

CORRECT

QUESTION 3

WHO WROTE 'WHERE EAGLES DARE'?

1) FLEMING
2) MACLEAN
3) FITZGERALD
4) INNES
5) FORBES

TYPE NUMBER OF YOUR CHOICE.
? 3

DO YOU WISH TO CHANGE YOUR ANSWER?
TYPE N FOR NO OR RETYPE YOUR
SELECTION IF YOU WISH TO CHANGE.
? N

YOUR ANSWER IS INCORRECT, JAMES.

COPY DOWN THE QUESTION
ON YOUR PIECE OF PAPER.

QUESTION 3

WHO WROTE 'WHERE EAGLES DARE'?

TYPE C WHEN YOU HAVE
WRITTEN DOWN THE QUESTION.
? C

QUESTION 4

WHO WROTE 'THE DAY OF THE JACKAL'?

1) HOOKER
2) FORBES
3) MACDONALD
4) MACLEAN
5) FORSYTH

TYPE NUMBER OF YOUR CHOICE.
‖
‖
‖
YOU HAVE SCORED 10, JAMES.

BYE

INTERROG

The final program is used by the teacher to investigate the student record file. The teacher has the option of looking at the results of all the students or requesting the results of selected students. Having elected to check individually, the teacher may continue to view individual records until the computer is instructed to halt the reviewing procedure. If the teacher does not have a list of students when using INTERROG, the computer informs the teacher if it is unable to locate a student, probably because the name has been misspelt, and then allows the teacher to continue to investigate other students.

Example of misspelling a name

TYPE IN THE STUDENT'S NAME.
LEAVE A SPACE BETWEEN CHRISTIAN
NAME AND SURNAME.
? LYNNE REDGRAVE

STUDENT'S NAME NOT ON FILE.
CHECK FOR INCORRECT SPELLING.

TYPE IN THE STUDENT'S NAME.
LEAVE A SPACE BETWEEN CHRISTIAN
NAME AND SURNAME.
? LYNNE REDGRAVE

YOU HAD BETTER CHECK THE SPELLING
WITH YOUR RECORDS LATER

DO YOU WISH TO INTERROGATE
ANOTHER STUDENT?
TYPE YES OR NO
? YES

Example printout of an interrogation of the Student Record File

DO YOU WISH TO INTERROGATE

A) AN INDIVIDUAL STUDENT
B) ALL STUDENTS

TYPE A OR B
? B

	TESTS				
NAME	1	2	3	4	5
ALAN LADD	*	15	14	*	13
RICHARD BURTON	10	12	*	*	14
JAMES MASON	10	*	10	11	18
SUSAN GEORGE	*	7	5	9	12
ANITA HARRIS	14	*	*	13	12
GEORGE COLE	18	19	20	*	17
PAUL NEWMAN	13	*	*	15	16
STEVE MCQUEEN	9	*	13	*	*
LYNN REDGRAVE	16	17	*	*	16
DUSTIN HOFFMAN	17	18	*	12	*

Example printout of an   DO YOU WISH TO INTERROGATE
interrogation of an
Individual Student Record   A) AN INDIVIDUAL STUDENT
B) ALL STUDENTS

TYPE A OR B
? A

TYPE IN THE STUDENT'S NAME.
LEAVE A SPACE BETWEEN CHRISTIAN
NAME AND SURNAME.
? STEVE MCQUEEN

		TESTS			
NAME	1	2	3	4	5
STEVE MCQUEEN	9	*	13	*	*

DO YOU WISH TO INTERROGATE
ANOTHER STUDENT?
TYPE YES OR NO
? YES

Program Listings:
Research Machines
380Z XDB

The following suite of programs contain two features which need to be mentioned. The first, which is permitted in many versions of Basic, is to omit the LET part of a statement which establishes a variable.

Example
30 LET $T = 0$ simply becomes   30 $T = 0$

The second feature is the replacing of the word PRINT by ? (a single question mark).

Example
90 PRINT "PLEASE TYPE IN YOUR NAME"

simply becomes

90 ? "PLEASE TYPE IN YOUR NAME"

Program SETSTUD
(student record
file)

```
10 REM SETTING UP STUDENT FILE
15 CLEAR 181,1
20 ?"HOW MANY TESTS ARE THERE TO BE?"
30 INPUT N
40 ?"HOW MANY STUDENTS IN THE FILE?"
50 INPUT S
70 OPEN #10,"O","STUDREC"
80 OPTION #10,"Q",0
90 PRINT #10,N
100 ?"TYPE IN NAMES OF STUDENTS."
110 ?"EXAMPLE  JOHN SMITH  WITH ONE SPACE"
120 ?"BETWEEN CHRISTIAN NAME AND SURNAME."
130 FOR I=1 TO S
140 ?"NAME ";I
150 INPUT N$
160 PPRINT #10,N$
170 FOR J =1 TO N
180 PRINT #10,"*"
190 NEXT J
200 NEXT I
210 ?"STUDENT FILE NOW COMPLETE."
220 CLOSE #10
```

Program QUEST
(question files)

```
10 REM  SETTING UP QUESTION FILES
20 CLEAR 181,1
25 C=1
30 ?"TYPE NAME OF QUESTION FILE."
40 ?"START WITH TEST1 AND THEN"
50 ?"TEST2 AND SO ON."
60 INPUT P$
70 ?
80 ?"NOW TYPE IN YOUR QUESTION"
90 ?"               ANSWER NUMBER"
100 ?"               NUMBER OF CHOICES"
110 ?"AND THE CHOICES TO SELECT FROM."
120 ?"WHEN ALL QUESTIONS ARE ENTERED"
130 ?"TYPE NONE IN RESPONSE TO  QUESTION. "
140 OPEN #12,"O",P$
150 OPTION #12,"Q",0
155 ?
156 ?
160 ? "QUESTION";C
170 INPUT Q$
180 IF Q$="NONE" THEN 330
190 ?"ANSWER"
200 INPUT A
210 ?"NUMBER OF CHOICES"
220 INPUT B
230 FOR J=1 TO B
240 ?"CHOICE ";J
250 INPUT C$(J)
260 NEXT J
270 PRINT #12,Q$
280 PRINT #12,A;",";B
290 FOR J=1 TO B
300 PRINT #12,C$(J)
310 NEXT J
315 C=C+1
320 GOTO 160
330 CLOSE #12
340 ?"QUESTION FILE ";P$;" IS"
350 ?"NOW SET UP."
```

Program STUDTEST (administration of test)

```
10 REM TEST PROGRAM
20 CLEAR 181,1
30 T=0
35 K=0
40 ?CHR$(12)
50 ?"YOU WILL NEED A PEN AND"
60 ?"A PIECE OF PAPER."
70 ?
80 ?
90 ? "PLEASE TYPE IN YOUR NAME"
100 ? "WITH A SPACE BETWEEN YOUR"
110 ? "CHRISTIAN NAME AND SURNAME."
120 ? "EXAMPLE: JOHN SMITH"
130 ?
140 INPUT M$
150 OPEN #11,"I","STUDREC"
160 OPTION #11,"Q",0
170 INPUT #11,N
180 INPUT #11,N$
190 ON EOF #11 GOTO 260
200 FOR J =1 TO N
210 INPUT #11,R$
220 NEXT J
230 IF N$=M$ THEN 250
240 GOTO 180
250 IF K=1 THEN 420 ELSE 440
260 IF K=1 THEN 350
270 ?
280 ?
290 ?"YOUR NAME DOES NOT APPEAR"
300 ?"TO BE ON RECORD.PLEASE"
310 ?"TYPE IT IN AGAIN.DON'T"
320 ?"FORGET THE SPACE."
330 K=1
340 GOTO 140
350 ?"YOU HAD BETTER CHECK"
360 ?"WITH YOUR TEACHER"
370 ?"AS THERE SEEMS TO BE"
380 ?"A PROBLEM."
390 ?
400 ?
410 GOTO 1270
420 ? CHR$(12)
430 ?"SORRY ABOUT THAT."
440 FOR I=1 TO 15
450 ZS=MID$(M$,I,1)
460 IF Z$=" " THEN 480
470 NEXT I
480 LET L$=LEFT$(M$,I)
485 CLOSE #11
490 ?
500 ? "WHICH TEST,";L$;"?"
510 ? "TYPE THE NUMBER PLEASE."
520 INPUT A
530 Y$="TESTN"
540 MID$(Y$,5,1)=RIGHT$(STR$(A),1)
550 OPEN #10,"I",Y$
560 OPTION #10,"Q",0
570 C=1
580 INPUT #10,Q$
590 ON EOF #10 GOTO 1030
600 INPUT #10,G,N
610 ? CHR$(12)
620 ?
630 ?"QUESTION ";C
640 ?
650 ? Q$;"?"
660 ?
670 FOR I=1 TO N
680 INPUT #10,B$
690 ? I;")  ";B$
```

```
700 NEXT I
710 ?
720 C=C+1
730 ? "TYPE NUMBER OF YOUR CHOICE."
740 INPUT X
750 ?
760 ?"DO YOU WISH TO CHANGE YOUR ANSWER?"
770 ?"TYPE N FOR NO OR RETYPE YOUR"
780 ?"SELECTION IF YOU WISH TO CHANGE."
790 INPUT F$
800 IF F$="N" THEN 820
810 X=VAL(F$)
820 IF X<>G THEN 890
830 T=T+1
840 ?
850 ? "CORRECT"
860 FOR J=1 TO 1500
870 NEXT J
880 GOTO 580
890 ?
900 ?
910 ? "YOUR ANSWER IS INCORRECT,";L$;"."
920 ?
930 ?"COPY DOWN THE QUESTION"
940 ?"ON YOUR PIECE OF PAPER."
950 ?
960 ?"QUESTION ";C-1
965 ?
970 ?Q$;"?"
980 ?
990 ?"TYPE C WHEN YOU HAVE"
1000 ?"WRITTEN DOWN THE QUESTION."
1010 INPUT G$
1020 GOTO 580
1030 CLOSE #10
1040 OPEN #11,"U","STUDREC"
1050 OPTION #11,"Q",0
1060 INPUT #11,N
1070 INPUT #11,N$
1080 ON EOF #11 GOTO 1210
1090 IF N$=M$ THEN 1140
1100 FOR K=1 TO N
1110 INPUT #11,R$
1120 NEXT K
1130 GOTO 1200
1140 FOR J=1 TO N
1150 L=LOC(11)
1160 INPUT #11,R$(J)
1170 IF J<>A THEN 1190
1180 PRINT #11@L,RIGHT$(STR$(T),LEN(STR$(T))-1)
1190 NEXT J
1200 GOTO 1070
1210 CLOSE #11
1220 ?CHR$(12)
1230 ? "YOU HAVE SCORED";T;",";L$;"."
1240 ?
1250 ?
1260 ?
1270 ? "BYE"
```

**Program
INTERROG
(viewing of test
results)**

```
10 REM INTERROGATING STUDENT FILE
20 CLEAR 181,1
30 R$(1)="*"
40 R$(2)="*"
```

```
50 R$(3)="*"
60 R$(4)="*"
70 R$(5)="*"
80 ? CHR$(12)
90 ?"DO YOU WISH TO INTERROGATE:"
100 ?
110 ?"A) AN INDIVIDUAL STUDENT"
120 ?"B) ALL STUDENTS"
130 ?
140 ?"TYPE A OR B PLEASE."
150 INPUT A$
160 T=0
170 OPEN #10,"I","STUDREC"
180 OPTION #10,"Q",0
190 INPUT #10,N
200 IF A$="A" THEN 220
210 GOTO 290
220 ?
230 ?
240 ? "TYPE IN THE STUDENT'S NAME."
250 ? "LEAVE A SPACE BETWEEN CHRISTIAN"
260 ? "NAME AND SURNAME."
270 INPUT P$
280 A=1
290 ?CHR$(12)                                  TESTS"
300 ?"
310 ?"      NAME                    1    2    3    4    5"
320 ?"      ====                ==================="
330 INPUT #10,N$
340 ON EOF#10 GOTO 480
350 IF A<>1 THEN 370
360 IF P$<>N$ THEN 440
370 T=1
380 FOR J=1 TO N
390 INPUT #10,R$(J)
400 NEXT J
410 PRINT USING 420;N$,R$(1),R$(2),R$(3),R$(4),R$(5)
420 !'LLLLLLLLLLLLLLLLLLL'RR 'RR 'RR 'RR 'RR
430 GOTO 470
440 FOR S=1 TO N
450 INPUT #10,R$
460 NEXT S
470 GOTO 330
480 CLOSE #10
490 IF T=1 THEN 560
495 ? CHR$(12)
500 ?
510 IF Q=1 THEN 580
520 ?"STUDENT'S NAME NOT ON FILE."
530 ?"CHECK FOR INCORRECT SPELLING."
540 Q=1
550 GOTO 160
560 IF A<>1 THEN 700
570 GOTO 600
580 ?"YOU HAD BETTER CHECK THE SPELLING"
590 ?"WITH YOUR RECORDS LATER."
600 ?
610 ?
620 ?
630 ?"DO YOU WISH TO INTERROGATE"
640 Q=0
650 ?"ANOTHER STUDENT?"
660 ?"TYPE YES OR NO"
670 INPUT F$
680 ?
690 IF F$="YES" THEN 160
700 ?
710 ?
720 ?
```

Basic

In order to make file handling available in Basic it is necessary to have a backing store facility. This could take the form of several large disk units being attached to the mainframe computer and available to remote users, working from a terminal; or, in the case of microcomputers, of their own smaller systems of backing store such as floppy disks or tape cassettes.

The discussion of file handling so far has been concerned solely with accessing information held in files with the object of selecting relevant items and printing them out (e.g. the information retrieval system). If we now consider the assessment function of the computer it is apparent that not only do we need to read information from a file, but we wish to **write information to a file** as well. (When the student completes a test the result must be stored in the student record file.) Reading from a file is fairly straightforward in most versions of Basic with file handling capabilities, and it is only when writing to a file is encountered that problems arise with some of the versions. To illustrate this, the updating of the student record file will be described, using Southampton BASIC on a terminal linked to an I.C.L. mainframe and using Extended Disk BASIC on the RM 380Z.

The student record file is called STUDREC and, in these examples, contains 10 names and positions for 5 test results for each student. At the beginning of the file is a number which identifies the number of tests involved, in this case 5. The record file could be interpreted as having the following format.

```
5
ALAN LADD
*
15
14
*
13
RICHARD BURTON
10
12
*
*
14
JAMES MASON
*
*
10
11
18
etc.
```

Southampton BASIC

The following program segment shows how the problem of updating the student record file could be accomplished using Southampton BASIC. It has also been included to illustrate writing to a file, which the reader may wish to use, not necessarily within the context of assessment. It is assumed that the student, JAMES MASON, has completed TEST1 and scored 10 and the variable T holds his score, the string variable M$ holds his name and the variable A holds the number of the test. These are inserted at the beginning of the program segment in the form of LET statements, but in the real application they would have been derived from INPUT statements and the scoring mechanism within the test administering program.

Program Segment

```
10 LET A = 1
20 LET T = 10
30 LET M$ = "JAMES MASON"
40 FILES STUDREC,UPDATE
50 SCRATCH #2
60 READ #1,N
70 WRITE #2,N
80 FOR I = 1 TO 10
90 READ #1,N$
100 FOR J = 1 TO N
110 READ #1,R$(J)
120 NEXT J
130 IF N$()M$ THEN 220
140 WRITE #2,N$
150 FOR K = 1 TO N
160 IF K()A THEN 190
170 WRITE #2,T
180 GOTO 200
190 WRITE #2,R$(K)
200 NEXT K
210 GOTO 260
220 WRITE #2,N$
230 FOR L = 1 TO N
240 WRITE #2,R$(L)
250 NEXT L
260 NEXT I
270 END
```

Sets up the 2nd file called UPDATE.
Reads the number at the beginning of file 1 (STUDREC) and places it at the beginning of file 2. (N is the number of tests involved.)
Reads a name from file 1.

Reads N test results from file 1.

Writes a name into file 2 (the name of the student taking the test).

Writes the student's score into file 2.

Writes the other results of the student taking the test, into file 2.

Writes a name into file 2 (the names of students not taking the test).
Writes the results of students not taking the test into file 2.

The Files	STUDREC	UPDATE
	5	5
	ALAN LADD	ALAN LADD
	*	*
	15	15
	14	14
	*	*
	13	13
	RICHARD BURTON	RICHARD BURTON
	10	10
	12	12
	*	*
	*	*
	14	14
	JAMES MASON	JAMES MASON
→	*	→ 10
	*	*
	10	10
	11	11
	18	18
	SUSAN GEORGE	SUSAN GEORGE
	*	*
	7	7
	5	5
	9	9
	12	12
	ANITA HARRIS	ANITA HARRIS
	14	14
	*	*
	*	*
	13	13
	12	12
	GEORGE COLE	GEORGE COLE
	18	18
	19	19
	20	20
	*	*
	17	17
	PAUL NEWMAN	PAUL NEWMAN
	13	13
	*	*
	*	*
	15	15
	16	16
	STEVE MCQUEEN	STEVE MCQUEEN
	9	9
	*	*
	13	13
	*	*
	*	*
	LYNN REDGRAVE	LYNN REDGRAVE

16	16
17	17
*	*
*	*
16	16
DUSTIN HOFFMAN	DUSTIN HOFFMAN
17	17
18	18
*	*
12	12
*	*

Explanation of Statements

One major disadvantage of file handling in Southampton BASIC is that before another student can use the test program the files used to hold the student records must be renamed. The reason for this is that a test result cannot be simply inserted into the file STUDREC. To overcome this difficulty the student records have to be read one at a time from the file STUDREC and written to the file UPDATE. Before writing, each is checked to see if the student's name matches the student using the test program. If there is a match then the record is copied into file UPDATE, but the asterisk in the position of the test completed by the student is replaced by the result. When the transfer of records is complete, the file UPDATE would be the most up-to-date version of the student record file.

Before this procedure started, the file UPDATE did not exist. It is the opening of a file for writing that initializes the creation of the file and, as a file cannot be created using the name of a file already in existence, the process cannot be repeated. This means that someone, the teacher perhaps, has to transfer out of Basic into a command language in order to manipulate the names of the files. STUDREC would have to be destroyed, a copy of UPDATE created and given the name STUDREC, and then the file UPDATE would have to be destroyed. An I.C.L. machine using the command language MAXIMOP would use the following instructions in MAXIMOP to accomplish the renaming of the files.

←BYE ⎫ FINISHED⎭	Come out of the BASIC system.
11.56.30←ERASE STUDREC	Destroy the file STUDREC.

11.56.39←EDIT UPDATE,STUDREC
←Z
	Make a copy of UPDATE and
	    call it STUDREC. Z finishes
	    the process.

11.56.49←ERASE UPDATE	Destroys the file UPDATE.
11.56.58←COND ⎫ CONDENSING ⎭	Tidy up the disk.
11.57.13→SOBS	Re-enter the Basic system.
←OLD TEST OK	Call up the test administering program.
←RUN	Set the program running for the next student.

The FILES statement has already been mentioned but it requires elaboration from the point of view of file names in excess of four characters. If STUDREC is used as a file name, the computer will accept it in the FILES statement but when it searches for the file it will only use the first four letters. This means that a FILES statement with both STUDREC and STUDRED as file names is not possible.

When writing to a file, the name of the file is given in the FILES statement but the file must not already exist on the disk storage device. The statement SCRATCH #2 then sets up the file UPDATE ready for writing. Information can now be written into the file using either a WRITE statement or a PRINT statement. If a WRITE statement is used the format of the information in the newly created file will be suitable for accessing via a READ statement at a later date. The PRINT statement would produce a format similar to that achieved as output on a terminal printout.

Examples
IF A$ = "ALAN LADD", B = 15 and C = 19

1 60 WRITE #1,A$,B,C

would appear in the file like this
ALAN LADD,15,19

2 70 PRINT #2,A$,B,C

would appear in the file like this
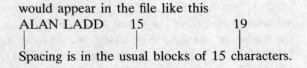
ALAN LADD   15   19

Spacing is in the usual blocks of 15 characters.

Research Machines 380Z Extended Disk BASIC

The following program segment shows how the updating of the student record file is carried out using Extended Disk Basic (XDB) on the Research Machines 380Z microcomputer. Exactly the same case as before will be considered, that is the student is JAMES MASON, who has just completed TEST1 and scored 10. The variables that hold this information, M$, A and T, will not appear as LET statements, as the program segment is a straight selection of statements from the program STUDTEST, given earlier, and therefore it will be assumed that they have been typed in by the student or calculated by the program earlier. An explanation of the statements will follow the program segment but several points need mentioning first in order to make the program segment easier to follow.

Firstly, there is only one file mentioned, the reason being that XDB allows the programmer to write to a file that already exists. This means that the student's test result can be inserted into the file STUDREC without having to use any temporary files such as UPDATE. A second point is that the writing to the file STUDREC takes place in XDB and this means that no manipulation of the files has to be carried out between tests. A student can complete a test, the student record be updated, and then a second student can come along, type RUN, and proceed with another test. (Or the original student can type RUN and try a different test.) Finally, at the time of writing the suite of programs, there was a minor "bug" in XDB which did not allow the defined use of the update mode according to the manual. Therefore, two small alterations are present in the program segment which it may be possible to remove later when Research Machines sort out the "bug".

The Program Segment

20 CLEAR 181,1	Clear string space for one file unit
,,	to be opened.
,,	
1040 OPEN #11,"U","STUDREC"	Open file unit 11 called STUDREC in the update mode.
1050 OPTION #11,"Q",0	Removes the quotation marks when writing to a file.
1060 INPUT #11,N	Read a number from file unit 11.
1070 INPUT #11,N$	Read a name from file unit 11.
1080 ON EOF #11 GOTO 1210	
1090 IF N$ = M$ THEN 1140	
1100 FOR K = 1 TO N	
1110 INPUT #11,R$	Read a score from file unit 11.
1120 NEXT K	
1130 GOTO 1200	
1140 FOR J = 1 TO N	
1150 L = LOC(11)	Sets L equal to the byte address of the beginning of the next input.
1160 INPUT #11,R$(J)	Read a score from file unit 11.
1170 IF J⟨⟩A THEN 1190	A = number of test completed.
1180 PRINT #11@L,RIGHT$(STR$(T),LEN(STR$(T)) − 1)	Write the student's score at byte address L.
1190 NEXT J	
1200 GOTO 1070	
1210 CLOSE #11	Close the file unit 11.

Explanation of Statements

Extended Disk Basic is capable of supporting many input/output devices (console, printing device, reader, punch, disks) and as a result it is necessary to direct an input/output operation to a specific device. In order to do this, each device is given a unit number. The console is 0, the printing device is 2, the reader device 3, and the disk device the numbers 10–255. The reason for a range being given to the disk device is so that each file can be associated with an individual unit number. This association is made by the OPEN command. If, for example, an INPUT statement is written in the program without a unit number then it defaults to the console.

Example

10 INPUT A$	10 INPUT #3,A$
Input would be expected from the console.	Input would be expected from the reader device.

The OPEN instruction also informs the microcomputer to initialise the input/output device ready for operation. One further characteristic is included in the OPEN statement and that determines the mode in which the device can be used. There are four modes I (input only), O (output only), R (random mode) and U (update mode), the last two referring to disk units only.

Example
1040 OPEN #11,"U","STUDREC"

This would initialise the disk device, associate the file STUDREC with the unit number 11 and set the format for the unit to be in the update mode. The update mode should function in the following way. Each output operation should begin at the same byte address in the file as the preceding input operation, and each input operation should begin at the first unprocessed byte address from the previous input/output operation. This means that if you read a record and identify it as that of the student user, you may write the student record (including the new test result) into the file and it should replace the original record. At present it is necessary to use the LOC statement to ensure that the record does overwrite at the correct byte address, but this problem should soon be corrected by Research Machines.

It is necessary to allocate dynamic space in the internal storage of the microcomputer for the maximum number of files to be opened at any one time. This is achieved by using the CLEAR statement. As each file unit requires 181 bytes of storage while the file is open, the CLEAR statement would be used in the following way.

For only 1 file unit open at any one time	CLEAR 181,1
For two file units open simultaneously	CLEAR 362,2
For three file units open simultaneously	CLEAR 543,3
etc.	

The OPTION statement is used to remove the quotation marks from any character string output to a file.

Example
1050 OPTION #11,"Q",0

The zero on the end tells the micro to omit any string delimiters on output. If there is no OPTION statement used to determine what character should be used to delimit character strings, it will default to using quotation marks.

The CLOSE statement causes the unit number to be disassociated from the disk file and allows the dynamic unit space to be released for reuse.

12 LIBRARY: a library monitoring system

This chapter describes a library monitoring system which has been used successfully in a school using batch processing and a telephone link to a mainframe computer.

The computerised library monitoring system makes use of both reading from a file and writing to a file. Like the test system it utilises a suite of programs.

Before the Computer

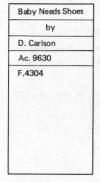

Baby Needs Shoes
by
D. Carlson
Ac. 9630
F.4304

Fig 12.1

READER'S TICKET
Name
Form

Fig 12.2

Inside each book is a ticket held in a cardboard pocket. On it is recorded the name of the book, the author of the book, the accession number, and the classmark (Fig. 12.1). Each student is issued with a ticket pocket bearing the name of the student, and his/her form (Fig. 12.2). These tickets are stored in a box, by the form, with a separate compartment for each form.

When a book is taken out, the ticket is transferred from the book to the student's ticket pocket, and the book is date stamped. When the book is returned, the process is reversed and the ticket is transferred to the book, before it is returned to the shelves.

However, this system, for us, had several drawbacks.

1 Until the book was returned, it was not possible to tell whether it was overdue, especially since the upper school had no library lesson and, therefore, there was no opportunity to keep track of the time a book had been out.

2 At times, the tickets kept on the counter were interfered with. Thus, people only apparently held books, or tickets were removed from the pockets.

3 From time to time large numbers of ticket pockets and their contents were accidentally tipped or dropped onto the floor, resulting in lots of loose tickets and no owners.

4 Whenever all the books were called in, for example for a stock-check, there would always be a number of students who would deny having the books, then or ever. Because of **2** and **3** above it was often difficult to insist that the student was at fault.

5 Reserving a book was a problem, partly because no single person had a complete overview of the operation of the system. We found ourselves having to check returned books against a reservation list which had to be continually updated and which proved time consuming. Because of problem

1 above, when a book might not be returned for weeks, a borrower might have to wait a very long time before the reserved book appeared.

After the Computer

The computerised system was considered first of all as a means of overcoming problem **5**, the reservation of books, although it was soon realised that such a system could overcome many of the other problems as well.

A program which would allow us to do the following things was duly prepared:

A To let the librarian know who has a book out at any one time by providing a typed list, which includes a code reference to the book. This allows the librarian to tell an individual which book he/she has (Fig. 12.3).

B To give a complete list of overdue books and the names/forms of the students holding them (Fig. 12.4). It is also possible to request a list of overdue books for any one form (Fig. 12.5).

C To let the librarian know who has a particular book out (Fig. 12.6).

This is useful for making reservations, and for returning lost books to the students who have them out. Students who lose books do not always ask the librarian if one has been handed in; they simply accept the fact that the book is lost. At the same time, under the old system, the librarian who receives a lost book doesn't know who to return it to without checking the students' ticket pockets (about 700).

The books are identified by their accession number (each new book is given a new number indicating that it was the 90th, 91st, 92nd book, and so on, to be put into the library). This number is on the catalogue card and recorded in an accession register.

When a student takes a book out, the following information is typed into the computer:

1 Date taken out.
2 House/Form number code (e.g. 2PA11)
3 Accession number.

The computer stores this information.

When a book is returned, the accession number is typed into the computer and this information is deleted from the records.

At any time, the librarian can ask who has book (identified by its accession number), who has a book and what, and who has an overdue book.

Because the computer is not readily accessible, and other demands are made on it during the day, the data described above is recorded on sheets (Fig. 12.7) and the information is typed into the computer at the end of each day.

Undoubtedly the system would be improved if there was a terminal on-site to dispense with the time lag between data collection and typing the information into the computer. At the same time, the possibility of error would be reduced since the data would be handled only once instead of twice.

```
ORIEL GRAMMAR LIBRARY OPERATIONS SCHOOL SYSTEM (LOSS)
========================================================

TYPE TODAY'S DATE:-280678

WHAT DO?:-CHECKFORM:3PA:00

   THE FOLLOWING BOOKS ON LOAN TO FORM 3PA

   PUPIL.NO.        ACC.NO.        DUE IN.
   ---------        -------        -------

   20               03932          09/06/78
   15               07179          27/06/78
   15               07239          09/06/78
   21               07263          09/06/78
   05               07315          05/07/78
   24               07512          09/06/78
   30               07529          27/06/78
   34               07594          27/06/78
   34               07608          27/06/78
   10               07795          09/06/78
   17               08157          05/07/78
   21               08246          27/06/78
   27               08251          05/07/78
   32               08255          05/07/78
   27               08263          09/06/78
   26               08506          27/06/78
   18               08835          09/06/78
   07               08878          27/06/78
   09               08957          05/07/78
   09               08963          05/07/78
   14               09025          05/07/78
   11               09068          05/07/78
   12               09382          09/06/78
   16               09395          09/06/78
   17               09429          05/07/78
   08               09457          27/06/78
   32               09597          09/06/78
   28               09616          09/06/78
   15               09630          05/07/78
   14               09635          09/06/78
   13               09647          27/06/78
   13               09666          09/06/78
   02               09675          09/06/78
   04               09720          05/07/78
   35               09739          27/06/78
   30               10023          27/06/78

FINISHED.OK.
```

Fig 12.3

```
ORIEL GRAMMAR LIBRARY OPERATIONS SCHOOL SYSTEM (LOSS)
=======================================================

TYPE TODAY'S DATE:-280678

WHAT DO?:-OVERDUE:ALL

THE FOLLOWING BOOKS ARE OVERDUE:-

ACC.NO.        FORM           PUPIL NO.       DATE DUE IN
-------        ----           ---------       -----------

01006          1GR            09              27/06/78

01445          2GR            12              27/06/78

01581          2GR            19              27/06/78

03790          1GR            31              09/06/78

03932          3PA            20              09/06/78

04118          1PE            29              09/06/78

04156          2GR            08              20/06/78

04370          2GR            04              20/06/78

04434          1PE            22              09/06/78

04638          1GR            32              09/06/78

04731          2GR            22              09/06/78

04844          1PA            10              09/06/78

04883          1GR            32              27/06/78

05000          2GR            12              27/06/78

05030          2GR            09              09/06/78

05160          3FA            33              09/06/78

05234          2PA            04              27/06/78

05513          1PA            07              09/06/78

05706          3PE            14              19/06/78

05742          1PA            13              09/06/78

05748          2PA            08              27/06/78

05871          1GR            21              09/06/78

06017          2PA            27              09/06/78
```

Fig 12.4

```
ORIEL GRAMMAR LIBRARY OPERATIONS SCHOOL SYSTEM (LOSS)
=====================================================

TYPE TODAY'S DATE:-280678

WHAT DO?:-OVERDUE:3PA

THE FOLLOWING BOOKS ARE OVERDUE:-

ACC.NO.         FORM          PUPIL NO.       DATE DUE IN
-------         ----          ---------       -----------

03932           3PA           20              09/06/78

07179           3PA           15              27/06/78

07239           3PA           15              09/06/78

07263           3PA           21              09/06/78

07512           3PA           24              09/06/78

07529           3PA           30              27/06/78

07594           3PA           34              27/06/78

07608           3PA           34              27/06/78

07795           3PA           10              09/06/78

08246           3PA           21              27/06/78

08263           3PA           27              09/06/78

08506           3PA           26              27/06/78

08835           3PA           18              09/06/78

08878           3PA           07              27/06/78

09382           3PA           12              09/06/78

09395           3PA           16              09/06/78

09457           3PA           08              27/06/78

09597           3PA           32              09/06/78

09616           3PA           28              09/06/78

09635           3PA           14              09/06/78

09647           3PA           13              27/06/78

09666           3PA           13              09/06/78

09675           3PA           02              09/06/78

09739           3PA           35              27/06/78

10023           3PA           30              27/06/78

FINISHED.OK.
```

Fig 12.5

Fig 12.6

ORIEL GRAMMAR LIBRARY OPERATIONS SCHOOL SYSTEM (LOSS)

TYPE TODAY'S DATE: ← 280678

WHAT DO?: → CHECKBOOK:09647

BOOK WITH ACC. NO. OF 09647:-
ON LOAN TO NO. 13 IN FORM 3PA
DUE BACK ON 27/06/78

FINISHED.OK.

LIBRARY DATA COLLECTION
SHEET NUMBER 30

DATE 10-4-78

BOOKS OUT

ACC. NO.	FORM NO.	PUPIL NO.
08246	3 PA	2 1
09992	3 PA	1 3
09770	2 GR	0 2
09765	2 GR	0 2
10204	2 GR	1 9
08931	2 GR	0 5
08935	1 FA	1 5

DATE ON STAMP 24-4-78

BOOKS IN

ACC. NO.
07529
10023
10216
09635
09425
08484
05234
10632
09534

Fig 12.7

Operation of the System

1 The ticket pocket system continues to work. This provides a very useful visual check and it is necessary for working the reservation system.

2 Each student in each form is given a number. The numbers usually run from 1–32. On each student's ticket pocket is recorded his/her name, form/house, and computer number. The four house names are abbreviated so that

Paget becomes PA
Grenfell becomes GR
Perebourne becomes PE
Fastolf becomes FA

Examples

A first-year form—Paget House

Name	Form	House	Form Number
Mary Green	1	PA	1
Jill Jones	1	PA	2
Jenny Smith	1	PA	3

A second-year form—Perebourne

Peter Able	2	PE	18
Tim Brown	2	PE	19
Bruce Field	2	PE	20
Brian Hall	2	PE	21

A list of these names and numbers is kept by the librarian and posted at the service desk.

The code (e.g. 2PE 18) is used to identify to the computer a student and for the librarian to identify that student from the computer printout.

The Reservation System

RESERVATION CARD
Acc. No.
Form
Number
Held by
Form
Number

Fig 12.8

In order to reserve a book, the following process is followed.

The student consults the catalogue cards to see if the library has the book. On the catalogue card is recorded the accession number. This number is noted, and a reservation card (Fig. 12.8) is completed. This entails filling in the first three items: the accession number of the book (Acc. No), the student form (e.g. 2 PA), and that student's number in the form.

On receipt of the reservation card, the librarian makes the following request of the computer: "Who has book accession number 9647?" It will respond by explaining that the book is not on loan or will give the number, year group, and form of the borrower (Fig. 12.6).

The librarian fills in the lower half of the reservation ticket and places the card in the ticket pocket of the student who holds the book. When the book is returned the librarian will see the reservation when replacing the ticket in the book. The book is put on a reservation shelf to await collection.

Meanwhile, the reservation card is put in the ticket pocket of the student who reserved the book, so that, when the student inquires about the return of the book, the ticket pocket can be consulted, or it can be pointed out that the book is available during a transaction concerning another book.

Should a number of students reserve a popular book, it is a case of first come, first served. The process, however, is the same and can take account of any number requesting the book.

Example

1   Reservation card submitted (by a 2nd Person).
2   The computer is asked who has book number, e.g. 3610.
3   Computer response, e.g. 4 PA 2.
4   The reserved ticket is put in the ticket pocket of 4 PA 2.

(But a reservation card is already there.) The Second card is marked 2nd—a third would be marked 3rd, and so on—and both cards (1st and 2nd) are left in 4 PA 2 ticket pocket.

5   When the book is returned, both cards are put in the ticket pocket of the first student to reserve the book and when that student takes the book out, the student's reservation card is destroyed, leaving the second card, When the book is returned, the remaining reservation card is put into that student's ticket pocket to show that the book is now available.

13 The Computer/User Interface

Even to experienced terminal users, small operational problems do present serious difficulties. Usually there are ways, if you know how, to resurrect a program that has crashed. If not, then the program can always be restarted. But for inexperienced users any break in the expected program sequence can be confusing and cause dissatisfaction, even if the user survives to finish the program. Often the programmer sees no difficulty in his/her program, the routines and responses seem obvious, but for someone not so familiar with the program there may be many apparent options where the programmer has intended only one. Also, the way in which the program handles its user can have importance, in prompting responses, suggesting alternatives, or just being friendly. It is this meeting of user and program that we have referred to, as have others, as the computer/user interface.

Techniques to produce the smooth running of a program can be employed to handle all situations except machine failure and line errors (caused by the bad transfer of information), and interruptions such as these are more likely on time-sharing telephone systems. It is not necessary to provide program "traps" but it is desirable; the resulting program is better in use. Sometimes quite simple programs become much more complex once checks are inserted after all the input statements in the program. Careful thought is required to decide which is the best way to inform the user of the alternatives. We feel it is desirable to produce a booklet which provides such information as well as forewarning the user of the output that is produced.

The programs included in this book use a number of techniques, some quite simple, others not so. They include amongst others:

DRAKE The student responses are checked, and CON for continue.

GAS Student responses are checked and certain values are excluded from the program.

CHEM The responses to certain questions are checked, and all input is taken as character, with numerical values being converted from character.

MENU Student responses are checked; correction facility.

VERB AXA for ending the run at any stage.

CLDP A check for misspelling enables the student to repeat an answer if only a few letters are incorrect or the correct letters are in the wrong order.

JOEL   "Menu" of available files, instructions can be requested to avoid lengthy repetitions.

POPULATION   Checks made for suitable range of values for growth rate.

In all cases the aim is to produce a program which will handle any data that is input to it, and which continues running with appropriate comments. Hopefully, a student will be able to use the program without being overseen by the teacher. The programs presented here may not trap all the eventualities, it is difficult to do so, but we have reached a compromise which is acceptable to us. We have tried to demonstrate a range of techniques without making the programs too complex. With experience we now regard the computer/user interface with more importance and try to make the programs self-sufficient.

Computer Conversations

Inevitably, the dialogue between the student and the computer develops into a conversation, and consequently the computer, or rather the program, takes on a personality. This can be favourable or otherwise in its effect on the student. We give two short excerpts to illustrate just what is possible. The student's thoughts are given in brackets.

WHICH FACILITY ?
←

(What do we do now! Lets try typing A.)

← A LINE ERROR

(Hello, what's this? Could try A again.)

← A
WRONG DATA TYPE
←

(Better try a number I suppose.)

← 1
FACILITY 1, HAVE YOU READ THE INSTRUCTIONS ?
←

(No I haven't, better say no.)

← NO
DO YOU REQUIRE HELP ?
←

(Well, yes I do.)

```
←YES
SORRY, NO HELP AVAILABLE FOR FACILITY 1
WHICH FACILITY ?
←
```

(Here we go again. Let's try 2.)

```
←2 SSDDFERTY BREAK IN
BREAK AT LINE 90
←
```

(What do we do now? Try 2 again?)

```
←2
ILLEGAL COMMAND
←2
ILLEGAL COMMAND
←3
ILLEGAL COMMAND
etc.
```

Computers can be polite, and helpful as well.

```
PLEASE TYPE IN YOUR NAME
←JOHN
HELLO, JOHN. HOPE YOU FIND THIS PROGRAM USEFUL.
HAVE YOU READ THE INSTRUCTIONS ?(YES OR NO)
←NO
WOULD YOU LIKE THE INSTRUCTIONS PRINTED ?(YES OR NO)
←NO
O.K., JOHN. WE'LL START
THE FACILITIES ARE NUMBERED 1 TO 5. TYPE
THE FACILITY YOU REQUIRE.
←A
PLEASE TYPE A NUMBER 1–5, JOHN
←1
FACILITY 1
etc.
```

The first example is a situation that can all too easily arise. It is the programmer's responsibility to avoid such confrontations. Tenuous telephone links do have problems that the programmer can do little to overcome, but microcomputers are free from these. The program should be self-contained so that the student can be left with the minimum of oversight.

Converting Alphanumeric Input to Numeric

Some versions of Basic include automatic checks on data that is input during the running of a program. For example, if two data items are expected and only one is provided, then the second is requested before the program continues. Also, if three items are provided then a phrase such as "extra lost" is printed and the program proceeds using the first two input values.

The input statement has to specify the type of data that is expected, either numeric or character string. When the wrong type of data is provided then some versions of Basic will give a warning and ask for the correct type before proceeding. However, other versions of Basic do not do this and the program terminates because there is an error in the data type. Inexperienced users of packages can easily make this kind of error, O (letter) for 0 (zero), for example, and the program termination prevents smooth running.

An example of how this can be avoided is provided in the program CHEM. Here input data is taken as being character, so that a number or a letter can be typed in without error. The character is then converted to a numeric value. To do this two string handling functions are used. One is VAL, and it is used as in

1000 LET J = VAL(J£)

In the computer's code each character has its own internal value. The function VAL uses this value. If J£ is a character string then its value is the value of the first character. The characters 0–9 have the numeric values 0–9 as well; letters and special characters have higher values. If the number provided by the student is only one digit long (i.e. 0–9), then this is all that is needed, but if it is 10, 11, 12 then a test is required to see if the character string is two characters long.

1010 IF LEN(J£)<2 THEN 1030

The function LEN(J£) takes the value of the number of characters in J£ i.e. if J£ = "RED" then LEN(J£) = 3. If the length of the string is greater than or equal to 2 then the value of the first two characters is calculated.

1020 LET J = J∗10 + VAL(J£[2,2])

J∗10 is the value of the first character multiplied by 10, because it is now the tens digit, and added to it is the units digit VAL(J£[2,2]). The VAL function takes the value of the part of J£ starting at the second character and finishing at the second character, i.e. the second character: Some examples of how this works are given here.

Character string	Numeric value in CHEM
6	6
A	33
ABC	$33 \times 10 + 34 = 364$
1	1
12	$1 \times 10 + 2 = 12$
12ABCH	$1 \times 10 + 2 = 12$

If there are more than two characters then only the first two are considered.

Once the value J has been calculated it has to be checked to see if it is in the usable range.

1030 IF J<1 OR J>20 THEN 980

Line 1020 is the invitation to type in a chemical number which is repeated if the number is inappropriate. Chemical numbers are only in the range 1 to 20. A similar process occurs when the test number is chosen

```
1050 PRINT "WHICH TEST DO YOU WANT TO DO ?";
1060 INPUT I£
1070 LET I = VAL(I£)
1080 IF LEN(I£)<2 THEN 1100
1090 LET I = I*10 + VAL(I£[2,2])
1100 IF I = 0 THEN 1160        An inference is to be made.
1110 IF I = 99 THEN 1220       Student wishes to end.
1120 IF I<1 OR I>11 THEN 1050  No such test number.
```

However, as was mentioned earlier in the description of CHEM, if the programmer is certain that the student will use only numbers for input then this "character conversion" is unnecessary and the program becomes much simpler. The checks on the value of the test number would still be needed.

Checking Input Data for a Range of Values

Sometimes the model on which a program is based can not be complete; that is, some situations have to be excluded. Two such examples are the French verbs chosen in VERB, and the formula used in GAS. Originally, VERB was intended to allow students to practise any regular French verbs. A list of suitable verbs from which the student might choose was provided, but a facility was included in the program to accept any regular French verb whether in the list or not. Included in the program was a list of irregular or unacceptable verbs. The verb chosen was checked against these and if the verb did not appear on the list it was accepted. It soon became clear that a definitive list of irregular present tense verbs was impossible to construct and that the allowance of any verb (based on a series of checks for the length of the word and whether it had an IR/ER/RE ending) was more of a programming achievement than a useful facility. The decision was taken to restrict the allowable verbs to 5 of each type, this being a generous number of verbs to practise on.

The formula that is used in GAS is not an exact model, but it gives a good approximation within a range of values. The inappropriate values must be excluded from the calculations. This is done at two places in the program.

```
380 PRINT "TEMPERATURE IN CELSIUS"
390 INPUT T
400 LET T = T + 273
410 IF T> = L THEN 440
420 PRINT "TEMPERATURES BELOW";(L - 273);"ARE UNRELIABLE"
430 GOTO 380
```

If unsuitable values of T are input, then the message is printed and T is asked for again. Later the volume values are checked.

```
490 PRINT "INPUT VOLUME";
500 INPUT V
510 IF V> =0.5E-1 THEN 540
520 PRINT "VOLUMES BELOW 0.05 ARE UNRELIABLE"
530 GOTO 490
```

Again a new value of V is requested if necessary.

A similar programming technique is used when certain values have a special significance. The program MENU takes its data in numeric form and checks for certain values. One hundred and forty nine food items are referenced in the program by code numbers. The code 151 is used to signal the end of the input menu and 152 enables the student to abort the menu entry. Checks are made at two points.

```
180 and 510   INPUT Q(I, 1)
190 and 520   IF Q(I, 1) = 151 THEN 270
200 and 530   IF Q(I, 1) = 152 THEN 990
```

Later a wider check takes place.

```
1100 IF Q(I, 1)>0 AND Q(I, 1)<150 AND Q(I, 1) = INT(Q(I, 1)) THEN 1140
1110 PRINT Q(I, 1); " IS AN UNKNOWN CODE. TYPE CODE, WEIGHT AGAIN"
```

The food code is checked to make sure that it lies in the range 1 to 149 inclusive, and also that it is given as a whole number (integer). If it is, then the integer part of the number is equal to the number itself, e.g.

integer part of 5.6 is 5
but the integer part of 7 is 7

As the program is run it may become necessary to check, or to change, the value of some of the input items. We run this program on a teletype linked by telephone to a remote computer, and sometimes, because of a faulty signal, it is uncertain just what values have been accepted by the program. This doesn't happen very often, but it needs to be handled when it does. For this reason facilities are built into the program to enable the student to check any input items, and to change them if necessary. Further checks are made on the answers to the questions, which can be repeated.

```
270 PRINT "DO YOU WISH TO CHECK ANY ITEMS ?(YES/NO);
280 INPUT C£
290 IF C£< >"YES" AND C£< >"NO" THEN 270
300 IF C£ = "NO" THEN 380
310 PRINT "TYPE ITEM NO. ";
320 INPUT C
330 IF C>O AND C<I AND C = INT(C) THEN 360
```

The last line makes sure that the item number is allowable.

Again questions are asked and the answers examined.

```
380 PRINT "DO YOU WISH TO CHANGE THE MENU ?(YES/NO)";
390 INPUT A£
400 IF A£<>"YES" AND A£<>"NO" THEN 380
410 IF A£<>"YES" THEN 670
420 LET N=I
430 PRINT "TYPE IN ITEM NO. ";
440 INPUT I
450 IF I>0 AND I<N+1 AND I=INT(I) AND I<50 THEN 480
460 PRINT "INCORRECT ITEM NO. ";
470 GOTO 430
```

Whenever a question is asked, the student is prompted to provide an answer which the program can handle. If another answer is given, then the question is asked again. To leave the program, a pair of questions must be answered in the manner indicated by the prompts.

```
990 PRINT "DO YOU REQUIRE A NEW MENU ?(YES/NO)";
```

and

```
1030 PRINT "DOES ANYONE ELSE WISH TO USE MENU ?(YES/NO)";
```

There is one form of check which is not made in this program. It would be possible to take all the input as character and convert the numeric values from these, ensuring that any number or letter typed in would be accepted. Most versions of Basic do check the data type (numeric or character) and give a message if there is an error. Southampton BASIC then asks for the data item to be typed in again. With this safeguard it is not essential to put a check in the program.

The Student's Control of the Program

Although the computer dictates the sequence of events there are occasions when the student can be allowed to have some say in the proceedings. If the student is asked to provide an answer to a question or to perform a task before continuing, then it can be useful to let the student say when he/she is ready to carry on. If mistakes are made, and it is inevitable that they will be made, or if for some reason the program has to be terminated before it is complete, then there needs to be a clear way to come out of the program. The first of these two examples of student control can be illustrated with reference to the historical package DRAKE, the second occurs in several of the programs but VERB is used here.

At a number of places during the run of DRAKE, the student is asked to plot positions on a map in the booklet provided to accompany the program.

A Captain's Log also has to be completed by the student, while the program is running, providing a record of the events on the voyage. When the instruction PLOT/LOG is issued it is accompanied by the message TYPE CON TO CONTINUE. A check on the input is used to repeat the message if anything other than CON is typed. The student can then perform the PLOT/LOG without the pressure of responding to the computer, or trying not to miss further printed information, and only continuing when ready to do so.

The program VERB may be used for practice with French verbs, and if the student decides that he/she has done enough, then in order to exit from the program the student may type AXA in reply to any of the questions asked. Whenever this response is given the program is directed to its end sequence which prints out the student's score and then stops. There may be good reason to suggest that all the programs used have the same pattern of responses for leaving a program, so that experience of the computer dialogue can be built up.

The programs in this book do not exhibit uniformity, but use a number of different techniques. For example, the teletype version of CHEM uses the code number 99, the micro version uses STOP, and MENU requires the food code 152. GAS needs STOP to be typed when a new gas is asked for and GRAD asks the user a number of questions on the route to its exit. The student, of course, must be informed of these devices and the information can be provided in the student booklet, or as instructions printed during the program run.

Use of Scoring Systems

The element of competition arises quite naturally in the program packages. Whether the student competes against other students or against the computer is a decision for the instigator of the program, as is the form of scoring and the level of marks awarded. The competition can be "friendly", with the computer giving a nominal score at the end of a run, or it can be serious, with marks being stored away for reference by the teacher to check the student's progress. Whatever use is made of the score the effect is to encourage the student to take the questions and decisions in the program seriously.

In DRAKE the student chooses answers from options provided. The marks are awarded on the basis that Drake's actual decisions should score the highest, not that there are "best" decisions. The scoring in VERB is much simpler; a mark is credited for every correct answer, and the number correct out of the total attempted is printed at the end of the run. These scores are for the student's benefit, not necessarily for the teacher.

The testing package STUDTEST gives the student's score at the end of the test and also inserts this score in a student file. The student file can be examined for the class scores or for an individual's progress.

**The Polite
Computer**

It has already been mentioned that the tone of the conversation that occurs between the computer and the user can be off-putting, especially when the user has little experience of computer packages. Often the computer has to acknowledge an incorrect answer and inform the student how to correct the error. It is the intention of the packages that the student should gain some benefit from the exercise and so the computer responses should be as helpful as possible. It is also possible to let the student down gently. For example, in the program DRAKE the choice of answer (A) to DECISION 1 produces the response

(A) PROBABLY AN UNWISE DECISION . . .

and then the "correct" course of action is explained.

Another example of the correction dialogue can be seen in the program VERB. The response to an incorrect input answer is, for example,

INCORRECT. REMEMBER,
THE ELLE ENDING FOR ER VERBS IS E.
TRY AGAIN.

The student receives some assistance and is then allowed to answer again. Only if this second answer is incorrect is the correct answer given to the student. For example,

INCORRECT.
IT SHOULD BE PORTE.

A further and more complicated illustration of this technique concerns checks for misspellings in the vocabulary program CLDP, which will be described in greater detail later. This program also includes a number of different responses, instead of just one, to give variety to the computer dialogue. Replies to correct and incorrect answers will be drawn from a stock of responses. For example, WELL DONE; THAT'S RIGHT; BAD LUCK. THE ENGLISH WORD IS —; SORRY. INCORRECT. — IS THE ENGLISH WORD.

**Options for
Answers**

To ask the student a blunt question is to invite a multitude of answers. Of course the program can be made to examine the responses for all reasonable answers, but this may be impractical, and there may be some unreasonable answers. One way to remove this problem is to prompt the answer, either directly or indirectly, by the way in which the question is phrased. For example, in GAS the question

CONTINUE ?

invites the answer YES or NO. In CHEM the prompt is given.

DO YOU WISH TO TRY ANOTHER CHEMICAL (YES OR NO) ?

The student's reply is checked and the question is repeated if it is neither YES nor NO.

A similar situation arises in DRAKE, when after the scene has been set the decision point is reached. There must be an infinite number of ways that the student could express his/her views, but attention is narrowed to several possible courses of action and the student is permitted to choose from them. The student can then reply, for example, A, B or C, and the programmer's task is much simpler. The multiple choice answer technique seems to be the ideal computer solution, even when numerical answers are asked for, and many students are familiar with this form of questioning anyway.

The Presentation of Output

An element of the programs which has immediate impact on the user is the layout of the output data. It certainly helps the user if the important information is easily readable amongst all the output. On paper a long printout might be inconvenient if it has to be searched through repeatedly. Blank lines printed between groups of data, or underlining, or rows of asterisks to break up continuous output, are used in some of our programs. In MENU blank lines are put either side of the menu table, the screen is blanked to focus the students attention in VERB, and underlining is used under the column headings in GRAD.

The visual effect is, perhaps, even more important in programs to be run on a visual display screen. A Research Machines 380Z, for example, displays on 24 lines of printing at a time, and instruction displays or tables have to be designed with this in mind. The package POPULATION produces a table and this has been boxed in to separate it from the dialogue. While the student is waiting for a particularly long search when using the information retrieval program JOEL a message

```
* * * * * * * * * * * * * * * * * * *
* SEARCH IN PROGRESS *
* * * * * * * * * * * * * * * * * * *
```

informs him just what is happening. The search is terminated by the message

FINISHED

A great deal of programming time can be taken up with lining up tables and ensuring that words are not broken at the end of lines. Obviously the TAB and PRINT USING instructions play an important part in output layout.

Another problem was encountered in the design of the animation in MATRIX. The timing of the sequence contributes greatly to the overall effect, and delay loops were used. For example

```
90 FOR J = 1 TO 2000:NEXT J
```

gives the student time to read the instructions.

During the matrix multiplication process, the numbers involved are moved about the screen and the arithmetic symbols placed in position. The speed at which this happens can be varied to suit the programmer's tastes, and those of the students. Again FOR ... NEXT loops are used, and for convenience are put on the same line of the program (this is allowed in RM 380Z 12K BASIC).

Deciding on the point at which running instructions are given in the program is not always easy. At the beginning seems an obvious answer, but sometimes they need to be repeated. When the output is on a continuous roll of paper then the student can turn back to instructions that have already been given. On a visual display screen this can not be done. Instead a provision can be built into the program to enable the student to ask for instructions at any point. Also, where the student has options these may be requested at any time, in the form of a "menu".

In the program JOEL, information can be retrieved from a number of different data files, and one has to be specified. After each enquiry is complete the program can return to the list of data files and their code numbers so that another choice can be made, or it can continue with the chosen file.

When the microcomputer version of CHEMICAL runs, the student will probably not remember all the tests that are displayed on the screen at the start of the run. To help, the "menu" of tests can be requested at any point, and then the testing can be continued. Of course, the information can be presented in a booklet for reference, but the immediacy of a screen display does have advantages.

Learning French Vocabulary

The learning of French words for everyday objects can be accomplished in many ways, the use of a computer being just one more. It can, however, offer some advantages which may not be possible with conventional methods. When the student comes to test his/her learning, the computer will respond immediately to answers, offering a limited amount of help and as a last resort the correct answer. This immediate response obliges the student to think through each answer and to determine whether it is correct at the time of testing. The computer can also act as a new stimulus for vocabulary learning, while at the same time allow the teacher to be employed with other students not involved with vocabulary testing. The package uses a technique often employed in language teaching.

The Package: CLDP This consists of a picture (Fig. 13.1), which would be given to the student perhaps for homework, with the directive to look up as many French words as possible relating to objects in the picture. When ready to attempt the test, the student is given a short passage which has certain words omitted and a number appearing in the spaces. The student reads the passage and then attempts the vocabulary test. The computer asks the student to supply each word in turn for the corresponding numbered space. At the end of the test the computer supplies the student with a score in the form of a percentage. If the wrong word is supplied at the first attempt, the student is informed of the English word for the object and given a second opportunity to supply the correct word. If still unable to produce the correct word, the student is told what the word should be

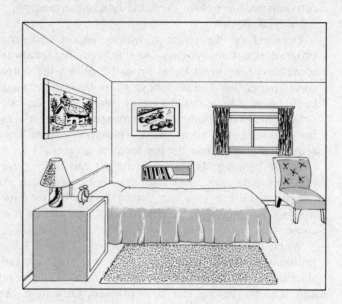

Fig 13.1

The Computer/User Interface

Any form of test which does not operate on a multiple choice basis presents the problem of trying to anticipate the possible answers that may be supplied by the student. In the French vocabulary test it is hoped that the correct word will be offered by the student but some attempt must be made to anticipate incorrect spelling of the correct solution. One way would be to try and include as many as possible incorrect spellings, within reason, of the correct word and then compare the student's answer with each in turn. The compilation of this list of incorrect spellings could be very time consuming and may be incomplete. The program CLDP which administers the test approaches the incorrect spelling problem in a rather more analytical way.

It makes the assumption that incorrect spelling results from four possibilities:

1) Adding extra letters
2) Omitting letters
3) Reversing two letters
4) An incorrect letter (e.g. GARCONS AND GARSONS).

In 1) and 2), the computer takes the word supplied by the student and the correct word read from a data statement and determines which has more letters. For words under seven letters in length, only a 1 letter difference is allowed and for words containing more than six letters a 1 or 2 letter difference is allowed. In the case of 1 extra letter, it removes 1 letter at a time from the longest word and compares what is left with the other word. In the case of 2 extra letters, it removes all combinations of two letters from the longest word and then compares each with the shorter word. The above method will therefore check the four possibilities of incorrect spelling caused by adding or omitting 1 or 2 letters. For case 3), if, after checking the lengths of the two words, it is found they have the same number of letters but are not the same word, then the computer checks to see if two of the letters are reversed. It works its way from left to right reversing two letters at a time and compares the result each time with the word offered by the student. In case 4), where the two words are of the same length, the computer takes the correct word from the data statement and replaces each letter in turn by all the letters of the alphabet and compares each possibility with the student's answer.

The Program Instructions for Checking Incorrect Spelling

The character string handling of ICL–CES BASIC enables both dissection and concatenation of a string variable to be performed. Most of the checking for incorrect spelling is achieved by use of the following statements.

SEG$(A$,N)   The segment of A$ from the Nth character to the end.
SEG$(A$,N,M) The segment of A$ from the Nth character to the Mth character.
SUB$(A$,N)   The Nth character of A$.
SUB$(A$,N,M) The substring of A$ of length M characters from the Nth.

Example: Reversing two letters

(*Note.* The range of variable names [e.g. A$,B$,C,D] can be increased by placing a number after the letter.)

If A$ is the correct word and happens to be TABLEAUX
and the loop counter I has the value 5:

```
8210 LET Z1$ = SUB$(A$,I)           Z1$ would contain E
8220 LET Z2$ = SUB$(A$,I + 1)       Z2$ would contain A
8230 LET D1$ = SUB$(A$,1,I – 1)&Z2$&Z1$&SEG$(A$,I + 2)
```

giving

D1$ = TABL &A & E & UX

D1$ would then contain TABLAEUX because the & symbol joins the character strings together. The computer would then compare D1$ with D$ (the student's response) and, if they matched, would inform the student of incorrect spelling.

The program also uses the statements LEN(A$) and CHR$(V) and they have the following significance:

LEN(A$) The number of characters in A$.
CHR$(V) The character whose character code is V (for the alphabet A = 33, B = 34 through to Z = 58)

Example: Replacing a letter

8010 LET P1 = LEN(A$)   The numeric variable P1 would contain the number 8 for A$ = TABLEAUX.
8280 LET D1$ = SUB$(A$,1,W − 1)&CHR$(V)&SEG$(A$,W + 1)

If A$ = TABLEAUX and W = 4 and V = 41, then D1$ would contain

D1$ = TAB & I & EAUX = TABIEAUX

D1$ would contain A$ apart from the letter L being replaced by I.

Program Summary

10–86	Student's instructions.
90–100	Ask for and accept student's name.
110–150	Ask for, accept and find required set of words.
160–190	Read word in English and French.
220	Ask for student's answer.
250–300	Accept answer and check for Q and AXA.
320	Is the answer correct ?
330	Enter subroutine for spelling errors.
360–565	Print responses.
590–660	Adjust scoring.
670	Return to beginning of loop for next word.
675–690	Print student score.
700–830	Select data words.
1000–1030	Data words.
8000–9800	Subroutine for spelling checks.
8030	Check for correct length of answer.
8040, 8050	Check for 1 letter extra or missing.
8060	Check for less than 7 letters.
8070, 8080	Check for 2 letters extra or missing.
8200–8250	Check for reversal of two letters.
8260–8310	Check for one letter wrong.
8400–8660	Find extra or missing letter.
8800–9080	Find extra or missing 2 letters.
9200–9250	Error message, chance to have another go.
9800	Return from the subroutine.
9998–9999	End with message.

VOICI LA (1)......DE CHRISTOPHE. ELLE EST TRES BIEN
RANGEE. CHRISTOPHE A FAIT SON (2)......AVANT DE
PARTIR POUR L'ECOLE. LES (3)......SONT TIRES.
AU-DESSOUS DE LA FENETRE IL Y A UN (4)......
COMFORTABLE. IL Y A UN TAPIS SUR LE (5)......,
UNE ETAGERE AVEC DES (6)......ET UN (7)......SUR
CHAQUE MUR. DANS UN DES DEUX TABLEAUX ON VOIT
UNE MAISON AVEC UNE GRANDE (8)......SUR LE TOIT.
DANS L'AUTRE ON VOIT DEUX (9)......DE COURSE. A
COTE DU LIT SE TROUVE UNE TABLE DE NUIT SUR
LAQUELLE ON PEUT TROUVER UNE (10)......ET UN
REVEIL-MATIN. IL EST (11)......HEURES DE
L'APRES-MIDI. CHRISTOPHE VA BIENTOT RENTRER
DE L' (12)......

Fig 13.2 The passage with the words omitted

CLDP:
Sample Run

NOTE. IF YOU MAKE A MISTAKE TYPING IN AN ANSWER
OR YOU CHANGE YOUR MIND, WHEN THE NEXT ARROW
APPEARS, RETYPE YOUR ANSWER. IF YOU ARE HAPPY
WITH YOUR ANSWER THEN PRESS THE LETTER Q
AND THEN THE ACCEPT KEY.
'Q' IS NEXT TO THE ACCEPT KEY.

NOTE. IF YOU WISH TO STOP THE PROGRAM AT ANY TIME, TYPE
AXA WHEN AN ARROW APPEARS.
WHAT IS YOUR CHRISTIAN NAME?
← SID
WHICH SET? TYPE 1, 2, 3, 4, 5, 6 OR 7.
← 1
* * * * * * *

WHAT SHOULD 1 BE?
← CHAMBER
← Q
I THINK YOU MAY HAVE MADE A SPELLING MISTAKE SID.
HAVE ANOTHER TRY.
← CHAMBRE
← Q
CORRECT.
* * * * * * *

WHAT SHOULD 2 BE?
← LIT
← Q
THAT'S RIGHT.
* * * * * * *

WHAT SHOULD 3 BE?
← RIDEUAX
← Q
I THINK YOU MAY HAVE MADE A SPELLING MISTAKE SID.
HAVE ANOTHER TRY.
← RIDEAUX
← Q
WELL DONE!
* * * * * * *

WHAT SHOULD 4 BE?
← FAUTEIL
← Q
I THINK YOU MAY HAVE MADE A SPELLING MISTAKE SID.
HAVE ANOTHER TRY.
← FAUTEILLE
← Q
BAD LUCK. THE ENGLISH WORD IS ARMCHAIR.
TRY AGAIN.
← FAUTEIL
← FAUTEUIL
THAT'S RIGHT.
* * * * * * *

WHAT SHOULD 5 BE?
← PLANCHER
← Q
CORRECT.
* * * * * * *

WHAT SHOULD 6 BE?
← LIVRES
← Q
WELL DONE SID.
* * * * * * *

WHAT SHOULD 7 BE?
← TABLEAU
← Q
WELL DONE!
* * * * * * *

WHAT SHOULD 8 BE?
← CHIMNEEQ
← CHEMINEE
CORRECT.
* * * * * * *

WHAT SHOULD 9 BE?
← VOITURES
← Q
THAT'S RIGHT.
* * * * * * *

```
WHAT SHOULD 10 BE?
←LAMPE
←Q
THAT'S RIGHT.
*******

WHAT SHOULD 11 BE?
←QUATRE
←Q
CORRECT.
*******

WHAT SHOULD 12 BE?
←ECOLE
←Q
WELL DONE
```

PROJECT FINISHED. THANK YOU FOR TRYING SID.
YOUR MARK IS 93.75%.

Program Listing:
ICL-CES BASIC

Note If 7 pictures and 7 sets of words are to be used with the program, then the 12 French words and 12 English words for each set, must be inserted in the program as DATA statements. The words to set 2 must start at statement number 1100, set 3 at 1200, set 4 at 1300, and so on. The words to set 1 occur in statements 1000–1030 and can be used as an example for setting up the other sets.

```
10 PRINT "NOTE. IF YOU MAKE A MISTAKE TYPING IN AN ANSWER"
20 PRINT "     OR YOU CHANGE YOUR MIND,WHEN THE NEXT ARROW"
30 PRINT "     APPEARS,RETYPE YOUR ANSWER.IF YOU ARE HAPPY"
40 PRINT "     WITH YOUR ANSWER THEN PRESS THE LETTER Q"
50 PRINT "     AND THEN THE ACCEPT KEY."
55 PRINT "     'Q' IS NEXT TO THE ACCEPT KEY."
60 PRINT
70 PRINT "NOTE.IF YOU WISH TO STOP THE PROGRAM AT ANY TIME, TYPE"
80 PRINT "     AXA WHEN AN ARROW APPEARS."
85 PRINT
86 PRINT
90 PRINT "WHAT IS YOUR CHRISTIAN NAME?"
100 INPUT C$
105 IF C$="AXA" THEN 9998
110 PRINT "WHICH SET? TYPE 1, 2, 3, 4, 5, 6 OR 7."
130 INPUT X$
140 IF X$="AXA" THEN 9998
150 ON VAL(X$) GOTO 700,720,740,760,780,800,820
160 LET T=0
170 FOR U=1 TO 12
180 LET R=0
190 READ A$,B$
200 PRINT "*******"
210 PRINT
220 PRINT "WHAT SHOULD ";U;"BE?"
230 GOTO 250
240 LET R=1
250 INPUT D$
```

```
260 IF D$="AXA" THEN 9998
270 INPUT E$
290 IF E$="Q" THEN 310
300 LET D$=E$
310 LET M=0
320 IF D$=A$ THEN 360
330 GOSUB 8000
340 IF M=1 THEN 360
345 IF R=1 THEN 560
350 GOTO 450
360 ON U GOTO 370,390,410,390,370,430,410,370,390,390,370,410
370 PRINT "CORRECT."
380 GOTO 570
390 PRINT "THAT'S RIGHT."
400 GOTO 570
410 PPINT "WELL DONE!"
420 GOTO 570
430 PRINT "WELL DONE ";C$;"."
440 GOTO 570
450 ON U GOTO 490,490,460,520,490,520,520,490,520,490,460,490
460 PRINT "NO ";C$;". THAT'S WRONG."
470 PRINT "THE ENGLISH WORD IS ";B$;". TRY AGAIN."
480 GOTO 540
490 PRINT "SORRY. INCORRECT. ";B$;" IS THE ENGLISH WORD."
500 PRINT "HAVE ANOTHER GO."
510 GOTO 540
520 PRINT "BAD LUCK. THE ENGLISH WORD IS ";B$;"."
530 PRINT "TRY AGAIN."
540 IF R=1 THEN 560
550 GOTO 240
560 PRINT "WRONG. THE WORD IS ";A$;"."
565 GOTO 670
570 IF R=1 THEN 630
580 IF M=1 THEN 610
590 LET T=T+4
600 GOTO 670
610 LET T=T+3.5
620 GOTO 670
630 IF M=1 THEN 660
640 LET T=T+2
650 GOTO 670
660 LET T=T+1.5
670 NEXT U
675 PRINT
676 PRINT
680 PRINT "PROJECT FINISHED. THANK YOU FOR TRYING ";C$;"."
690 PRINT "YOUR MARK IS ";INT(T/48)*100;"%."
695 STOP
700 RESTORE 1000
710 GOTO 160
720 RESTORE 1100
730 GOTO 160
740 RESTORE 1200
750 GOTO 160
760 RESTORE 1300
770 GOTO 160
780 RESTORE 1400
790 GOTO 160
800 RESTORE 1500
810 GOTO 160
820 RESTORE 1600
830 GOTO 160
1000 DATA CHAMBRE,BEDROOM,LIT,BED,RIDEAUX,CURTAINS,FAUTEUIL,ARMCHAIR
1010 DATA PLANCHER,FLOOR,LIVRES,BOOKS,TABLEAU,PICTURE
1020 DATA CHEMINEE,CHIMNEY,VOITURES,CARS,LAMPE,LAMP
1030 DATA QUATRE,FOUR,ECOLE,SCHOOL
```

```
8000 LET M=0
8010 LET P1=LEN(A$)
8020 LET P2=LEN(D$)
8030 IF P1=P2 THEN 8200
8040 IF P1-P2=1 THEN 8400
8050 IF P1-P2=-1 THEN 8600
8060 IF LEN(A$)<7 THEN 8090
8070 IF P1-P2=2 THEN 8800
8080 IF P1-P2=-2 THEN 9000
8090 GOTO 9800
8200 FOR I=1 TO P1-1
8210 LET Z1$=SUB$(A$,I)
8220 LET Z2$=SUB$(A$,I+1)
8230 LET D1$=SUB$(A$,1,I-1)&Z2$&Z1$&SEG$(A$,I+2)
8240 IF D$=D1$ THEN 9200
8250 NEXT I
8260 FOR W=1 TO P1
8270 FOR V=33 TO 58
8280 LET D1$=SUB$(A$,1,W-1)&CHR$(V)&SEG$(A$,W+1)
8290 IF D1$=D$ THEN 9200
8300 NEXT V
8310 NEXT W
8320 GOTO 9800
8400 LET Y1$=A$
8410 LET Y2$=D$
8420 GOTO 8630
8600 LET Y1$=D$
8610 LET Y2$=A$
8620 LET P1=P2
8630 FOR J=1 TO P1
8640 LET D1$=SUB$(Y1$,1,J-1)&SEG$(Y1$,J+1)
8650 IF D1$=Y2$ THEN 9200
8660 NEXT J
8670 GOTO 9800
8800 LET Y1$=A$
8810 LET Y2$=D$
8820 GOTO 9030
9000 LET Y1$=D$
9010 LET Y2$=A$
9020 LET P1=P2
9030 FOR K=1 TO P1-1
9040 FOR L=K TO P1-1
9050 LET D1$=SUB$(Y1$,1,K-1)&SEG$(Y1$,K+1,L)&SEG$(Y1$,L+2)
9060 IF D1$=Y2$ THEN 9200
9070 NEXT L
9080 NEXT K
9090 GOTO 9800
9200 PRINT "I THINK YOU MAY HAVE MADE A SPELLING MISTAKE ";C$;"."
9210 PRINT "HAVE ANOTHER TRY."
9220 INPUT I$
9225 IF I$="AXA" THEN 9998
9226 INPUT J$
9227 IF J$="Q" THEN 9230
9228 LET I$=J$
9230 IF I$=A$ THEN 9250
9240 GOTO 9800
9250 LET M=1
9800 RETURN
9998 PRINT "PROGRAM STOPPED."
9999 END
```

14 Classroom and Computer Management

Class management will be affected by a number of factors:

1 Quantity of hardware available To a large degree the class management problems that arise stem from limited hardware. The use of some programs, for example drill exercises or instruction programs, can prove difficult to organise. If all of a class cannot have access to a running program at the same time it means that the teacher will have at least two groups to manage.

2 Quality of hardware available A terminal with only hard copy facilities may rule out the use of some programs by the whole class. Dependence on a visual display unit with no hard copy facility will in some cases affect the time taken to run a program because students have to copy data from the screen. The time factor is increased where each student has to run the program to obtain some data.

3 Access to hardware Do you have to move the hardware to the class, or do you move the class—or some part of it—to the hardware? Is the hardware in a reasonably sized room or in a restricted area?

4 The nature of the program Some programs determine the size of the group (where the group may be one person). Others are versatile in this respect, allowing use by individuals, small groups or large classes.

5 The user's familiarity with the computer If a student has not run a program before there will be a number of things that have to be explained. For example, that any user input has to be followed by pressing the ACCEPT/RETURN key, how to use the shift key (if that is necessary), how to change a response before the ACCEPT/RETURN key has been pressed.

6 The availability of supervision for the computer user/s The teacher's management burden can be alleviated considerably if another teacher can adopt this responsibility.

Given that limited hardware, access to it and the nature of the program all affect the number of users, there are several user arrangements to consider. The computer might be used by

1 Individuals. This would involve the use of the computer by only one or two students during a lesson, each working independently of the other and engaged in an activity which not all of the members of the class are expected to undertake.

2 Small groups of students who run a program without reference to the teacher.
3 Small groups in which the teacher is a participant.
4 A whole class which functions as a single unit under the direction of the teacher.
5 A whole class in which the students function as individuals, taking it in turns to run the program.

From the point of view of reducing the teacher's management problems, arrangement **4** offers the most easily controlled situation. The program CHEMICAL which has been run on a Research Machines 380Z using a large television screen lends itself well to a teacher-led discussion concerning the testing of an unknown substance and the deductive processes associated with making an inference. At the same time, it does mean that the students' direct contact with the computer, something which many people consider to be an important spin-off of computer-assisted learning, will be limited. CHEMICAL has certain advantages in this respect because it is a versatile program. It would be reasonable to expect students to be encouraged to run the program themselves sometime after the class lesson.

Although at first sight the prospect of individual class members running programs does not seem to be a viable proposition, there may well be opportunities to do this. It may be the case that one or two members of the class would benefit from drill exercises. In this event, little pressure would be put upon the resource, but it may mean that the student concerned will miss some other aspect of the work. Some teachers have expressed an interest in developing programs to assist in a remedial context where the group size is very small and where the problem of the rest of the class getting ahead does not exist. Another possibility is in the context of resource-based learning. In this situation the student might be encouraged to run a program which yields information or an experience which is pertinent to only his or her studies.

Arrangement **5,** where a whole class functions as individuals, is perhaps a more attractive prospect, but not without its difficulties. The program will need to demand a relatively limited input and student/computer dialogue. The output will also need to be limited and the overall running time brief. This will ensure that everyone can obtain some output during a lesson, perhaps a table of results printed on paper.

The use of small groups does, to some extent, overcome the problem of limited hardware, allows reasonable student contact with the computer, and of course encourages student interaction, often of a co-operative nature. It also creates problems. It is sometimes desirable that a group should not run a program in the presence of the rest of the class. The noise generated by discussion might prove to be a distraction to the others or they might simply "give the game away". Whatever the reason, it is possible that the class will have to be split. This raises the question of supervision. It may be difficult to arrange for the class and the computer group to be supervised simultaneously. Even if it is possible the teacher's attention may be split between setting up the exercise, briefing the computer users, and teaching the rest of the class. It doesn't follow that the problem cannot be overcome. But it is there to be solved.

The second problem that can arise from group work is the need to construct a program of work which will accommodate those who have not yet had a chance to run the program and those who have completed the exercise. DRAKE and VILLAGE were prepared for use by small groups, and the question of class management was approached differently in each case. Francis Drake was a topic which embraced the whole of the man's career. Because it was divided into a number of sub-topics and the students encouraged to work at their own speed, the members of the class were soon engaged at several points. The result was that a bottleneck was avoided at the point where the simulation was to be used. It meant that activities and supporting material had to be prepared well in advance and enough to cater for those in the habit of working fast. It was essentially a linear arrangement, with exercises both before and after the simulation.

An alternative scheme of work might be viewed as a circle composed of segments, each segment representing a different exercise and entry being possible at any point. Village was embedded in such a work program (Fig 14.1). It can be seen that a decision to allow small groups to run a program might have implications for the preparation of materials and lesson organisation beyond that required for the computer exercise itself.

Some computer exercises depend upon the student having been briefed by the teacher prior to the running of the program. Many programs will be self-contained in this respect but, where it is necessary, time has to be found to do the briefing, although the problem can sometimes be overcome by preparing booklets which serve this purpose. Where a large number of students are expected to run a program over a relatively short period of time, careful preparation and briefing will pay dividends. MENU and POPULATION are programs which might be used in this way. In both cases the class should be told what to expect, perhaps being given a short demonstration before being asked to run the program themselves. They should be familiarised with the aims of the project and the operational procedures. They must also know what is expected of them once they have obtained their results.

When running MENU there is a tremendous temptation to take advantage of all that newly realised computing power immediately. A more sensible approach would be to encourage the students to prepare a relatively modest menu at first. Unfamiliarity with the keyboard and operating procedures and lack of manual dexterity all serve to increase the time taken to complete a run. A large menu probably means a lot of impatient students waiting for their turn. The package POPULATION requires each student to run the program three times. It does not follow that these runs have to be completed one after the other. Each student should get one set of results and then go back to the computer on two more occasions. This ensures that everyone is involved as quickly as possible.

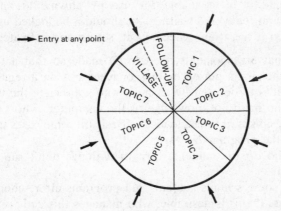

Entry at any point

Fig 14.1

A mode of operation that is often employed is that of batch processing. Here the demands of the users are specified on suitably prepared forms and these keyed in by one person and the results returned to the user. To do this effectively a printer is essential. In this way a user can take advantage of the program without having to queue to use the terminal. The requests of students can be taken in one lesson and the results returned in the next. It probably means that the processing will have to be done after school and this raises the questions of who should do it and how to ensure that the computer is free. From a class management point of view batch processing has certain attractions, but it also sacrifices an opportunity to use the computer exercise as a motivator.

Many computer exercises, especially the simulations, will have to be followed by a discussion between the students and the teacher. This will be done to establish that the aims of the package have been achieved. In some cases the aims of the package will only be achieved at this point, where students can compare their individual results, as in the case of GAS, and draw conclusions from their collected evidence. During the discussion the teacher should expect to develop some of the issues that have been raised and to clarify points which the students have had difficulty in understanding. The question arises as to how and when this discussion should take place. Should it be with every group as it finishes a run or should it be delayed until all the members of the class have run the program? If the whole class is involved in a simulation at the same time this question does not arise, but where it does the teacher is faced with another management problem which has to be solved.

In the light of the potential demands on the computer, it is plain to see that if these become substantial considerable attention has to be paid to managing the resource itself. Among the questions that will need to be answered are these:

1 Who is to be responsible for it in its various roles?
2 Where is it to be located?
3 Even if it is portable, is moving it around the school desirable?
4 What measures will need to be made for its security?

Should it be available for use by anyone at any time—sitting in a classroom ready and waiting—or should it be locked up so that when it is to be used it has to be wheeled out, set up and activated?

5 What arrangements need to be made so that a teacher can book the computer for a period or two, or reserve it on a regular basis?
6 If it is to be used by teachers who appreciate the value of the programs but who have no knowledge of the computer, who switches it on and off, changes disks or tapes, loads the Basic (in some cases the correct Basic), and loads the programs?
7 Who do the students turn to if things don't run as smoothly as they should?
8 In some schools students run programs after school or in private study periods. If this is desirable, who manages this activity?
9 If a substantial clerical task is taken on, for example a library monitoring system, who sees that this does not conflict with the other demands for computer time?

Throughout this chapter an attempt has been made to highlight some of the problems that can arise when a school purchases a microcomputer or obtains an on-line terminal. The solutions to these problems will depend very much on the staff and the school environment. There is no ready-made formula for organising the computer day; and at the end of that day, which can be quite late, the solutions to many of the problems will depend on the interest and enthusiasm of those concerned.

Index